Long Life Prayer

for

H. H. 17TH GYALWA KARMAPA
URGYEN TRINLEY DORJE

Naturally arising Dharmakaya,
unchanging and ever-present,
Karmapa, You appear as the Form
Kaya's magical illusion.
May Your Three Secret Vajras
remain stable in the realms
And Your Infinite Spontaneous
Activity blaze in glory.

written by

His Eminence Gyaltsab Rinpoche

VAJRA EDITIONS
Book Series

comprise oral teachings given by Khenchen Thrangu Rinpoche.
They present the view and practices of the Vajrayana.

They are reproduced through
the inspiration of H.H. Karmapa,
the blessing of Khenchen Thrangu Rinpoche
and the guidance of Ven. Lama Karma Shedrup

This series is dedicated
to their long life and prosperity.

Zhyi-sil Cho-kyi Gha-tsal
Publications

VAJRA EDITIONS

MEDICINE BUDDHA
teachings

by

KHENCHEN THRANGU RINPOCHE

Acknowledgements

We would like to thank the Very Venerable Khenchen Thrangu Rinpoche for giving these teachings, Lama Yeshe Gyamtso for translating them, Venerable Lama Tashi Namgyal and the staff of Shenpen Osel who transcribed, edited and first published these teachings and Michelle Martin for translating the sadhanas and sutra.

Mudras modelled by Ven. Lama Karma Shedrup.

These teachings on the Medicine Buddha Sadhana and the Medicine Buddha Sutra by Khenchen Thrangu Rinpoche are reprinted from *Shenpen Osel, Volume 4, Numbers 1& 2.*

Reprinted by arrangement with Shenpen Osel, Seattle, www.shenpen-osel.org

Reproduced with permission by Zhyisil Chokyi Ghatsal Publications. PO Box 6259 Wellesley St, Auckland, New Zealand email: inquiries@greatliberation.org website: www.greatliberation.org

Contents

Biography of Thrangu Rinpoche	*ix*
Foreword	*xi*
Preface	*xiii*
Mahamudra Lineage Prayer	*xix*

Medicine Buddha Teachings

Introduction to the Practice — 1

Medicine Buddha Sadhana — 13

—*The Preliminaries* — 13

—*Visualization* — 28

—*Offerings* — 44

—*Praises* — 60

—*The Mantra and Blessings* — 65

—*Conclusion of the Practice* — 68

Mudras — 81

Medicine Buddha Sutra 99

—*Twelve Extraordinary Aspirations for the
Benefit of Sentient Beings* 99

—*The Benefits of Hearing and Recollecting
the Medicine Buddha's Name* 112

The Correct View Regarding Both Deities
and Maras 135

Somehow Our Buddha Nature Has Been Awakened,
and We Are Very Fortunate Indeed 153

A Stream of Lapis Lazuli
—*Medicine Buddha Sadhana (English)* 158

—*Short Menla Practice* 173

—*Shorter Menla Practice* 174

The Twelve Great Aspirations of the
Medicine Buddha 175

Notes 179

Glossary of Terms 191

Index 209

Meditation Centre Information 217

Long Life Prayer for Thrangu Rinpoche 218

Biography of Thrangu Rinpoche

T he lineage of the Thrangu Rinpoche incarnations began in the fifteenth century when the Seventh Karmapa, Chodrak Gyatso visited the region of Thrangu in Tibet. At this time, His Holiness Karmapa established Thrangu Monastery and enthroned Sherap Gyaltsen as the first Thrangu Rinpoche, recognizing him as the re-established emanation of Shuwu Palgyi Senge, one of the twenty-five great siddha disciples of Guru Padmasambhava.

Khenchen Thrangu Rinpoche is the ninth incarnation of this lineage and was born in Kham, Tibet in 1933. When he was four, H.H. the Sixteenth Gyalwa Karmapa and Palpung Situ Rinpoche recognized him as the incarnation of Thrangu Tulku by prophesying the names of his parents and the place of his birth.

He entered Thrangu monastery and from the ages of seven to sixteen he studied reading, writing, grammar, poetry, and astrology, memorised ritual texts, and completed two preliminary retreats. At sixteen under the direction of Khenpo Lodro Rabsel, he began the study of the three vehicles of Buddhism while staying in retreat.

At twenty-three he received full ordination from the Karmapa. When he was twenty-seven, Rinpoche left Tibet for India at the time of the Communist invasion. He was called to Rumtek, Sikkim, where the Karmapa had his seat in exile. At thirty-five, he took the geshe examination before 1500 monks at Buxador monastic refugee camp in

Bengal, and was awarded the degree of Geshe Lharampa. On his return to Rumtek he was named Abbot of Rumtek monastery and the Nalanda Institute for Higher Buddhist studies at Rumtek. He has been the personal teacher of the four principal Karma Kagyu tulkus: Shamar Rinpoche, Situ Rinpoche, Jamgon Kongtrul Rinpoche and Gyaltsab Rinpoche.

Thrangu Rinpoche has travelled extensively throughout Europe, the Far East and the USA. He is the abbot of Gampo Abbey, Nova Scotia, and of Thrangu House, Oxford, in the UK. In 1984 he spent several months in Tibet where he ordained over 100 monks and nuns and visited several monasteries. He has also founded Thrangu Tashi Choling monastery in Boudhnath; a retreat centre and college at Namo Buddha east of the Katmandu Valley, and has established a school in Boudhnath for the general education of lay children and young monks. He also built Tara Abbey in Katmandu. In October of 1999 he consecrated the college at Sarnath which will accept students from the different traditions of Buddhism and will be open to Western students as well.

Thrangu Rinpoche, a recognised master of Mahamudra meditation has given teachings in over twenty-five countries and is especially known for taking complex teachings and making them accessible to Western students.

More recently, because of his vast knowledge of the Dharma, he was appointed by His Holiness the Dalai Lama to be the personal tutor for the recently escaped Seventeenth Karmapa Urgyen Trinley Dorje.

Ven. Lama Karma Shedrup Cho Gyi Senge Kartung

Foreword

Thrangu Rinpoche is one of the greatest masters of our present time and through his immense compassion and vast wisdom has taught this commentary, which not only explains the Medicine Buddha teachings and practice but also tantric practice in general, which we are very fortunate indeed to receive.

The teaching and publication of commentaries such as this in the West is a sign of the increasing development of western Buddhism and its students to receive such profound healing and purification practices. I am extremely pleased about.

While Buddhahood is our aim and the ultimate purpose of the Medicine Buddha sadhana, in order to achieve this we need conducive conditions on a relative level, such as a healthy body and a clear and stable mind which due to the vast and beneficial aspirations of the Medicine Buddha can be brought about through this practice.

The practices and methods of tantra are well known for their effectiveness and swift results. However they are very much dependent on confidence and diligence in one's practice. It is my wish this will increase through gaining more understanding of their meaning and relevance as explained here. Therefore I encourage all students involved with Vajrayana practices to read and study this commentary for the benefit of themselves and all sentient beings.

May this merit cause the life and teachings of the great masters to flourish and remain for many eons benefitting limitless sentient beings.

K. S. Kastung

Karma Choeling Buddhist Monastery
66 Bodhisattva Road
RD 1 Kaukapakapa
New Zealand

Preface

All of the Buddha's teachings can be subsumed under the two categories of shamatha and vipashyana—calm abiding and insight. In the Hinayana traditions of Buddhism the intention of the vipashyana teachings is to establish the lack of true existence of the individual— sometimes called one-fold egolessness, the selflessness of the individual, the identitylessness of the individual—and the lack of true existence of gross phenomena or things. The intention of the vipashyana teachings of the first half of the Mahayana teachings—the second turning of the wheel of dharma—is to extend this understanding to include the lack of true existence even of the most subtle phenomenon, including atoms and subatomic matter and energy, time, and all forms of consciousness itself. These two understandings together are referred to as two-fold egolessness, the selflessness of the individual and the selflessness of phenomena, and are both included in the terms shunyata or emptiness.

The second half of the Mahayana teachings—the third turning of the wheel of dharma—goes on to teach that emptiness is not simply a mere nothingness, nor merely the other side of the coin of interdependence, nor even simply a state beyond all conceptuality. The third turning teaches that this emptiness—while lacking any limiting characteristics, such as color, shape, size, location, substance, or gender, and being empty of all cognitive and emotional obscurations—is not empty of its own nature, the radiant clarity of mind and reality, which we refer to as clear light, in which all the positive qualities of intelligence, wisdom, compassion, skilful means, devotion, confidence, etc., inhere as one undifferentiable quality. Various manifestations of this quality arise out of the clear light nature in the form of the deities of the Vajrayana tradition such as the Medicine Buddha, Vajrayogini, Tara, or Chenrezig. And although it is said from the standpoint of relative truth that these deities actually do exist as individual beings who can be supplicated, they exist as such because, and only because, the qualities that they embody were already inherent in the clear light nature, the Buddha nature, of their own minds when they were confused sentient beings, just as they inherently exist today in the minds of all confused beings.

The essential nature of all deities can be better understood by understanding the essential nature of their body, speech, and mind. The body of the deity is the union of appearance and emptiness and emerges in the practitioner's experience when the experience of perceiver and perceived is purified. What is it purified of? Grasping and fixation. Grasping or clinging to a self, and fixating on an other. In the words of Guru Rinpoche, "Perceiver and perceived when purified are the body of the deity, clear emptiness."

The speech of the deity is the union of sound and emptiness. We all know that sound is intangible, but sounds without the experience of their emptiness have tremendous power to hurt us, to insult us, to exalt us, to exhilarate us, etc. But when sounds and verbal communications are experienced as mere sounds, as the union of sound and emptiness, their power over us dissolves and we experience perfect equanimity.

The mind of the deity is the union of awareness and emptiness. The experiences of the five sense consciousnesses and of the mental consciousness give rise to a constantly changing kaleidoscope of thoughts, mental afflictions, and subtle dualistic perceptions which have the power, in the absence of the experiential understanding of their emptiness, to involve us in the most outrageous, outlandish, though sometimes very subtle, melodramas of the mind. But when their essential emptiness is recognized, and one ceases to welcome and reject, they dissolve or are self-liberated in their own place, the space of empty awareness. All deities share these three aspects of the essential nature—which we also call Mahamudra or dzogchen—and all practitioners who practice deity meditation with sufficient diligence and perseverance will come to realize this very same nature—the body, speech, and mind of the deity—in themselves as they become the deity.

At the same time, each deity has its own particular relative blessing. If one meditates on Chenrezig, ultimately one will realize Mahamudra or dzogchen, and attain Buddhahood. But in the short run, one will experience a strengthening of one's loving kindness and compassion. If one meditates on Green Tara, ultimately one will attain enlightenment, but in the short run, one will experience freedom from fear and mental paralysis, the increased ability to accomplish one's objectives, and an increase in active compassion. If one meditates on Manjushri, in the end one will attain enlightenment, but in the short run one will experience an increase in intelligence, insight, and wisdom. If one meditates on the Medicine Buddha, one will eventually attain enlightenment, but in the meantime one will experience an increase in healing powers both for oneself and others and a decrease in physical and mental illness and suffering. Whether or not we have a very strong motive to attain Buddhahood, we all desire these sorts of relative objectives, so deity meditation provides tremendous incentive for the practice of dharma.

And yet deity meditation is just another version of shamatha and vipashyana. When one meditates on the form, the attire and other attributes, the entourage and environment, and the internal mandala of a deity, and when one recites the deity's mantra, one is practicing shamatha; and when one realizes that all that one is meditating on is mere empty appearance, one is practicing vipashyana. But because meditation on the deity and on the union of the deity and one's own root lama instantly connects one with the empty clear light nature—which is the essence of the deity, the guru, and the lineage, as well as being one's own essential nature—the power of this form of shamatha to purify the mind of the practitioner of the mental obscurations blocking his or her insight is immeasurably greater than that of ordinary tranquillity meditation on mundane objects like the breath or a flower or a candle flame. And since the forms upon which one is meditating are mere mental fabrications, their emptiness is more immediately apparent than, say, the emptiness of something like the Jefferson Memorial or the Washington Monument.

This is all possible because of the special quality of the Vajrayana, which takes enlightenment as the path, rather than seeing it merely as a goal. Through the three processes of abhisheka, which ripens the mental continuum; oral transmission, which supports one's practice; and the teachings, which liberate, one is connected directly to the enlightened state transmitted by the guru and the lineage. Thereafter, when one practices or merely brings to mind those teachings, one is instantly reconnected with that compassionate primordial awareness, and this constant reconnecting then becomes one's path, bringing with it the rapid purification of mental defilements and the rapid accumulation of merit and wisdom. The recognition of this connection is the uncovering of one's own wisdom. If it goes unrecognised, it still exists in the practitioner's mental continuum as a seed, which will gradually ripen according to conditions.

The teachings here on the Medicine Buddha, which comprise the first half of this book present the stages of practice of the Medicine Buddha Sadhana. In it Khenchen Thrangu Rinpoche elucidates not only the details of this particular practice, but also many of the basic principles of tantric theory and practice in general: the notion of deities and Buddha realms, the principles of samayasattva and jnanasattva, the principles of emanating and gathering, and the use of offerings to cultivate qualities, to mention a few. For anyone engaged in any Vajrayana practice, this teaching is very useful in understanding the foundations of tantric practice, and a garden of delights. In addition, Rinpoche describes and explains the mudras in the sadhana and gives a particularly lucid description of the five wisdoms associated with the five Buddha families, describing them as five aspects of intrinsic awareness or as five aspects of the wisdom of a Buddha.

The second half of this book consists of Rinpoche's teachings on the *Medicine Buddha Sutra,* by the Buddha Shakyamuni. In these teachings Rinpoche explains the twelve aspirations; the benefits of hearing, recollecting, and reciting the name of the Medicine Buddha; the meaning of deity in Vajrayana Buddhism; the nature of the four maras and the transcendence of obstacles in the path; and the four qualities of a good intention.

—*Lama Tashi Namgyal*

Vajradhara

The Mahamudra Lineage Prayer

Great Vajradhara (Tib. Dorje Chang), Tilopa, Naropa,
Marpa, Milarepa, Lord of Dharma, Gampopa
Knower of the Three Times, omniscient Karmapa,
Holders of the four greater and eight lesser lineages,
Drigung, Taglung, Tsalpa, these three, glorious Drukpa
   and others
Masters of the profound path of Mahamudra,
Unequalled protectors of beings, the Dakpo Kagyu
I supplicate you, the Kagyu gurus. I hold your lineage.
Grant your blessing that I may follow your example.

Detachment is the foot of meditation, as is taught
To this meditator who is not attached to food and wealth
Who cuts the ties to this life, grant your blessing
That I have no desire for honor and gain.

Devotion is the head of meditation, as is taught
The guru opens the gate to the treasury of oral instruction.
To the meditator who continually supplicates you
Grant your blessing that genuine devotion is born within.

Non-distraction is the body of meditation, as is taught.
Whatever arises, is fresh, the nature of realization.
To the meditator who rests simply in naturalness,
Grant your blessing that my meditation is free from
   conceptualization

The essence of thought is dharmakaya, as is taught
Nothing whatsoever, it arises as everything.
To the meditator for whom all arises in unceasinging play.
Grant you blessing that I realize samsara and nirvana as
   inseparable.

Through all my births, may I never be separated
   from the perfect guru
And always enjoy the splendor of dharma.
Perfecting the qualities of the paths and stages,
May I swiftly attain the state of Vajradhara.

MEDICINE BUDDHA

teachings

*In the Cascade Mountains in Washington, in June of 1999, the Very
Venerable Khenchen Thrangu Rinpoche led an eight-day retreat to
teach the Medicine Buddha Sadhana and Medicine Buddha Sutra.
Rinpoche gave the teachings in Tibetan; they were orally translated by
Lama Yeshe Gyamtso. The following is an edited transcript.*

Introduction to the Practice

A Practice that is Extremely Effective in the Removal of Sickness

I am delighted to have this opportunity to be here, to study the Medicine Buddha practice and to talk about dharma. As usual, I begin teaching sessions with the short lineage supplication that begins with the words "Great Vajradhara." We use this supplication because it is the one most often practiced at the seats of the Kagyu tradition and by Kagyu practitioners elsewhere. It was composed by Pengar Jampal Zangpo, the foremost disciple of the Sixth Gyalwang Karmapa, Thongwa Dönden, and the root guru of the Seventh Gyalwang Karmapa, Chödrak Gyamtso. After receiving instructions from the Sixth Gyalwang Karmapa, Pengar Jampal Zangpo went to Sky Lake in the north of Tibet to practice. In the middle of this lake, there was an island called Semodo and on that island there was a mountain with a cave in it. In this cave in utter isolation he practiced for eighteen years. The isolation there is complete, because it is very difficult to get to that island except in the middle of winter. He practiced, therefore, in total isolation for eighteen years and developed extraordinary realization of Mahamudra. This lineage supplication, which he composed after that period of retreat, is regarded as containing the essence and blessing of his realization, which is therefore why we use it. So when you chant it, please do so with faith and generate strong devotion for the root guru and the other gurus of the lineage, such as Vajradhara, Tilopa, Naropa, and so forth.

When you receive instruction in dharma, the motivation with which you do so is extremely important. Recognize that the instructions you are receiving are a basis for your practice of dharma, and that your practice of dharma is of great benefit. This benefit is not limited to you alone or only to a few—yourself and a few others—but ultimately the benefit of your practice will be enjoyed by all beings who fill space. Therefore, when you receive teachings in the beginning, do it with that recollection and with the motivation that by receiving these instructions, by meditating on and supplicating the Medicine Buddha, by studying his sutra, and so on, you are receiving them and will practice them so that you can bring about the liberation of all beings.

So in order to receive the teachings properly, please generate the attitude of bodhicitta, which is necessary for the practice of dharma in general, and particularly for the practice of something like the Medicine Buddha.

We might think that there is something of a contradiction between the motivation with which we might practice the Medicine Buddha and the motivation of bodhicitta. We might think that fundamentally we are practicing the Medicine Buddha in order to benefit our own bodies, whereas the motivation of bodhicitta is the wish to benefit all beings. But in fact there is no contradiction, because, in order to be effective in benefiting other beings, we need to accomplish an excellent samadhi or meditative absorption; and in order to accomplish that, together with the insight and realization that it brings, we need to have a stable practice. In order to have a stable and profound practice, we need to be physically and mentally healthy or comfortable, because by being comfortable in our body, and comfortable in our mind, we will be free of obstacles to diligence in practice and free of obstacles to the cultivation of meditative absorption. So therefore, we are practicing the Medicine Buddha in order to attain states of mental and physical health or balance, not merely for our own benefit, but for the benefit of others as well.

There is, therefore, no contradiction between the motivation you might have for practicing the Medicine Buddha and your motivation for practicing dharma in general. We practice dharma in order to attain Buddhahood, and we practice the Medicine Buddha in order to attain that same goal. We may be practicing it specifically in order to attain a state of mental and physical health in this life, but when we practice the Medicine Buddha in this way, we are not really limiting our motivation to our attainment of mental and physical health, because by means of that practice we can accomplish great benefit for ourselves and others; and we can successfully complete our practice of dharma in the sense of attaining Buddhahood.

Furthermore, by practicing the Medicine Buddha, we not only achieve health in this life but we cause ourselves to be blessed by the Medicine Buddha throughout all future lives as well. And through cultivating the stages of the practice of the Medicine Buddha—the generation stage and the completion stage—we not only achieve benefit for ourselves, but we are actually cultivating the potential to benefit others. And by doing these practices we actually bless the environment and all the beings in that environment.

The practice of the Medicine Buddha is fundamentally a mental practice, a practice of meditation. Now, you might wonder how something you are doing primarily with your mind could affect your body. How could practicing the Medicine Buddha preserve your physical health or alleviate physical sickness? You might think that the mind and body are fundamentally unrelated, and that therefore the practice of meditation cannot affect our bodies. In fact, our bodies and minds are extremely interrelated. The body supports or is the container for our mind, but the body is also based upon or supported by the mind. Therefore, the practice of meditation does affect your body and your physical state. Specifically, in the meditation practice of the Medicine Buddha, in addition to visualizing the Medicine Buddha in front of you, you are also visualizing your own body as the body of the Medicine Buddha. These and other visualizations, and the recitation of the mantra and so forth, which initially or primarily seem only to affect the mind, do, therefore, eventually affect the body as well.

We practice fundamentally with our minds, but this practice does affect and benefit both the mind and the body. As is generally taught, what we identify as our mind consists of eight different consciousnesses, or functions of consciousness. These arise the way they do because of the connection between body and mind. For example, one of the eight consciousnesses is the eye consciousness, the visual consciousness. This consciousness is a function of three things: its object, which is visible forms; its organic support, which is the eye as an organ of vision; and the consciousness, which is the mind functioning in connection with these two. Now, the point of this is that the visual consciousness never arises in isolation from an object and an organic support. It arises *because* the organic support is capable of detecting its appropriate object—in this case, visible form. Therefore, because the object, the organ, and the consciousness are so intimately interrelated or interconnected, the transformation of any one of these will necessarily affect the aspect or manner of the other two. Therefore, just as when an object is changed, that affects the visual consciousness of that object in dependence upon the organ; and when the organ is changed, that affects the visual consciousness and therefore the perceived objects; in the same way, when the consciousness is transformed, as it is through the practice of meditation, that affects the perception of objects and the organic support itself.

In the same way, our other senses arise as consciousnesses in connection with their objects and their organic supports. Based upon the organ of the ear, there arises what is called the ear consciousness or hearing, which experiences its object, audible sounds. In dependence upon the organic support of the nose, there arises the nose consciousness, which detects smells. In dependence upon the organ of the tongue, there arises the tongue consciousness, which detects tastes. And in dependence on the organic support of the body and the nerves of the body, there arises the body consciousness, which detects or experiences tactile sensations. All of these consciousnesses arise or are generated by the presence of an object which is encountered by its appropriate organ. Sometimes they arise based upon the organ itself experiencing the sensation, but in any case, the sensations of the five senses that we experience are functions of the organs and the objects experienced by these organs, which generate appropriate consciousnesses. Because the consciousness pervades the experience of its object and the experience of the organ itself, if the consciousness is transformed, or one's mode of experience of consciousness is transformed, into pure appearance, then the appearances of the objects, and also of the organs themselves, will become pure or sacred. It is in this way that the practice of this form of meditation can benefit not only your mind but also your body.

In addition to the five sense consciousnesses, the sixth consciousness, which is the mental consciousness, also arises in connection with physical experience. Now, according to the Abhidharma, the mental consciousness does not rely exclusively upon a specific physical organ support the way the five sense consciousnesses do. The condition that leads to the arising of the mental consciousness is the previous moment of that consciousness itself. Generally speaking, this arises to some extent on the impressions produced by the physical experience of the senses. So, indirectly, we could say that the organ support for the mental consciousness is the momentum of all of the consciousnesses connected with sense experience. But the mental consciousness itself is that which generates and experiences all of the varieties of emotion and thought that we know—attachment, aversion, bewilderment, apathy, pride, jealousy, feelings of joy and delight, feelings of sadness, feelings of faith and compassion, etc.—all of these different emotional states and all of the thoughts connected with them are varieties of experiences of the sixth or mental consciousness. Now, as these various thoughts and emotions pass through our minds, they transform and influence that consciousness itself. But not only that—they also affect the five sense consciousnesses. For example, when you are very sad and you look at something, you will perceive it as sad, or as unpleasant. If you look at the identical object when you are happy, you will see the same thing as pleasant. And if you look at it when you are angry, you will see, again, the same object as entirely different. This is a very simple example of how the mental consciousness in particular and our mind in general affects our experience of sense objects and the sense consciousnesses and the sense organs themselves.

Of the eight consciousnesses, the most evident in our experience are these six consciousnesses, or six functions: the five sense consciousnesses and the mental consciousness. But there are, in addition to these, two other functions of mind, which are called stable or underlying consciousnesses or functions. These are the seventh consciousness, which is the subtle mental affliction, and the eighth consciousness, which is called the all-basis. The seventh consciousness, the consciousness which is the root of mental affliction, refers to the subtle, fundamental misapprehension of an existent self, the fixation on a self. This fixation is itself the root of samsara. It is not, however, regarded as an unvirtuous or negative thing in itself. It is morally neutral. But because it is ignorance and the basis of further ignorance, it is regarded as the most fundamental and important thing to be abandoned or relinquished. In fact, we could say that the teachings of Buddhadharma are mainly about how to abandon this fixation on self. It is for that reason that there is so much emphasis in Buddhadharma on the meditations on selflessness, emptiness, and so forth. Through these meditations one can realize selflessness, through which one relinquishes the kleshas, through which one attains liberation.

The meditation upon selflessness, however, and specifically the meditation upon the lack of true existence of the personal self,[1] does not consist of trying to imagine or convince yourself that you are nothing whatsoever. It is done, especially in the visualization practices of the generation stage of tantra, by replacing your solid sense of your own existence with something else. In the case of the Medicine Buddha practice, you relinquish the thought, "I am me, I am the person I think I am," and replace it with the thought, "I am the Medicine Buddha." The primary technique in the meditation consists of imagining yourself to be the Medicine Buddha, conceiving of yourself as the Medicine

Buddha. By replacing the thought of yourself as yourself with the thought of yourself as the Medicine Buddha, you gradually counteract and remove the fixation on your personal self. And as that fixation is removed, the power of the seventh consciousness is reduced. And as it is reduced, the kleshas or mental afflictions are gradually weakened, which causes you to experience greater and greater well-being in both body and mind.

The eighth consciousness is the all-basis consciousness, so called because it is the ground on which habits, both good and bad, accrue. We experience things the way we do because of the habits we have accumulated. As we accumulate good habits we have positive experiences, and as we accumulate bad habits we have negative experiences. The fundamental reason for our immersion in samsara is the accumulation of bad habits, some more virulent than others. The process of getting ourselves out of samsara consists of gradually weakening the bad habits and strengthening the good habits. For example, when we begin to practice, we have no confidence whatsoever that we really are the Medicine Buddha. We have a strong negative habit of regarding ourselves as whomever we regard ourselves to be. But through cultivating the technique and attitude of regarding ourselves as possessing the body, the speech, the mind, the qualities, and the blessings of the Medicine Buddha, then these natural qualities within us will increase.

The main practice in Vajrayana consists of the generation stage, the cultivation of the practice of regarding oneself as a deity. From an ordinary point of view, we might regard this as useless. We would think, "Well, I am not a deity. What use is there in my pretending to be a deity?" But in fact, the root of samsara is the habit of impure perception. By regarding oneself as a deity one gradually purifies, weakens, and removes that habit and replaces it with the positive habit of pure perception. It is for this reason that the meditation upon oneself as a deity is considered so important.

In most religious traditions, the deities of that tradition, when they are related to or imagined, are imagined in front of one. Then, visualizing the deity or deities as being present in front of one, one prays to them, and by doing so hopefully one receives their blessing, which benefits one in some way. In the Vajrayana tradition, however, we regard the blessing and the power and the qualities of the deities as being innate, as being within one's own mind. This innate presence of the wisdom and blessings of the deities in our own minds is called the unity of the expanse and wisdom, or the unity of space and wisdom. Of course, it is true that when we look at our minds, we have mental afflictions, we have thoughts, we have all kinds of suffering and problems. But at the same time we always have the innate potential to transcend these. And the reason why we have this innate potential is that the nature of the mind and the nature of everything that arises in the mind is emptiness. Regardless of what is passing through our mind, our mind is always a boundless space of emptiness.

The innate potential of our minds lies in the very fact that our minds are empty. Because our minds are empty, all of the problems and sufferings and defects that arise in our minds can be removed or purified, because they too are empty. This emptiness of the mind is not absolute nothingness; it is not a static or dead or neutral emptiness, because, while emptiness is indeed the nature of the mind, the nature of that emptiness is wisdom—it is the innate potential for the arising of all qualities. In Buddhist scriptures this innate potential is called Buddha nature.

Now, the process of working with our life situation through practice in tantric Buddhism consists first of acknowledging that one's own basic nature is that potential, that Buddha nature, and then of meditating upon its presence within one by regarding oneself as a deity. The form of the deity is the embodiment or expression of that potential, that unity of emptiness and wisdom, within one. It is through regarding oneself as the deity that defects are gradually eradicated and qualities gradually revealed. The primary technique of visualization is to visualize ourselves as the deity, because the potential to transcend our problems is innate rather than external to us. Therefore, our main practice in meditation upon deities is the self-generation of the deity, visualizing oneself as the deity.

If you ask is this the only way in which we work with deities, the answer is no. We also visualize deities in front of us. Now, in the common tradition[2] of Buddhism, as is found in the scriptures of the Theravadin tradition and so on—which I cannot read in the Pali but have read in Tibetan translation—we find an extensive presentation by the Buddha that there is no external deity to be relied upon, that the path consists fundamentally of eradicating one's own kleshas, thereby eventually attaining the state of an arhat or arhati without remainder. Thus in the sutras of the common vehicle, the state of liberation is presented as freedom from all kleshas, limitations, and attachment, but not particularly as an abiding wisdom.

However, in the sutras of the Mahayana, and especially in the teachings of the Vajrayana, it is clearly taught that once someone attains full liberation and Buddhahood, they do not become nothing. The process of purification finally reveals, and therefore there remains, an enduring wisdom that is of the nature of nonconceptual compassion. The attainment of Buddhahood, the path through which it is attained, really begins with the generation of bodhicitta, which is the intention to attain liberation so that one can bring all beings to the same state. Because that is the motivation with which the path is begun, when the result, which is Buddhahood, is attained, the result of that path is naturally spontaneous, impartial, and nonconceptual compassion. Therefore, we regard Buddhas as having an awareness that is responsive to the needs of beings, and therefore as being open and accessible to our prayers and supplication. For that reason, while we primarily visualize ourselves as deities, we also visualize the deities as present in front of us.

We supplement the visualization of ourselves as the deity with visualizations such as imagining the actual wisdom deities themselves dissolving into ourselves again and again, by means of which we receive their blessing. Sometimes we visualize the deity in front of us, separate from ourselves, thinking that rays of light from the deity's heart engulf and pervade us, granting the blessing of the deity. And sometimes we visualize that rays of light, which embody the blessing of that deity in front of us, strike all beings, removing their obstacles, increasing their longevity, wisdom, and so on. All of these visualizations are methods by which we arouse the compassion of all Buddhas and cause their blessings to enter into ourselves and others.

All the yidams and deities used in meditation have the same fundamental nature and are utterly pure. Nevertheless they have different appearances, which reflect the different activities that they embody and engage in. These different activities are primarily determined by the individual aspirations they made at the time of their initial generation of bodhicitta. For example, in the case of the Medicine Buddha, there is a specific set of aspirations, as there is in the case of the bodhisattva Avalokiteshvara or the bodhisattva Arya Tara. It is primarily for this reason that deities manifest in their varied appearances— sometimes appearing as male, in which case they primarily embody upaya or method; sometimes appearing as female, in which case they primarily embody prajna or wisdom; sometimes appearing as peaceful, sometimes appearing as wrathful, and so on. In the case of the Medicine Buddha, at the time of his initial generation of bodhicitta—with which act he began the path that culminated in his attainment of Buddhahood—his primary motivation was to remove all suffering of beings in general, but especially to remove the physical and mental sufferings of beings caused through the imbalance of the elements, which we know of as mental and physical illness. This was his primary motivation or aspiration throughout the three periods of innumerable eons during which he gathered the accumulations of merit and wisdom that culminated in his attainment of Buddhahood as the Medicine Buddha. Therefore, as the Medicine Buddha, he possesses extraordinary ability and engages in extraordinary activity to pacify sickness. Whether you access this activity through visualizing yourself as the Medicine Buddha, or through arousing the compassion and activity of the Medicine Buddha as conceived of as external to yourself, in either case, the practice of the Medicine Buddha is supremely effective in the removal of sickness.

The practice of the Medicine Buddha comes primarily from the uncommon tradition of the Vajrayana, which means that the transmission of the practice is done using three processes called the empowerment, which ripens; the instruction, which frees; and the reading transmission, which supports. The function of empowerment, the formal ceremony or ritual of empowerment, is to introduce you to the practice and to the process of visualization and so forth, which will make up the practice. The function of the instruction, which frees, is to give you complete access to the practice by means of telling you literally how to do it—what you do with your body, what you say with your speech, and what you think with your mind. The function of the reading transmission, which supports, is to transmit the blessing of the lineage of the practice which serves to consecrate or bless your practice in the form of sound. Because the lineage has been transmitted as the sound of the words of its transmission, when the reading transmission is given to you, you simply listen to the sound and think that by doing so you receive the blessing of the lineage.

With regard to the empowerment, you should understand that the Medicine Buddha practice is not solely a Vajrayana practice. Like the practice of Mahamudra, it is a combination of Vajrayana [tantra] and sutra. For example, while we could say that Mahamudra is primarily taught in the Vajrayana, it is also found in certain sutras, such as the *Samadhiraja Sutra,* and so forth. In the same way, this practice of the Medicine Buddha is a combination of what the Buddha taught about the Medicine Buddha in the sutras of the Medicine Buddha and in various tantras. Because it is connected with Vajrayana, it is most appropriate to receive the empowerment to enhance the practice; but because it is also connected with the sutras, it is acceptable to do the practice without the empowerment as well. When you are receiving the reading transmission, there is no particular visualization you need to do. Maintain the motivation of bodhicitta for receiving the transmission, and think that simply by hearing the sounds of the words you receive the transmission or blessing of the lineage of this practice.

To give you a support for your visualization of the Medicine Buddha when doing the practice, you can obtain an image of the Medicine Buddha.

OM

AH

HUM

Medicine Buddha Sadhana

*The Great King of Medicine Is Active in Pacifying
the Suffering of Beings*

The Preliminaries

I *am now going to start going through* the text itself, the liturgy for the practice, so that you will understand how to do it. As you will have noticed, the first part of the Medicine Buddha practice is the lineage supplication, which consists of the supplication of the principal Medicine Buddha, the seven accompanying Medicine Buddhas, the sixteen bodhisattvas, and finally, the holders and propagators of the teachings of the Medicine Buddha. The purpose of reciting this supplication at the beginning of the practice is to invoke and receive at the very beginning of the practice the blessing of the Medicine Buddha through the power of your faith in and devotion to the deity and to the lineage of this teaching.

The supplication begins with one line in the language of Sanskrit:

NAMO BEKENDZE MAHA RADZAYE

This means, "Homage to the great king of medicine." The initial homage to the Medicine Buddha as the great king of medicine is done in Sanskrit because the source of the teachings of the Vajrayana in particular, and of the Buddhadharma in general—the original sutra and tantra teachings of the Buddha Shakyamuni—were given primarily in Sanskrit. Moreover, the mahasiddhas, bodhisattvas, and shravakas of India also primarily used Sanskrit as their dharma language. Therefore, in order to maintain a connection with the source of the tradition, and because the Sanskrit language itself is held to bear great blessing, the initial supplication is made in Sanskrit, after which follows the main body of the supplication of the Medicine Buddha in Tibetan.

The first stanza of the supplication is addressed to the principal Medicine Buddha, and is based on the Buddha Shakyamuni's presentation of the Medicine Buddha's initial motivation for his path and the aspirations he made in connection therewith, as recorded in the sutras on the Medicine Buddha.[3]

> *You are endowed with an oceanic treasury of qualities*
> *   and merit;*
> *By the blessing of your inconceivable compassion*
> *You calm the suffering and torment of sentient beings.*
> *I supplicate you, Light of Lapis Lazuli.*

The meaning of the stanza is that, because of the quality and special nature of his initial motivation and ensuing aspirations, the Medicine Buddha very quickly accumulated vast amounts of merit, as a result of which, while on the path and finally at the time of fruition or Buddhahood, he came to embody a vast treasury of qualities associated with awakening. Therefore, because of his initial compassionate motivation and because of the qualities of his awakening, he possesses inconceivable blessing, by virtue of which, in accordance with his aspiration and motivation, he is active in pacifying the sufferings of beings. So in chanting the beginning of the supplication, you mention him by name, referring to him as the Light of Vaidurya.

The second stanza is also addressed to the Medicine Buddha, and it continues from the presentation in the first. In the first stanza you were essentially praising the fact that he embodies extraordinary merit and qualities as a result of his extraordinary motivation and aspirations. Upon his initial generation of bodhicitta the Medicine Buddha made twelve particular aspirations. In connection with these, the benefits of recollecting the name of the Medicine Buddha begin to be specified in the second stanza.

> *Those bound by very intense greed*
> *Are born in the hungry ghost realm.*
> *If they hear your name, they are born human*
> *   and take delight in generosity.*
> *I supplicate you, victorious Menla.*

Recollection of the name means keeping the name of the Medicine Buddha in mind by having an attitude of faith and devotion to the Medicine Buddha. The stanza says that even someone who, as a result of intense greed, is destined to be reborn as a preta or hungry ghost, if such a person hears the name of the Medicine Buddha, they will be reborn as a human being and will delight in generosity. In that way, you supplicate the Medicine Buddha by referring to the power or blessing of his name.

The next stanza gives a second benefit of recollecting and hearing the name of the Medicine Buddha.

> *Violating morality and abusing others,*
> *Beings are born in the hell realms.*
> *Hearing your name, they'll be born*
> *   in the higher realms, it's said.*
> *I supplicate you, King of Medicine.*

Those who violate moral commitments and who actively harm or abuse others will be reborn in the hell realms. This refers to those who have no interest in maintaining the dharma commitments they have undertaken, who have no interest in benefiting others, and who are only interested in harming them. But if even such a person hears the name of the Medicine Buddha, they will be reborn in higher realms. By simply hearing the name of the Medicine Buddha, their inherent capacity for virtue will be awakened and they will gradually become interested in acting appropriately and benefiting others. Changing their course of action, they will not be reborn in a lower realm.

The next stanza describes a third benefit of hearing or recollecting the name of the Medicine Buddha.

> *Whoever by repeated dissension and slander*
> *Creates deep schisms and takes life,*
> *Hearing your name, they cannot harm others.*
> *I supplicate you, King of Medicine.*

Those who are naturally jealous, competitive, and arrogant, and as a result, find themselves always trying to produce dissension; who, when seeing that others are friendly and harmonious, automatically try to create discord; who create schisms where there is harmony and discord even to the point where it leads to loss either of their own life or the lives of others; even someone with this jealous, competitive, and arrogant nature—if they hear the name of the Medicine Buddha, will be unable to cause harm. Unable to cause harm means that their mindset and their attitudes will change. They will cease to be jealous, cease to be arrogant, and will gradually find themselves unwilling and therefore unable to intentionally bring this kind of harm to others.

There are two sutras principally concerned with the Medicine Buddha. One is the *Sutra of the Medicine Buddha*, which is concerned with the principal Medicine Buddha, his twelve aspirations, and the benefits of recollecting his name. The second is the *Sutra of the Eight Medicine Buddhas*, or the *Sutra of the Eight Medicine Buddha Brothers*. The Medicine Buddhas referred to in this sutra are the previously mentioned principal one and seven others who form his retinue. The next stanza in the supplication is concerned with the other seven Medicine Buddhas. They each have their own individual aspirations. Some of them have made eight aspirations; some have made four. And the recollection of their names brings benefits similar to those brought about by the recollection of the name of the principal Medicine Buddha.

> *Excellent Name, Appearance of Stainless Fine Gold,*
> *Glorious Supreme One Free of Misery,*
> *Resounding Dharma Melody,*
> *King of Direct Knowledge, King of Melody,*
> *And King of Shakyas, I supplicate you all.*

These seven Buddhas are named Tshen Lek, or Excellent Name; Ser Zang Dri Me Nangwa, or Appearance of Stainless Fine Gold; Nya Ngen Me Chok Pal, Glorious Supreme One Free of Misery; Chö Drak Yang, Resounding Dharma Melody; Ngön Khyen Gyalpo, King of Direct Knowledge; Dra Yang Gyalpo, King of Melody; and Shakya Gyalpo, King of the Shakyas.

The next stanza is a supplication to the other deities in the mandala[4] of the Medicine Buddha. These are not listed in their entirety, but each set of deities is mentioned briefly and a few of the names of each set are mentioned.

> *Manjushri, Kyabdröl, Vajrapani,*
> *Brahma, Indra, the Four Kings of the Four Directions,*
> *The twelve great Yaksha chiefs, and others,*
> *I supplicate you, entire and perfect mandala.*

The first class of deities after the eight Medicine Buddhas are the sixteen bodhisattvas. Here three of them are mentioned: Manjushri, Kyabdröl, and Vajrapani. The next class are the ten protectors of the world, or of the directions, of whom two are mentioned, Brahma and Indra. The next class are the four great kings of the four directions, who are also protectors, not mentioned here by their individual names.

Finally there are the twelve yaksha chieftains, or yaksha generals, and they too are just mentioned as a class. The last line of the stanza indicates that this is the supplication of the entire mandala of the Medicine Buddha.

Up to this point you have supplicated the principal Medicine Buddha and his retinue, and in doing so have supplicated the body of the Medicine Buddha and the mind or the emanations of the Medicine Buddha. What remains is to supplicate the speech of the Medicine Buddha; having supplicated the Buddhas and bodhisattvas of the mandala, you next supplicate the dharma.

> *The Sutra of the Seven Tathagatas' Aspirations,*
> *And the Sutra of the Medicine Buddha,*
> *the treatise by the great abbot Santarakshita,*
>   *and so forth,*
> *I supplicate all the volumes of the genuine Dharma.*

Mentioned first are the two sutras taught by the Buddha Shakyamuni about the Medicine Buddha: the *Sutra of the Aspirations of the Seven Tathagatas,* which means the seven Medicine Buddhas in the retinue, and the *Sutra of the Medicine Buddha,* which is the principal Medicine Buddha. Mentioned in the same stanza are the shastras,[5] which also form part of the scriptural source for the Medicine Buddha tradition. These are referred to by mentioning as an example the treatise of the great abbot Santarakshita, which is one of the oldest or original sources of the Medicine Buddha practice. And then you chant, "I supplicate the genuine dharma in the form of books." The reason for this is that in general, of course, dharma exists in the form of the written word. But it has a special significance in the case of this mandala. The self-generation—the form of the Medicine Buddha with which you identify your own body—is the Medicine Buddha alone, without retinue. But the front visualization is the Medicine Buddha surrounded by all the rest of the mandala. The first circle of the mandala immediately surrounding him consists of the other seven Medicine Buddhas and the volumes of the dharma as the eighth member of the retinue. During this supplication you visualize the Medicine Buddha seated in the sky in front of you in the center of a fully opened eight-petalled lotus and surrounding him, on each of the seven petals other than the one directly in front of him, the seven other Medicine Buddhas. On the lotus petal directly in front of the principal Medicine Buddha, you visualize the volumes of the dharma, the sutras, and so forth, that present his practice.

The next stanza of the supplication supplicates the lineage of this practice.

> *Bodhisattva Santarakshita, Trisong Deutsen, and others,*
> *Translators, scholars, kings, ministers, bodhisattvas,*
> *and all genuine lamas of the lineage,*
> *Powerful One of the Dharma, and others, I supplicate you.*

First mentioned are those who first brought this tradition of the Medicine Buddha from India to Tibet. Where it says bodhisattva, it means the abbot Santarakshita, who bestowed this teaching on many students, including the Tibetan dharma king Trisong Deutsen, who is mentioned next. Then supplicated are all of the translators of Tibet and the panditas of India who enabled this tradition to spread to Tibet through translating it, teaching it, explaining it, and so on. Next are supplicated all of the other inheritors of this tradition, bodhisattvas who took the form of dharma kings, ministers and so on. Finally, all the gurus of the lineage of this practice are supplicated, and in particular one's own root guru. This supplication was composed, and the practice in general was edited, by the learned and accomplished master Karma Chagmey Rinpoche, and so he supplicates his own root guru, Chökyi Wangchuk, by name here.

The final stanza of the supplication dedicates the power of the supplication to the ends that you wish to achieve.

> *Through the blessing of this supplication,*
> *May all variety of disease and dangers of*

this life be pacified.
At death, may all fear of the lower realms be allayed.
Grant your blessing that we are then born in Sukhavati.

The stanza reads, "Through the blessing of supplicating in this way,"—which means by the blessing of supplicating the Medicine Buddha, his retinue of Buddhas, bodhisattvas, and protectors, and all the teachers of the lineage, with devotion—"in the short run may the various diseases, dangers, and fears be pacified, and at the time of death, after all fear of being reborn in the lower realms has been pacified, grant your blessing that we may be born in Sukhavati, the land of great happiness and great bliss." You are expressing your wish here to be protected from suffering both in the short term and in the long term. In the short term you are asking to be protected from sickness and various other dangers—from whatever can go wrong—in this life. In the long term, you are asking that you not be reborn in lower states or in lower realms, and that, once the danger and fear of being reborn in the lower realms have been transcended, you may achieve rebirth in Sukhavati, the realm of Amitabha. That completes the lineage supplication.

After the lineage supplication comes the taking of refuge and the generation of bodhicitta, which, as necessary preliminaries, are always recited at the beginning of any Vajrayana practice. Each has a specific function. The function of taking refuge is to prevent your practice from becoming an incorrect path. The function of generating bodhicitta is to prevent your practice from becoming an inferior path. In the case of this practice, each of these aspects—refuge and bodhicitta—occupies two lines of a four-line stanza.

NAMO *to the sources of refuge, the three jewels*
And the three roots, I go for refuge.

The first line of the refuge identifies the sources of refuge, and they are two: the three jewels and the three roots. The three jewels, which are the common sources of refuge,[6] are the Buddha, in whom one takes refuge by accepting him as a teacher and an example; the dharma, in which one takes refuge by accepting it as a path; and the sangha, in which one takes refuge by accepting the sangha as companions and guides on that path. Identifying the three jewels as the initial source of refuge indicates that by taking refuge in them you are freeing yourself from the possibility of an incorrect path.

Then there are the uncommon sources of refuge, which are unique to Vajrayana. They are known as the three roots: the gurus, who are the root of blessing; the yidams or deities, who are the root of attainment; and the dharmapalas, or dharma protectors, who are the root of activity. First of these are the gurus, who are the root of blessing. Blessing refers to the power of dharma—that which in dharma is actually effective, that actually brings the result of dharma. Obviously in practicing we need that effectiveness—that power or blessing of dharma—to enter into us. The original source of this blessing, of course, is the Buddha, who first taught the dharma in this particular historical period. Unfortunately, we do not have the ability in this life to meet the Buddha or hear the Buddha's speech directly. But we do have the opportunity to practice his teachings and to attain the same result we could have attained had we met the Buddha, because the essence of his teachings—and therefore the blessing or effectiveness of his teachings—has been passed down through the lineage, beginning with the Buddha himself and culminating with our own personal teacher or root guru. Therefore, the first source of refuge in the Vajrayana are root and lineage gurus—and, especially the root guru—who are the source of the blessing of dharma.

The second source of refuge in the Vajrayana, the second root, are the yidams, the deities, who are the sources of attainment or siddhi. While the guru is the source of the blessing and effectiveness of dharma, the guru cannot simply hand you the result or attainment of dharma practice. The source or root of that attainment is your practice. And your practice is embodied by the yidam or deity which is the basis of that practice. This means that you attain the result of dharma practice through engaging in the techniques of visualizing the body of the deity and engaging in the generation and completion stage practices which are associated with that deity. In this specific instance, the yidam is the Medicine Buddha. By identifying with the body of the Medicine Buddha, you attain the result, the attainments or siddhis, associated with the Medicine Buddha, which include the pacification of sickness and other sufferings.[7] The reason why these deities are referred to as *yidams*, which literally means mental commitment, is that in order to practice dharma you have to have a clear direction and strong focus in the technique and method of practice. The idea of yidam is that a certain practice and, in the case of Vajrayana a certain deity, is identified by you as that practice to which you commit yourself, that direction in practice which you will take. A yidam is the deity about which you think, "I will practice this. I will come to attain this result."

The third Vajrayana source of refuge, the third root, are the dharmapalas, the protectors, who are the root of activity. Activity here means the protection of your practice from obstacles, so that you can successfully complete it and bring it to the appropriate result, so that you will be able to benefit others effectively in a way that is in accordance with the practice. In order to achieve these ends you need this blessing of activity or protection. This is gained chiefly from specific bodhisattvas who take the form of protectors, and, in certain cases, dakinis. In the specific case of the Medicine Buddha, when the Buddha taught the Medicine Buddha sutras, there were certain deities who committed themselves to protecting these teachings and all practitioners of these teachings, including even those who merely recollect the name of the Medicine Buddha. These protector deities are represented in the mandala, and they include the twelve yaksha chieftains, the four great kings, the ten protectors of the world, and so on. In this way, you are taking refuge by accepting the Buddha as a teacher; his teachings, the dharma, as a path; the sangha as companions and guides on that path; and you are taking refuge by requesting the blessings of the gurus, attainment through the yidam, and the protection of the dharmapalas and dakinis. That is the taking of refuge, which serves to protect your practice from becoming an incorrect path.

Next comes the generation of bodhicitta, which serves to protect your practice from becoming an inferior path.

> *To establish all beings in Buddhahood,*
> *I awaken the mind of supreme enlightenment.*

It is true, of course, that our basic motivation for practicing is that we all wish to be free from suffering. This wish to be free from suffering is good. But it is often somewhat limited, which is to say that it is somewhat selfish, and it is often somewhat petty or small-minded in scope. The idea behind generating bodhicitta is to recollect that all beings without exception wish to be happy in exactly the same way and to exactly the same degree as we do. If you bring that to mind fully, then your aspiration to attain freedom for yourself will expand and become an aspiration to bring all beings to that same freedom. This aspiration has to be a long-term aspiration. It is not enough simply to aspire to free beings from a certain type of suffering, or to free them from the suffering they are undergoing now, or to free them from this year's suffering. For it to be the aspiration of bodhicitta, which is the fullest and most extensive motivation, you must have the attitude of wishing to establish beings in a state that will permanently free them from all suffering. Now, the only way that you can actually make beings permanently happy is to bring them to a state of full awakening, to Buddhahood. So ultimately, the only way to protect beings from suffering is to establish them all in awakening, because they simply will not be happy until they have attained it. If you understand this—that all beings wish to be happy just as much as we do and that none of us can be happy until we attain awakening—then you will naturally give rise to bodhicitta, which is the intention to bring each and every being to a state of full and perfect awakening. Bodhicitta also includes within it, of course, the aspiration to be of any other assistance you can to beings along the way to accomplishing that ultimate goal. So it is not limited to any specific form of assistance.

If bodhicitta has been genuinely generated, then your motivation for practice will be reflected in your thinking, "I am practicing in order to bring all beings to awakening; I am not practicing merely because I am afraid of my own suffering or because I wish to protect a few others from suffering or because I wish to protect all others from a few types of suffering." In that way your motivation for the practice of the Medicine Buddha becomes bodhicitta, which is the attitude: "In order to bring all beings to a state of Buddhahood I must first attain the state of the Medicine Buddha in order to be able to do so effectively, because in my present state I cannot effectively protect or benefit others."

The refuge and the generation of bodhicitta are followed by the blessing or consecration of the place and the materials of practice.

From the expanse of primordial purity come forth
Clouds of offerings filling the earth and sky
With mandalas, articles of royalty, and goddesses.
May they never be exhausted. **PUD DZA HO.**

The reason for this stage of the practice is that at any given moment we have an impure perception[8] of and an impure attitude towards ourselves, towards others, and towards the environment as a whole. The more we invest in that impure perception or attitude—in the perception of things as impure—the worse our situation will become, and the more attachment and aversion and apathy we will find ourselves generating. The remedy for this is simply to change our attitude and to regard things as pure. Initially, of course, this takes some conscious effort. But by regarding things as pure, you will gradually start to perceive things as pure, which will purify the habitual tendency to perceive them as impure.

At this point the liturgy reads, "Clouds of offerings emanated from the primordially pure expanse fill the sky and the earth." You imagine that the place in which you are practicing is a completely pure realm filled with every imaginable type of pleasant offering substance. This realm and these offerings, although you are imagining them, are not imaginary. They have been there from the very beginning, which is why it says in the liturgy "emanated from the primordially pure expanse." From the very beginning, this is how things actually are, how things actually have been. You are not creating them by imagining them, nor are you fooling yourselves by imagining them. It is rather that our present mode of perception is like being in the midst of a nightmare from which we hope to wake up; and when we wake up from it, we will see things as they are. It is important to understand that you are imagining things to be what in fact they really are.

The offering substances contained in this pure realm include such things as offering mandalas, the seven articles of royalty, and various other kinds of offerings that are specified in the liturgy, together with gods and goddesses who present them, and so on. All of these offerings are inexhaustible; they are unlimited in amount, they are perfect in quality, they do not just disappear, and they never get used up. This section is both the consecration of the offerings and the consecration of the place of practice. And the attitude with which this is done is that you are starting to purify your otherwise impure perception of your environment—of your body, of your mind, and of all the other materials and implements in your environment.

Following the consecration of the offerings is meditation on the four immeasurables. The four immeasurables are four attitudes that are to be cultivated without limit, which is why they are known as immeasurable, or unlimited. Unlimited means no limit on "how much" and no limit on "for whom." The first immeasurable, in the usual enumeration, is love. Immeasurable love means no limit on how much love and how much compassion you generate, and especially no limit on for whom you generate it.

> *May all beings be happy and free of suffering.*
> *May their happiness not diminish.*
> *May they abide in equanimity.*

Intrinsic to all four of these attitudes is impartiality. When enumerated separately, impartiality is the fourth of the four immeasurables—love, compassion, empathetic joy, and impartiality. However, when you actually practice them, you need to begin with the cultivation of impartiality. We all have some degree of love, some degree of compassion, and some degree of empathetic joy. But in order to make these genuine and to make them immeasurable we need to cultivate impartiality, which is why it is to be cultivated first. When we say that we all have some degree of love, we mean that we all wish that some beings be happy and possess causes of happiness. We all also have some degree of compassion—we all wish that some beings be free from suffering and the causes of suffering. The problem is that we generally wish these things only for certain beings and do not particularly care about what happens to other beings. Although our love and compassion are indeed love and compassion, they are partial; and because they are partial, they are impure and incomplete. If you cultivate impartiality, they become unlimited—which means that they become perfect. So the first stage in the cultivation of the four immeasurables is to cultivate impartiality towards beings, which means cultivating the attitude that you have the same amount of love and the same amount of compassion for all beings. And then, on that basis, you can strengthen the attitude of love—the desire that beings be happy and possess causes of happiness—and by strengthening it you will strengthen that attitude towards all beings in general. If you do not cultivate impartiality in the beginning, by strengthening your love for some you may generate aggression for others. Therefore, you need first to cultivate impartiality, and then, on the basis of impartiality, to cultivate the other three—love, compassion, and empathetic joy. However, in the text they are listed in the usual order, which places impartiality—here referred to as equanimity—at the end.

Essentially love consists of wanting others to be happy, and compassion consists of wanting others not to suffer. These two attitudes, of course, are excellent. But if they are present without any way to bring about what you wish—if your love is without any way to bring about the happiness of beings and your compassion is devoid of any way to remove the sufferings of beings—then they will actually become a cause of greater suffering and sadness for you. You will be more sensitive to the sufferings of others because of your attitude, but will feel unable to help. And so, instead of just the other being suffering, two beings will suffer—you will suffer as well. If, however, the attitudes of love and compassion include the understanding of how you can actually bring about happiness and freedom from suffering, then these attitudes do not become sources of depression. Therefore we expand the attitude of love from "may all beings be happy" to "may all beings be happy and possess causes of happiness," and expand the attitude of compassion from "may all beings be free from suffering" to "may all beings be free from suffering and free from causes of suffering." While you cannot confidently expect to be able to make all beings happy on the spot, you can gradually cause beings to accomplish or accumulate causes of happiness and to avoid and get rid of causes of suffering. And because you understand that in the long term you will be able to make beings happy and free beings from suffering, then these attitudes of love and compassion become not only confident but actually joyous. In this way, the effect of love and compassion is no longer sadness and depression but empathetic joy, which is the third immeasurable. In this way, you train or cultivate the four immeasurables as a preliminary for meditation on the Medicine Buddha.

Now to apply the four immeasurables to the specific context of the Medicine Buddha practice: Since the primary cause of suffering in this case is the physical affliction of sickness, and since that is the initial focus of this practice, you can focus on that in your meditation on the four immeasurables. Thinking that it is in order to remove the sickness of beings that you are praying to the Medicine Buddha, meditating upon the Medicine Buddha, reciting the Medicine Buddha's mantra, and so on, you could formulate the four immeasurables in the following way: Immeasurable love would be the attitude, "May all beings possess the happiness of well-being and the causes of that." Immeasurable compassion would be, "May all beings be free from sickness and the causes of sickness." Immeasurable empathetic joy would be rejoicing in the well-being of others and in their freedom from illness. And immeasurable impartiality would be generating these aspirations and attitudes not merely for those you know, such as your own friends and family, but for all beings without exception.

When you do the Medicine Buddha practice with the intention and aspiration to benefit yourself and others in this way, sometimes you will perceive an evident benefit: Either you or someone else will be freed from sickness in a way that you identify as a result of your practice. This will give you greater confidence in the practice. At other times, no matter how much you practice and how hard you pray and how many mantras you say, you will not perceive any evident benefit. And this will cause you to doubt the practice, and you will think, "Well maybe it doesn't really work." But you need to remember that the benefit of this practice is not like the direct physical effect of the function of a machine, such as something that emits a laser beam. There is always a result from doing this practice, but the way in which the result will manifest is not absolutely definite. So in your attitude towards the results of practice, you need to have a long-term focus. In that way you can keep the practice focused on the four immeasurables. That completes the preliminaries to the Medicine Buddha practice.

Visualization

Now I am going to explain the actual visualization of oneself as the Medicine Buddha, which causes the blessing of the Medicine Buddha to enter into one, and the simultaneous visualization of the mandala of the Medicine Buddha in front of one, which serves as an object of one's supplication and a field for the accumulation of merit through making offerings.

The visualization is begun by purifying your perception of the entire world, including your own body and mind. This is done initially through the single recitation of the mantra of the pure nature or the mantra of the purity of dharmata:

OM SOBHAWA SHUDDHA SARWA DHARMA SOBHAWA SHUDDHO HAM

The meaning of the mantra reflects its significance. Following the initial syllable *Om*, the next word is *sobhawa*, which means the nature, and then *shuddha*, which means pure. Ordinarily the things that appear to us—the world of external appearances and our internal perceiving mind—appear to us as being impure because of the presence of the kleshas and other obscurations in our minds. What is meant here by the pure nature is that, although we perceive appearances and our minds in this impure way, this is not their actual nature. While they seem to be impure, in fact, in their nature, in and of themselves, they are pure. Following the statement "pure by nature," are the words *sarwa*, which means all, and *dharma*, which means things. So the mantra states that "all things are pure in their nature."

The term *dharma* usually has one of two meanings. One meaning is *sadharma* or the genuine dharma, the teachings of the Buddha, and the other meaning is thing, things in general, anything that can be known. Here it refers to things.

The mantra continues with the words *sobhawa shuddho* a second time and then *A Hum*. Because of the way that Sanskrit links words, the second *shuddha* and *A Hum* are joined together to become *shuddho ham*. Again *swabava shuddha* means pure in its nature or their nature; *A Hum* can mean self or the very embodiment of something. Here it is understood to mean that not only are all things pure in their nature, but that they are in and of themselves the very embodiment of that purity. So this mantra is essentially a statement of why the path can lead to the result. Because things are pure in their nature, because this purity is present within the nature of things, then it can manifest as experience and as a result—through taking that inherent purity as a path. For example, because sesame oil is present within sesame seeds, then by pressing the seeds you can extract the oil. If there were no oil present within the sesame seeds, you could not get oil, no matter how hard you pressed the seeds. Because the hidden nature of things is their purity, then by regarding things as pure, you can directly experience them as pure; you can directly experience their purity. The *swabawa* mantra is used here to point this out, and also to introduce or begin the samadhi which will culminate in the visualization of yourself as the Medicine Buddha.

Following the recitation of the *sobhawa* mantra, you say the Tibetan words, *tong pa nyi du jur*, which means that everything becomes empty or becomes emptiness.

Everything becomes emptiness.

This describes the beginning of the visualization. At this point you imagine that everything disappears, that everything becomes emptiness—not only in how it is but in how it manifests. However, it is important to remember that you are not pretending here that things are other than they are. You are using the imaginary dissolution of things into emptiness as an acknowledgment of the fact that things have been, from the very beginning,[9] empty in their nature.

The dissolution of ordinary impure appearances into emptiness is the first part of a two-step process that serves to counteract our usual superimposition of impurity onto appearances.[10] The second step is the emergence from or within that expanse of emptiness of the pure appearances which are the realm and palace of the Medicine Buddha.

*From its depth, this triple universe becomes
the exquisite palace, where*

The first step is to think that all of the impure appearances dissolve into emptiness, and the second is that from within that emptiness the realm and palace of the Medicine Buddha emerge. Now when you imagine that the place in which you are practicing has become the realm and palace of the Medicine Buddha, you do not limit this consideration to this world or to this planet alone. As it says in the liturgy, it is the entire billion worlds of this larger world system, or galaxy.

There are two ways that you can do this practice. The simplest way is to visualize yourself as the Medicine Buddha. The more elaborate way, which is indicated in the liturgy, is also to visualize the Medicine Buddha, surrounded by his retinue, present in front of you as well. It is easier for beginners to do the self-visualization alone; on the other hand, doing the front visualization as well gives one the opportunity to gather the accumulation of merit. In either case, in the midst of the realm of the Medicine Buddha, which you have visualized as emerging from the expanse of emptiness, there is a palace. This palace is square, and quite symmetrical. In the center of each of the four sides is a large gateway, each forming an entry into the palace. If you are doing the practice with both self and front visualizations, you need to visualize two palaces: one in the center of which you will sit as the self visualization; and one in front of you and somewhat elevated, which will serve as the residence for the front visualization.

> *On lion thrones, each with a lotus and moon disk on top*
> *Appear deep blue HUNGs, the seed syllable of myself and*
> *the main figure visualized in the front,*

In the center of the self-visualization's palace is a throne made of gold and jewels and other precious substances that is upheld by eight snow lions. The significance of the lion throne is primarily the sense of utter fearlessness—indicating the deity's freedom from fear and danger of any kind. On top of the throne is a fully opened lotus flower, on top of the center of which, lying flat, is a moon disc, on top of which you will be visualizing yourself seated in the form of the Medicine Buddha. In the center of the palace in the front visualization, you visualize a sixteen-petalled lotus, in the center of which you visual an eight-petalled lotus. In the center of the eight-petalled lotus, you visualize another lion throne, lotus, and moon disc seat, as in the self-visualization. There are eight- and sixteen-petalled lotuses in the front visualization because there will be additional Buddhas and bodhisattvas in those places.

Next, on top of the moon discs in both the front and self visualizations, you visualize a blue syllable [HUNG] HUM.[11] The HUM syllable on top of the moon disc in the self-visualization palace represents the essence of the mind or wisdom of the self-visualization deity, and the blue HUM on top of the moon disc in the front-visualization palace represents the essence of the mind or wisdom of the front-visualization deity. This particular syllable HUM is used because HUM is the sound of dharmata, the expression as sound of the nature[12] itself. It is blue because that is the color of the deity who will emerge from the syllable—the Medicine Buddha is blue, as is Vajradhara—but also because blue represents that which is unchanging and unfabricated.[13] Having visualized the syllables, you then visualize innumerable rays of light radiating from each of these syllables simultaneously. On the end of each ray of light are innumerable offering goddesses holding various offering substances which they present to all the Buddhas and bodhisattvas in all the directions throughout space. This vast array of Buddhas and bodhisattvas receives these offerings with pleasure, and as a consequence their nonconceptual compassion is aroused, which manifests as their blessings' coming back in the form of rays of blue light which dissolve into the HUM. Rays of light which went out bearing offerings are reabsorbed bearing blessings back into the two HUM syllables. Once again rays of light radiate outward from both HUM's simultaneously, this time purifying the entire external world, the entire universe, of everything in it that could possibly cause harm or suffering of any kind, and also purifying the mental continuums of all beings without exception of any kind of suffering or misery or cause of suffering. Then the rays of light are reabsorbed again into their respective HUM's. At that moment the syllables are instantly and simultaneously transformed into the Medicine Buddha.

from which, arises Menla, his body the color of
lapis lazuli and radiating light.

After this transformation, the self-visualized Medicine Buddha that you are identifying with is now considered your own body, and the front visualization is in front of you. The Medicine Buddha is a brilliant blue in color—the color of a precious stone called vaidurya, generally considered to be lapis lazuli. In appearance the Medicine Buddha is luminous and majestic and radiates innumerable rays of light primarily the color of his own body. Yidams can appear in a number of different ways—peaceful or wrathful and frightening; nirmanakaya or sambhogakaya in form, and so on. The Medicine Buddha is peaceful and in the nirmanakaya form.

> *He is clothed in the three dharma robes.*

Saying that he appears in nirmanakaya form means that, though some yidams appearing in sambhogakaya form wear lots of jewellery and silken robes and so on, the Medicine Buddha manifests in what is called the passionless appearance of a nirmanakaya Buddha, wearing only the three dharma robes commonly worn by the monastic sangha: the inner and outer upper robes and the lower skirt.

The Medicine Buddha has two arms.

> *His right hand in the mudra of supreme generosity*
> *holds an arura.*
> *His left hand in meditation mudra holds a begging bowl.*

His right hand is extended, palm outward, over his right knee in the gesture called supreme generosity. In it he holds the *arura*, or myrobalan, fruit. This plant represents all the best medicines. The position of his right hand and the *arura* which he holds represent the eradication of suffering, especially the suffering of sickness, using the means of relative truth. Sickness can be alleviated by adjusting the functioning of interdependent causes and conditions by the use of relative means within the realm of relative truth, such as medical treatment and so on. The giving of these methods is represented by the gesture of the Medicine Buddha's right hand.

His left hand rests in his lap, palm upward, in the gesture of meditative stability or meditation, which represents the eradication of sickness and suffering—and, indeed, the very roots of samsara—through the realization of absolute truth. From the point of view of either relative truth or absolute truth, the fundamental cause of sickness and suffering is a lack of contentment and the addictive quality of samsara. Therefore, to indicate the need for contentment, in his left hand he holds a begging bowl.

Because the mind of the Medicine Buddha is stainless and pure, his form reflects this in its excellence and physical perfection.

> *With the major and minor marks complete,*
> *he sits in the vajra posture.*

He is adorned by what are called the marks and signs, the primary and secondary indications of the awakening of a Buddha. In all aspects of his physical form—the crown protuberance, or *ushnisha*, the image of wheels on the soles of his feet, and so forth—the Medicine Buddha is identical to the Buddha Shakyamuni, with the single difference that the Buddha Shakyamuni's skin is golden in color, while the Medicine Buddha is blue. Because the Medicine Buddha is immersed in an unwavering samadhi of absorption within the realization of the nature of all things, and because this samadhi is utterly stable, he is seated with his legs fully crossed in the vajra posture. You visualize yourself in this form, and you visualize the front visualization in the same form as well.

Everything described up to this point—the palace, the throne, and the Medicine Buddha—pertains to both the self and the front visualizations. In the case of the front visualization, however, you will remember that the lion throne sits in the center of an eight-petalled lotus, which in turn sits in the center of a sixteen-petalled lotus. Now on seven of the eight petals of the eight petalled lotus, which surround the Medicine Buddha in the front visualization—on the seven petals other than the one directly in front of the Medicine Buddha—are the seven other Medicine Buddhas, the Buddha Shakyamuni and six others. As is the principal Medicine Buddha, they are all adorned by the thirty-two marks and the eighty signs of physical perfection which grace the body of a Buddha.

> *In particular, on the lotus petals of the front visualization*
> *Are the seven Buddhas, Shakyamuni and the others,*
> *and dharma texts.*

On the eighth petal, directly in front of the principal Medicine Buddha, is a volume of the dharma. The reason for this is that in the end it is the dharma that liberates us from samsara and from sickness. When we talk about the *sadharma*, or the genuine dharma, we are referring fundamentally to the third and fourth of the four noble truths: the truth of the cessation of suffering and the truth of the path leading to the cessation of suffering. The truth of cessation is the result of practice, which is the abandonment or transcendence of everything that is to be abandoned or transcended.[14] The truth of the path is the dharma we practice that leads to that transcendence. The dharma in essence is the experience and realization of the meaning of dharma[15] that is present within the minds of those who practice it and achieve its result. By extension, the dharma also refers to the tradition of passing on that meaning, and therefore one visualizes that meaning passed on from the Buddha down to the present day in the form of books on the petal directly in front of the Medicine Buddha visualized in front.

> *Surrounding them are the sixteen bodhisattvas,*
> *surrounding them are the ten protectors of the world,*
> *and the twelve great chiefs with their respective retinues.*
> *The four great kings are at the four gates.*

Surrounding the seven Medicine Buddhas and the volumes of dharma, are sixteen bodhisattvas on the petals of the sixteen-petalled lotus. These are the sixteen bodhisattvas who were the main recipients of the teachings of the Medicine Buddha sutras given by the Buddha. They all manifest in the sambhogakaya form, wearing ornate jewellery and so forth. Beyond the perimeter of that lotus, but still within the palace of the front visualization, are twenty-two other main deities, each of whom has a retinue. On the Medicine Buddha's right, forming a semicircle to the right of the principal deities, are the ten protectors of the directions—otherwise known as the ten protectors of the world. These are deities such as Brahma, Indra, and so forth. Likewise, forming a semicircle on the left side of the palace are the twelve yaksha chieftains or generals. Each of these figures is surrounded by a vast retinue of their own. Finally, in the four gates or gateways of the palace visualized in front are the four kings of the gods. They are visualized here because they are protectors of the Buddhadharma in general. Specifically whenever the Buddha taught, and especially whenever he exhibited miracles, he would emanate a magnificent magical palace like this one, and, to signify their function as protectors of his teachings, these four kings of the gods would guard each of the four gates as gatekeepers.

When you are practicing, if you can, visualize all of these deities. But if you cannot, do not be discouraged. Do not feel that somehow the practice has become ineffective or invalid because you cannot visualize each and every one of them. It is sufficient to generate as clear a visualization as you can of yourself as the Medicine Buddha and of the Medicine Buddha in front of you. If, in addition to that, you can visualize the seven additional Medicine Buddhas and the volumes of dharma, good. If, in addition to that, you can visualize the sixteen bodhisattvas, that is also good. But you should gauge the extent of the visualization to what you actually can do. In any case, the practice will be effective and will cause the blessing of dharma in general and the blessing of the Medicine Buddha in particular to enter you. It will serve its function and be effective, regardless of how you do the visualization. More important than how many deities you visualize is to understand what you are doing. And most important is to understand that by visualizing yourself as the Medicine Buddha you are not pretending to be something that you are not, and that by visualizing the Medicine Buddha and his retinue in front of you, you are not pretending that they are in a place where they are not. By definition, Buddhas are omniscient. Whenever someone thinks of them, brings them to mind, or supplicates them, they are aware of it and respond with their compassion and blessing. In the final analysis, the situation is identical to their actually being present anywhere they are thought of. Therefore, it is always appropriate to regard a Buddha that is present in one's mind as actually being present in front of one. When you think that the Medicine Buddha, together with his retinue, is present in front of you, it is really true that they are.

Visualizing yourself as the Medicine Buddha is also appropriate, because your fundamental nature—what you truly are—is Buddha nature. Buddha nature is essentially the potential to attain awakening. At some point in the future you will attain the same awakening or Buddhahood as the Medicine Buddha himself. By visualizing yourself as the Medicine Buddha, you are assuming the appearance of what fundamentally you are even now and what manifestly you will be upon your awakening. It is to acknowledge this truth that you assume the aspect of the body, speech, and mind of the Medicine Buddha, which is, therefore, entirely appropriate.

While it is entirely appropriate to visualize yourself as the Medicine Buddha and to visualize the Medicine Buddha and retinue in front of you, you may still have some hesitation or doubt that the visualization is anything more than just a visualization. This is understood, and therefore the next phase of the practice is designed to counteract that doubt. In order to alleviate any residual doubts you may have, you next invite the actual wisdom deities and dissolve them into the visualization.

From the three syllables in their three places and the
    HUNG *in their hearts,*
Lights radiate, invoking from the eastern

Buddha realms, countless
Wisdom deities which dissolve into myself and the one
visualized in front.

The first step in inviting the wisdom deities is to visualize in the three places of the self-visualized Medicine Buddha, in the three places of the Medicine Buddha visualized in front, and, if possible, in the three places of the rest of the deities in the retinue, the three syllables, OM AH HUNG. Inside your head you visualize a white OM, which is the essence of the body of the Medicine Buddha; in your throat a red AH, which is the essence of his speech; and in your heart a blue HUM, which is the essence of his mind. Visualizing these in the body of the self-visualized Medicine Buddha and in the bodies of the deities visualized in front, you then think that from these syllables rays of light of the corresponding colors—and most particularly rays of blue light from the HUM syllables in the heart centers of the deities—radiate. This radiation of light invites, from their individual Buddha realms, the deities of the mandala. Each of the eight Medicine Buddhas—the principle one and the seven Buddhas of the retinue—has his own realm, all of which are understood to be in the eastern direction.[16] From these different pure realms the eight Medicine Buddhas and their retinues of deities are invited and they all dissolve into you as the Medicine Buddha and into the front visualization. In practice you do not think that they immediately dissolve into you, but that they present themselves and are present in the sky in front of you, between the two palaces of the self and front visualizations.

Having described the visualization, you then recite a stanza that is an actual invitation to the deities to approach.

HUNG
The eight Menla brothers and all deities
without exception
I invite here to this place. Please rain upon us your
great blessings.

Bestow the supreme empowerment on those who are
worthy and faithful.
Dispel false guides and obstacles to long life.
NAMO MAHA BEKENDZE SAPARIWARA BENZA
SAMAYADZA DZA BENZA SAMAYA TIKTRA
LEN

First you invite the eight Medicine Buddhas together with their retinues, saying, "Please come to this place and rain down your great blessing upon me, the practitioner, and upon others." Then you ask that they, "Bestow the supreme empowerment upon me, the fortunate one, who has faith," and that, by so doing, they, "Please dispel obstacles, such as obstacles to life and longevity and other obstacles in general."

The mantra that follows seals and reinforces this act of invitation. The mantra means, "Great King of Medicine, together with your retinue, *vajra samaya jaja.*"[17] *Vajra samaya* means unchanging commitment or samaya. Here you are reminding these Buddhas of their commitment to liberate beings. From their initial generation of bodhicitta, up to and including the moment of their attainment of full Buddhahood, the motivation for their entire path was the wish to liberate beings. They therefore have an unchanging commitment—a vajra-like or indestructible samaya—to the liberation of beings. So when you say these words, *vajra samaya jaja*, you are saying to these Buddhas, "You must come here and bless me because you have committed yourself to do so." At that point, then, think with confidence that all of the wisdom deities of the mandala have actually come and are present in the sky in front of you.

The mantra that follows is *vajra samaya tiktralen. Vajra samaya* means unchanging commitment, and *tiktra* means to remain stable. With this mantra you are saying, "Through the power of your unchanging commitment to the welfare and liberation of beings, please dissolve inseparably into me and remain within me stably or permanently." At that point you think that all of the invited deities, reminded of their commitment and with their compassion aroused in that way, dissolve both into the self visualization and into the deities of the front visualization. And at that point think that your body, speech, and mind visualized as the Medicine Buddha and the body, speech, and mind of the Medicine Buddha have become indivisible.[18]

This dissolving of the actual wisdom deity into both the self and front visualizations is a remedy for one's habitual perception of things as impure or ordinary.

Having just dissolved the wisdom beings into oneself and into the front visualization—as a remedy for one's obscurations, one's wrongdoing, and one's conceptualization, we then receive empowerment. This phase of the practice is represented in the liturgy simply by the mantra:

OM HUM TRAM HRI AH ABHIKENTZA HUM

The visualization which accompanies the mantra is as follows: Once again you visualize the three syllables—OM AH HUM—in the three places of oneself as the Medicine Buddha and of the deities of the front visualization, and once again rays of light radiate from them—especially from the HUM in your heart—inviting this time the five male Buddhas of the five families with their retinues from their pure realms. The Buddhas are holding in their hands precious vases[19] filled with the ambrosia of wisdom, which they pour into you as the self-visualized Medicine Buddha through the aperture at the very center of the top of your head. The first part of this mantra—OM HUM TRAM HRI AH—represents this empowerment being administered by the five Buddhas simultaneously. OM represents Vairochana; HUM, Akshobhya; TRAM, Ratnasambhava; HRI, Amitabha; and AH, Amoghasiddhi.[20] Visualizing that this pure ambrosia fills your entire body, you think that it purifies all the wrongdoing, obscurations, and defilements of any kind whatsoever of your body, speech, and mind. The words *Abhikentza* mean empowerment.

Questions & Answers

Question: Does the Medicine Buddha ever have a consort and, if so, what is her name?

Rinpoche: In this case, because he is visualized in the form of a supreme nirmanakaya, he does not. There could be cases in which he is visualized in a sambhogakaya form with a consort in order to indicate the unity of upaya and prajna—it is possible, but I cannot think of an instance, and so I cannot say his consort's name is this or that.

Question: Rinpoche, in the visualization, there are eight petals and then sixteen petals around that. Petals aren't really that large and so it is difficult for me to visualize each of them containing a bodhisattva and his retinue. Is it like a window to their world or what is the best way to visualize this realistically?

Rinpoche: In pure realms flowers can get really big. But if it makes it easier to relate to, these are basically thrones that are somewhat connected with one another and that have the basic shape or style of flower petals.

Question: Rinpoche talked about the front visualization as being a field for the accumulation of merit. Why does the front visualization have something to do with accumulating merit?

Rinpoche: In this practice, as the liturgy indicates, merit is accumulated through paying homage and making various offerings—the mandala offering and the offering of praises and so forth—primarily to the front visualization. You accumulate merit by performing offerings to that in which you have absolute confidence, which is the actual Buddha. Therefore, it is easier to accumulate merit by making offerings to the front visualization, which you are perceiving as different from and possibly superior to yourself.

Question: When doing the mantra towards the end of the practice, do we focus our attention primarily on ourself and the mantra in our heart or do we alternate attention between the Buddha in front and ourselves?

Rinpoche: You apply it to both. You visualize the seed syllable and the mantra garland within the heart of both the self and front visualizations, and in both cases, you identify it as the embodiment of the wisdom or mind of the deity. Then normally you would think that rays of light radiate from the seed syllable and mantra garland in the heart of the self visualization. These rays of light strike and enter the hearts of the deities of the front visualization, arousing their compassion, causing rays of light to come from the front visualization and to dispel the sickness and suffering of all beings and so forth.

Question: I can't manage to visualize the front visualization and myself as the Medicine Buddha simultaneously. Should I alternate between them? Should I spend a chunk of time doing the front visualization and then come back to the self visualization for an amount of time?

Rinpoche: That's fine. You can go back and forth.

Question: Quickly or slowly or what?

Rinpoche: The best thing is to go back and forth as frequently as is comfortable.

Question: Rinpoche, does this particular sadhana have any special significance for you? Is this of special significance to the Thrangu lineage?

Rinpoche: This does not have any particular significance for me or my monastery, except that it is one of the three Medicine Buddha practices which is normally done in the Kagyu tradition as a whole. There is a long one, a medium one, and this one, which is the short one. We are practicing this one because it is the short one.

Question: What Tibetan word is being translating as "pure?"

Translator: *Takpa.*

Question: Is it always translated as "pure"?

Translator: By *me*, yes. A lot of people do a lot of different things; I cannot guarantee that they always call it "pure."

Question: Maybe Rinpoche could say what the word means.

Rinpoche: You can think of synonyms for pure as being "free of impurity," which by extension would mean "free of defect or imperfection." It would indicate that which is stainless, that which is perfect, flawless, and so on.

Question: Rinpoche, is there a particular significance for the light radiating from the eastern Buddha realms?

Rinpoche: In the sutras of the Medicine Buddha, the Buddha described their realms—the principal realm of the principal Medicine Buddha and the other realms of the attendant Buddhas—as all being in the east.

Question: When we visualize light going out to the universe, does that include everything? Rocks and trees and chairs and buildings?

Translator: At which point? During the creation of the deity or during the recitation of the mantra?

Question: During the recitation of the mantra.

Rinpoche: Yes. Initially, before the generation of the deity, you purify your perception of the entire universe by visualizing that it all dissolves into emptiness. Theoretically, from that point onward all impurity has ceased. But when you get to the repetition of the main mantra you can renew that purification by once again bringing to mind impure appearances and purifying them with the rays of light which emerge from the heart of the deity.

Question: Rinpoche, in other visualization practices, sometimes there's a sense of seeing one's own root teacher in the form of that deity. Is there anything like that in this practice?

Rinpoche: Yes, it is appropriate to identify the front visualization with your root guru. People relate to the front visualization in slightly different ways. If they feel particularly devoted to the Medicine Buddha, then they will primarily think of the front visualization as the actual Medicine Buddha. But they can also think of the front visualization as in essence their root guru.

Offerings

The next section of the practice is the accumulation of merit through making offerings. As indicated earlier, the self visualization presents offerings to the front visualization. Rays of light emerge from the heart of the self visualization. On the ends of these rays of light are offerings goddesses holding various offering substances, which they present to all the deities of the front visualization.

HUNG
Flowers, incense, lights, scents,
Food, music and so forth;
Forms, sounds, smells, tastes, touch, and all dharmas,
I offer to the deities.
May we perfect the two accumulations.
OM BENZA ARGHAM PADYAM PUPE DHUPE
ALOKE GENDHE NEWIDYE SHABDA RUPA
SHABDA GENDHE RASA SAPARSHE

TRATITSA HUNG

First they present a set of eight related offerings. First is drinking water, which is offered to the mouths of the deities. Second is water for washing or rinsing the feet, which is offered to the feet of the deities. Third is flowers, which are offered to the eyes of the deities. Fourth is incense, the scent of which is offered to the nose of the deities. Fifth is lamps, which are offered again to the eyes of the deities. Sixth is perfume, which is offered to the whole body of the deities. Seventh is food, offered to the mouths of the deities. And eighth is musical instruments symbolizing the sound of music, offered to the ears of the deities.

Offered with these eight offerings are the five offerings of pleasant things which are perceived by the five senses. These are beautiful forms, pleasant sounds, smells, tastes, and tactile sensations.

In general, offerings can be categorized into four types: outer, inner, secret, and ultimate. Outer offerings are essentially the offering of whatever is beautiful and pleasant in the external world. What is being presented to the deity here are all things in the external world that are appropriate and beautiful. By making these offerings, you gather the accumulation of merit. Therefore it says in the text, "By making these offerings to the deities, may we complete the two accumulations." The two accumulations are the conceptual accumulation of merit and the nonconceptual accumulation of wisdom. The making of the offerings themselves gathers or completes the conceptual accumulation of merit; when these offerings are made within the recognition of the ultimate unreality of the offerings, the offerer, and the act of offering—when there is recognition of the emptiness of the offerings, the emptiness of the offerer, and the emptiness of the act of offering—then the nonconceptual accumulation of wisdom is also completed.

Finally the offerings are presented at the end of the stanza with the offering mantras that denote them. The word *vajra* at the beginning of the mantra indicates that the nature of the offering substances is emptiness. Then the individual offerings are named in order, and finally *tra ti tsa,* or *pra ti cha,* means individually to each. So to each of the deities the offerings are presented.

At this point in most Vajrayana practices the outer offerings would be followed by the inner, secret, and ultimate offerings. The inner offering is generally the offering of some kind of torma. Torma is referred to in this context as an inner offering because the offering of it is a way to increase your samadhi, your meditative absorption, which is an internal phenomenon. The secret offering is the offering of the unity of bliss and emptiness, which is made in order to induce or stabilize this recognition in the practitioner. In the same way, the ultimate offering, the offering of the recognition of the ultimate nature itself, is made in order to stabilize that recognition in the practitioner. Here these offerings are not given because this practice, while it is Vajrayana in tradition, tends to follow the sutras in style. Therefore, the offerings that follow are those which are commonly presented in the sutras themselves.

The next two sets of offerings presented are the eight auspicious substances and the eight auspicious signs or marks.

HUNG
The eight foremost auspicious substances,
The best royal white mustard seed, and the others,
I offer to the deity.
May the two accumulations be perfected.
MANGALAM ARTHA SIDDHI HUNG

The eight auspicious substances are so called because they are eight substances or things which are connected with the arising of dharma in this world. They are considered auspicious because they were significant in bringing about the arising of the teachings. The eight auspicious signs or designs appear on the body of a Buddha and are therefore considered auspicious.

The first of the eight auspicious substances is the conch shell. Immediately after the Buddha's awakening he realized that, although he himself had seen perfectly and completely the nature of all things, the dharmata—which is profound and tranquil and beyond all elaboration—he felt that were he to try to explain this to anyone else, they would be unable to understand it. So he resolved to remain in samadhi, alone in the forest. After he had remained in samadhi for forty-nine days, the god Indra, who was an emanation of a bodhisattva, appeared in front of the Buddha and offered him a white conch shell with its spiral going clockwise as an offering to encourage the Buddha to teach. It was in response to that first offering that the Buddha decided to turn the dharmachakra, or to teach the dharma. As a consequence of which beings have the opportunity to encounter the dharma and attain its results. For that reason, the conch shell with its clockwise swirl, is considered auspicious.

The second auspicious substance is yoghurt. This is connected with the Buddha's teaching in that in order to practice dharma properly we need to abandon or transcend two extremes in lifestyle or conduct. One of these extremes is hedonism, in which your goal and your endeavour is to seek as much pleasure as possible—including the acquisition of fine clothes, fine food, and so on. The problem with this extreme is that, if it becomes your goal or obsession, it leaves no time or energy for the practice of dharma. But we also need to abandon the other extreme, which is mortification of the body,[21] because the attempt to attain something through tormenting or depriving your physical body of what it needs does not lead to awakening, and in fact can slow down your progress towards the development of profound wisdom. In order to show by example that it is necessary to abandon the extreme of hedonism, the Buddha left the palace of his father, who was a king, and lived for six years on the banks of the Naranjana River in conditions of utmost austerity. But in order to show that one must also abandon the extreme of mortification, he accepted immediately before his awakening an offering of a mixture of yoghurt and extremely condensed milk, which was given to him by a Brahmin woman named Lekshe. Immediately upon his consuming this offering of yoghurt, all of the marks and signs of physical perfection which adorn the body of a

Conch Shell

Durva Grass

Bilva Fruit

Givam

Buddha, which had become somewhat indistinct during his years of austerity, immediately became distinct and resplendent.

The third auspicious substance is durva grass, which was offered to the Buddha by the grass-cutter and seller Tashi—meaning auspicious—shortly before his awakening, from which he made the mat-like seat on which he sat at the time of his awakening. Therefore, because it is connected with the Buddha's awakening, which is the event that transformed this period of history from a period of darkness into a period of illumination, durva grass is also considered an auspicious substance.

The fourth auspicious substance is vermilion. The origin of the auspiciousness of vermilion is this: When the Buddha was in the process of attaining awakening or just about to attain it, Mara appeared and, exhibiting various sorts of unpleasant magical displays in order to obstruct the Buddha, finally challenged him, saying, "You cannot attain awakening; you cannot do this." In response to which the Buddha said, "Yes, I can, because I have completed the two accumulations over three periods of innumerable eons." In response, Mara said, "Well, who is your witness? Who can you bring to prove this?"—in response to which the Buddha extended his right hand down past his right knee and touched the earth. The goddess of the earth then appeared out of the earth and, offering the Buddha vermilion, said, "I serve as witness that he has completed the two accumulations throughout these three periods of innumerable eons."

The fifth auspicious substance is bilva fruit. The origin of the auspiciousness of this fruit is that when the Buddha, while living in the palace compound of his father, the king of the Shakyas, first observed the sufferings of birth, aging, sickness, and death and resolved to attain freedom from them, he initially went to the root of a tree and practiced meditation there. During that time he developed a perfect state of shamatha, in acknowledgment of which the goddess or spirit of the tree offered him a bilva fruit.

The sixth auspicious substance is a mirror. The origin of the auspiciousness of the mirror is that when the Buddha had received and consumed the yoghurt which he was offered by the Brahmin woman Lekshe, his physical form, which had become emaciated from his six years of austerity, was restored to its full vigour and majesty, causing the thirty-two marks and eighty signs of physical perfection to be vivid and apparent, in response to which the goddess of form—which in this instance appears to be a goddess of the desire realm gods—appeared in front of the Buddha and offered him a mirror so that he could witness his own physical majesty and splendour.

The seventh auspicious substance is called *givam*, a medicinal substance that is derived from some part of the body of the elephant—possibly from the elephant's gall bladder. It is auspicious because it commemorates an occasion long after the Buddha's awakening when the Buddha's cousin, Devadata—who was always attempting to kill or otherwise harm the Buddha and had been doing so for many lives because he was afflicted with great jealousy of the Buddha—finally attempted to assassinate the Buddha by sending a mad elephant

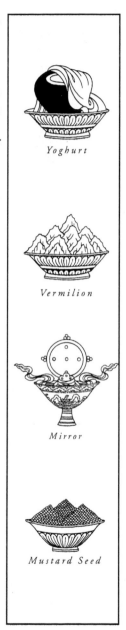

Yoghurt

Vermilion

Mirror

Mustard Seed

running out into the path where the Buddha was walking. The Buddha emanated ten lions from his ten fingers, which slowed the elephant down. The elephant then bowed to the Buddha and offered himself, including his body, to the Buddha. Since *givam*, which is an effective medicine, comes from the body of an elephant, it commemorates that occasion in which the Buddha conquered the aggression of the mad elephant.

The eighth auspicious substance is white mustard seed, which was offered to the Buddha by Vajrapani on one of the fifteen days during the Buddha's period of exhibition of miracles. At one time during the Buddha's lifetime there were six prominent non-Buddhist religious teachers in India. At one point they gathered together and, in order to attempt to discredit the Buddha, they challenged him to a competition of miracles. The Buddha accepted,[22] and the competition occurred at the beginning of what is now the first month of the Tibetan and Asian calendars. The Buddha's exhibition of miracles occurred from the first to the fifteenth day of the first lunar month. For the first eight days, the six other religious teachers competing were still present, but on the eighth day the Buddha scared them off in the following way: From the Buddha's throne the bodhisattva Vajrapani, accompanied by five fearsome *rakshasas,* emerged. Seeing that, the six *tirtika* teachers ran off as fast as they could and did not come back. For the remaining week the Buddha exhibited miracles alone without any competition. When Vajrapani emerged from the Buddha's throne, he offered the Buddha white mustard seed, which therefore commemorates this occasion.

These eight auspicious substances are seemingly common things, but they have great auspicious significance because each of them commemorates a specific occasion connected with the arising of dharma in this world, its teaching, its increase, and the demonstration of its power and benefit.

Thus, you offer the eight auspicious substances to the Medicine Buddha and his retinue, making the aspiration to complete the two accumulations by offering them. The mantra at the end of that stanza is *mangalam,* which means auspicious, and *artha siddhi,* which makes it the accomplishment of auspiciousness.

The next set of offerings are the eight auspicious signs or marks.[23]

> HUNG
> *The eight foremost auspicious symbols,*
> *The peerless royal vase and all others,*
> *I offer to the deity.*
> *May sentient beings perfect the two accumulations.*
> MANGALAM KUMBHA HUNG

In general, every Buddha is adorned with the thirty-two marks and the eighty signs, but of all of these, eight are foremost. These eight marks or shapes of these items resemble the shapes of particular parts of the Buddha's body, and have therefore come to serve as emblems of the Buddhadharma. The first of these is the parasol. The round shape of the parasol is like the beautifully round shape of the Buddha's head.

The second sign or symbol is the auspicious fish; the shape of the fish represents the shape of the Buddha's eyes when his eyes were half-closed in the posture of meditation. The third is the auspicious vase, which represents the Buddha's throat, in part because of the shape of his neck, but also because out of the throat of the Buddha emerges the sacred dharma which, like the ambrosia from a precious vase, satisfies all the needs of beings, assuages the thirst of samsara, removes suffering, brings happiness, and is inexhaustible.

The fourth is the auspicious conch, which in this case represents the speech of the Buddha. The conch is used as a musical instrument and as a horn to call people from a great distance. It is famous as having a resounding and clear sound. In the same way, the Buddha's speech is always of an appropriate volume and melody. If you are sitting close to the Buddha, his voice does not sound too loud, but if you are sitting very far away from him you can still hear it.

The fifth is the precious victory banner. The precious victory banner represents the fitting and beautiful quality of the Buddha's form in

Parasol

Vase

Victory Banner

Lotus

general, which is perfectly proportioned. All of his body parts are the right size for the rest of his body; it is not as though he has a huge head and his arms are too short or his legs are too short or anything like that. His body is perfectly proportioned.

The sixth one is the glorious knot,[24] which represents the Buddha's heart or mind. This doesn't mean that he literally has the design of the glorious knot on his chest. It means that his mind or his heart knows everything completely and clearly, without limitation.

The seventh is the lotus, which represents the tongue of the Buddha, which is supple, fine, and slender. With it he can speak clearly. In whatever he wants to say his enunciation is perfect; also his tongue and saliva improve the taste of all food.

The eighth is the auspicious wheel, which is actually found as a design on the souls of the Buddha's feet—the image of a golden wheel. This represents his turning of the wheel of the dharma, by means of which beings are liberated.[25]

Because these eight marks or signs are images that naturally occur on a Buddha's body or resemble certain qualities of the Buddha, then they have become embodiments in and of themselves of auspiciousness and goodness. Therefore, it is believed that to keep them in your home, or to wear them on your body, brings auspiciousness.

In this sadhana we offer these eight shapes or signs to the deities in order to bring about the auspiciousness of them, and by offering them we accumulate great merit, through which inauspicious circumstances that inhibit the dharma practice of the practitioner, and of beings in general, are averted. While offering we make the aspiration that by these offerings all beings without exception will perfect the two accumulations: the conceptual accumulation of merit and the non-conceptual accumulation of wisdom.

The mantra at the end of this stanza is *mangalam kumbha hum. Mangalam* means auspicious; *kumbaha* means vase. The vase is used here to indicate all eight of these signs or shapes. Because it represents the shape of the Buddha's throat, and because it was out of the Buddha's throat originally that the dharma issued forth, the vase is considered of foremost importance.

The next offering is the offering of the seven articles of royalty, which are seven possessions,[26] literally speaking, things [and types of animals and people] that are always found in the entourage of a chakravartin; a certain type of monarch who rules over an entire world or universe.

> HUNG *The sources of pleasure, the seven*
>   *precious articles,*
> *The most excellent royal one, the jewel,*
>   *and the others,*
> *I offer to the deity.*
> *May I perfect the two accumulations.*
> **OM MANI RATNA HUNG**

A chakravartin appears during the best or finest periods of history, during what is called a fortunate eon or period. The seven articles of

Fish

Conch

Glorious Knot

Wheel

royalty distinguish a chakravartin from any other monarch; however the true internal meaning of these seven articles is that they represent, or correspond internally to the seven limbs of the path of awakening, which are seven qualities that all Buddhas and bodhisattvas possess as factors of their attaining awakening. So when you make this offering to the deities, you think that externally you are offering the seven articles of royalty as representations of the seven aspects of the path to awakening.

You present these offerings to all the deities of the mandala visualized in front, making the aspiration that by doing so you will complete the two accumulations—the conceptual accumulation of merit and the nonconceptual accumulation of wisdom.

The first of the seven articles of royalty is the precious jewel, which corresponds to the virtue of faith. A bodhisattva must possess abundant and excellent faith to serve as ground for the development of all good qualities. The meaning of this is that if one has faith, then all other qualities, such as meditative stability, diligence, insight into the meaning of dharma and so on, will definitely arise, and on the basis of their arising, one will be able to eradicate all that is to be transcended or abandoned.

The second branch of awakening is knowledge or insight, prajna. Of the seven articles of royalty, this knowledge corresponds to the precious wheel, which enables the chakravartin to be victorious against any kind of invasion or warfare. In the same way, it is knowledge, or prajna, that enables one to conquer the kleshas and ignorance.[27]

The third branch of awakening is samadhi or meditative absorption, which serves as the necessary ground for knowledge or prajna. If prajna is grounded in samadhi, then it will be stable, tranquil, effective, and appropriate or correct. If it is not grounded in samadhi then prajna goes off the track, becomes incorrect and runs wild, so that it actually is more of a problem than a benefit. The third article of royalty is the consort of the monarch. The consort serves to keep the monarch on track, to pacify and tame the monarch. So therefore, the consort corresponds to samadhi.

The fourth branch of awakening is joy, which arises from the correct presence and application of both samadhi and prajna. Joy here refers, for example, to the joy of the attainment of the first bodhisattva level, which is called the Utterly Joyful. Of the seven articles of royalty, joy corresponds to the precious minister. In most enumerations this is a minister who gives wise council to the monarch and therefore promotes joy. Sometimes it is also called the precious householder, which is the subject of the monarch who also brings appropriate advice.

The fifth limb of awakening is diligence and this corresponds to the precious excellent horse. Just as an excellent horse enables the monarch to travel anywhere they wish to go with great speed, in the same way the possession of diligence enables the bodhisattva to cultivate the qualities of samadhi and prajna, and, through cultivating them, to eradicate the kleshas and to increase all positive qualities.

The sixth article of royalty is the precious elephant. The significance of this elephant is that it is extremely peaceful and tame, so it represents, from among the seven limbs of awakening, the faculty of mindfulness, which is a mind kept tranquil and always consciously aware of what is going on in the mind and what one's actions are.

The seventh and last limb of awakening is equanimity, a state of mind in which the bodhisattva is free from the afflictions of attachment to some things and aversion to other things. Through the faculty of equanimity, the bodhisattva overcomes the warfare of the kleshas. Of the seven articles of royalty, it is represented by the precious general, because the precious general overcomes all warfare and aggression. So these are the seven articles of royalty, which are offered as symbols of the seven limbs or factors of awakening.

Externally one is symbolically offering the seven articles of royalty, but internally one is offering the seven limbs of awakening. Offering the seven limbs of awakening means cultivating these virtues within oneself. By cultivating them within oneself, one enters the true and genuine path leading to awakening, which is the most pleasing of all things to all Buddhas and bodhisattvas. The cultivation of these and other virtues is the ultimate or true offering to Buddhas and bodhisattvas, which is why they are offered at this point.

The mantra used to complete this offering refers to the first of the seven articles, the precious jewel. *Mani* means jewel and *ratna* means precious.

The next offering, which completes the main section of the offerings, is the offering of a mandala.

> HUNG *The foremost of all, Mount Meru*
> *With its four continents and subcontinents*
> *I offer to the deity.*
> *May the two accumulations be perfected.*
> OM RATNA MANDALA HUNG

In general, of course, we make these offerings in order to gather and complete the accumulation of merit. We do not make them for the benefit of the Buddhas and bodhisattvas, who are their ostensible recipients. Buddhas and bodhisattvas are not particularly pleased by the presentation of offerings or displeased by their absence. The only real reason for making offerings is that the person making them gathers the accumulation of merit by doing so. We make offerings for our own benefit,[28] and it is how it affects us that is important. Offerings are not limited to that which you can actually physically assemble around you as offering substances. Offerings can be of any of three types, which are called actually assembled, mentally emanated, and produced through the power of aspiration. Actually assembled offerings are physically present and under your power to offer. Mentally emanated offerings are offerings that you imagine, that you do not actually have physically present before you, but that you can imagine clearly enough to offer in your mind. Offerings offered through the power of aspiration are things that are so vast and limitless that you cannot even encompass them in your mind or imagine them, but you can at least make the aspiration to offer them to the Buddhas and bodhisattvas. It is said that any of these three types of offerings will all produce the accumulation of merit. We use the offering of the entire universe as a mandala because the vastness of it produces great merit.

Specifically mentioned are the central mountain, Mount Meru, together with the continents surrounding it. These together, along with everything that goes with them, make up the mandala, which is considered the principal among all offerings. In detail, the offering consists of Mount Meru, which includes on top of Mount Meru the second of the desire god realms—enumerated from the bottom up—called the heaven or god-realm of the thirty-three. Surrounding Mount Meru are seven concentric rings[29] of golden mountains with lakes in between them. In these seven golden mountains and on their lakes live the gods of the first realm of the desire god realms and the four great kings—the same four kings who are guardians in the mandala of the Medicine Buddha. When you offer Mount Meru, you also think that you are offering all of the wealth of those god's realms. Outside those seven golden mountains are the four main continents with their eight subcontinents, which are the habitation of humans—all of the wealth, possessions, splendour, and beauty of which you offer as well. In short, you offer the world, indeed the whole universe, and all it contains to all of the deities, and you make the aspiration that by so doing, you complete the two accumulations and that you and the whole world be free from sickness.

After the fundamental offerings—the eight traditional offerings of water, flowers, incense, and so forth, and the offering of everything that is pleasing to the five senses—there have occurred four different sets of offerings: the eight auspicious substances, the eight auspicious signs, the seven articles of royalty, and finally the offering of the mandala. The next offering is the offering of ablution—of washing the bodies of the deities. This is done in order to create the auspicious basis for the removal of your own wrongdoing, your own defilements, and your own obscurations—the afflictive obscurations and the cognitive obscurations.

HUNG
With scented water

I bathe the sugata's body.
Although the deity is flawless,
This creates the auspicious connection for purifying
*   all wrongs and obscurations.*
OM SARWA TATHAGATA ABIKEKATE SAMAYA
SHRIYE HUNG

Here you think that from the heart of yourself visualized as the Medicine Buddha rays of light are emanated. On the tips of each of these rays are offering goddesses holding precious vases filled with ambrosia. With the ambrosia from these vases, they bathe the bodies of the primary Medicine Buddha, the seven other Medicine Buddhas, the sixteen bodhisattvas, and all of the other deities in the mandala. The words of the text say, "With scented water I bathe the sugata's body; although the deity is without stain, this creates the auspicious basis for purifying all wrongdoing and obscurations."

This offering of ablution is culminated with the mantra, *Om Sarwa Tathagata Abikekate Samaya Shriye Hung. Sarva* means all. *Tathagata* means tathagatas or Buddhas. And *abikekate* refers to this process which in some contexts means empowerment, but in this context means ablution. Through this offering you increase the splendour and majesty of the deities; therefore, there is the words *shriye*, which means splendid, majestic, or glorious.

The next offering, which goes along with ablution, is drying the bodies of the deities, which is done by visualized offering goddesses holding fine white cotton towels scented with perfume.

HUNG
With a scented, soft white cloth
I dry the victor's body.
Although you, the deity, are flawless,
This creates the auspicious connection for
*   freedom from suffering.*
OM KAYA BISHODHANI HUNG

You state in these two stanzas that you are not washing and drying the deities because they are dirty or have stains that need to be washed away, and so on; you are drying the bodies of the deities after washing them because it creates the interdependent cause of drying up or removing the suffering of all beings. Therefore, you make the aspiration that the suffering of all beings—especially the sufferings of physical sickness and mental affliction—be removed. *Kaya bishodhani* means the purification of the body.

Next is the offering of clothes or robes to the deities of the mandala.

> HUNG *With these beautiful saffron robes*
> *I clothe the victor's body.*
> *Although your body is never cold,*
> *This creates the auspicious connection for vitality to flourish.*
> OM BENZA WAYTRA AH HUNG

Having bathed and dried them, next we have to offer them appropriate robes. The robes that are actually mentioned in the first line of this stanza are those that are offered to the Medicine Buddha and to the seven Buddhas in his retinue, all of whom, since they are manifesting in supreme nirmanakaya form, wear only the beautiful saffron red and yellow robes which are worn by Buddhas. As the visualized goddesses offer the robes, you recite, "With these I clothe the Victor's body." As in the previous offerings, you are making this offering, not because the Medicine Buddha is in any danger of becoming cold, but in order to create the auspicious basis for benefiting yourself and others. Therefore, you say, "Although your body is never cold, this creates the auspicious basis for the flourishing of vitality and physical splendour." As a result of this offering vitality and physical splendour will arise in you and others through the power of your aspiration. Although not mentioned specifically in the liturgy, the clothing offered to the bodhisattvas is appropriate to their appearance [in sambhogakaya form]: elegant garments of multicolored silk and jewellery made of gold and jewels, and so on. The bodhisattvas are offered fine clothes and jewellery not because they are particularly attached to them, but because by offering them you create the auspicious basis for the increase of vitality. The word *vastra* in the mantra means robes or clothing or fabric.

Each of these sections—ablution, drying, and offering clothing—has its own particular significance. The fundamental significance of all three of them is indicated in connection with the second, where it says, "I make this offering in order to establish the auspicious basis for the removal of suffering." The point of making these offerings is to remove the suffering of beings, which is primarily accomplished on the level of auspicious interdependence by the second offering, drying. But to remove the suffering of beings you must first remove the causes of suffering, which are wrongdoing and obscurations. So therefore, drying is preceded by ablution, the symbolic function of which is to purify the wrongdoing and obscurations of all beings. Finally, once the suffering has been removed, what develops in its place is a state of mental and physical well-being—including physical vitality, splendour and health—and a state of wisdom and peace within the mind, the interdependent cause of the arising of which is established by the offering of robes and clothing, which is the third part.

Praises

Following the offerings come the praises. The praises are performed by imagining that offering goddesses emanated from the light rays from your heart sing the praises of the deities in the words of the liturgy with beautiful melodies. Praised are the qualities of body, speech, and mind of the Medicine Buddha and his retinue. These praises are not done in order to please the Medicine Buddha; Buddhas and bodhisattvas are not pleased by praise nor displeased by its absence. One performs the praises to remind oneself, the practitioner, of the qualities of the deities. This increases one's devotion and one's resolve or desire to attain the state of the deities, which increases one's diligence in practice.

The praises consist of three stanzas. The first is a praise of the Medicine Buddha. The second is a praise of the other seven Medicine

Buddhas and the sixteen bodhisattvas. And the third is a praise of the remaining deities of the mandala, including the ten protectors of the ten directions, the twelve yaksha chieftains, and so forth.

The first stanza is addressed to the Medicine Buddha.

> HUNG
> *Your body is like a mountain, the color of lapis lazuli.*
> *You dispel the suffering of illness in sentient beings.*
> *Surrounded by a retinue of eight bodhisattvas,*
> *Holder of Medicine, precious deity, I praise and*
> *prostrate to you.*

The first line praises the appearance of his body or form: "The color of your body is like a mountain of lapis or vaidurya," which is to say that in appearance his body is like the stainless mass of a blue jewel, like a lapis or vaidurya, and radiant with rays of light. So that is a praise of the majesty of his appearance. The second line is praise of his activity, and it says, "You remove the sufferings of sickness of all beings." Sufferings of sickness here refer expressly to the literal suffering of physical illnesses, but also by implication ultimately to the sickness and the suffering of the sickness of samsara itself, which the Medicine Buddha also dispels.

Having praised his appearance and activity, you then praise his retinue. Here the retinue referred to in the liturgy is not the retinue of the mandala; what is referred to here are the eight great bodhisattvas who exemplify the Mahayana sangha. These are not the same as the sixteen bodhisattvas in the mandala; in fact, not all eight of these eight primary bodhisattvas are among the sixteen, although some of them are. Generally speaking, when we talk about the sangha, there is the ordinary sangha of the common vehicle and the exalted sangha of the Mahayana, which is made up of bodhisattvas. These are exemplified by what are called the eight close offspring of the Buddha, eight great bodhisattvas such as Manjushri, Avalokiteshvara, Vajrapani, and so on.[30] Then in the last line you say, "I pay homage to and praise that deity who holds the precious medicine," which is another way of referring to the Medicine Buddha himself.

The second stanza of praise praises the three jewels in general, exemplified by the Buddhas, dharma, and sangha found in this mandala.

> *Excellent Name, Precious Moon, Fine Gold, Free of Misery,*
> *Resounding Dharma Ocean, Dharma Mind, Shakyamuni,*
> *The genuine dharma, the sixteen bodhisattvas, and others,*
> *To the precious three jewels, I offer praise and prostrate.*

First mentioned are the seven other Medicine Buddhas—Excellent Name, Precious Moon, Fine Gold, Free of Misery, Resounding Dharma Ocean, Dharma Mind, and Buddha Shakyamuni. Then, following that, is mentioned the dharma itself, visually represented in the mandala by the sutras and commentaries but also understood as being the essence of the path. Finally, for the sangha it mentions "the sixteen bodhisattvas, and so forth," which means all of the Mahayana sangha, as exemplified by the sixteen bodhisattvas found within this mandala. Then one completes the praise by saying, "I pay homage to and praise the three precious jewels."

The final stanza is a praise to the remaining deities of the mandala and to all others who are associated with the mandala.

> *To Brahma, Indra, the Great Kings,*
>   *the Protectors of the Ten Directions,*
> *The twelve yaksha chiefs and all their assistants,*
> *Vidyadharas and rishis of medicine, divine and human,*
> *To the deities of ambrosial medicine,*
>   *I offer praise and prostrate.*

First mentioned are Brahma and Indra, who are two among the ten protectors of the ten directions; and then the four great kings; the twelve yaksha generals or chieftains, together with their retinues; and then finally all of the holders of the knowledge of medicine and those who have mastered medicine, who here are referred to as Vidyadharas and rishis of medicine, both those living in the realms of the gods and those living in the realms of humans. In short, one pays homage to and praises all of the deities of this mandala of ambrosial medicine.

All of the stages of the practice so far—the visualization of the bodies of the deities, the dissolution of the wisdom deities into them, the presentation of offerings and of praises to the deities—are aspects of the practice of the generation stage. In general, generation stage practice needs to have three characteristics: clear appearance or clarity of appearance, stable pride, and recollection of purity. What is meant by clear appearance is simply that there be a clear and distinct visualization of whatever it is you are visualizing. Whether you are visualizing the Medicine Buddha alone, that is to say yourself as the Medicine Buddha and the Medicine Buddha in front of you, or in addition to that you are visualizing the seven other Medicine Buddhas surrounding the front visualization, or in addition to that you are visualizing the sixteen bodhisattvas, or in addition to that you are visualizing the entire mandala with the ten protectors and the twelve chieftains, and so on, in any case, whatever you are visualizing, clear appearance means that the appearance of the deities—the color, the shape, the ornaments and costumes and robes, the scepters and other things that are held in the hands, and so on—should be visualized in a way that allows your mind to remain stable and calm while nevertheless generating a clear and vivid image.

The second characteristic of generation stage practice is stable pride. Generally speaking, of course, pride is something we want to get rid of—it is a klesha. But here the word pride means something that is very necessary in Vajrayana practices. Pride means being free of the misconception that, in visualizing yourself as the Medicine Buddha or in visualizing the Medicine Buddha in front of you, you are pretending that things are other than what they are. Stable pride here means recognizing that, although you are meditating on the Medicine Buddha as a conscious act, nevertheless, that is what you actually are. It is acknowledging that you actually are the Medicine Buddha. In the case of the front visualization it is acknowledging or recognizing that the front visualization is the actual presence of the Medicine Buddha, right in front of you. So stable pride really refers to an attitude of confidence, trust and belief. It is important to recognize that when you do the self visualization and the front visualization you are not merely imagining something that is fictitious. You are not pretending that things are other than they are. When you make these offerings—admittedly mentally emanated—to the deities, you should reflect upon the fact that these offerings are actually occurring, they are actually taking their effect. By making these offerings, you are actually gathering the accumulation of merit. To the extent that you have this confidence in the validity and accuracy of the practice, you will have that much delight in it, that much devotion, and that much benefit.

The third characteristic of the generation stage is the recollection of purity. This has several meanings. Most obviously it means the recognition that the forms of the deities are wondrous and splendid, that the deities are not unpleasant in appearance, that they are not strange or of an inappropriate form; they are beautiful and pleasing in every way. But beyond that, it is the recognition that the nature of the deity's form is the embodiment of the deity's wisdom. The deities' bodies are not flesh and blood—coarse bodies like our own—nor are they inanimate solid objects, as though made of earth and stone or wood. They are the pure embodiment of wisdom, which means that they are the expression of emptiness in the form of a clear, vivid appearance. Practically speaking, when visualizing them, you should see them or imagine them as being a vivid appearance—with their distinct colors, ornaments, scepters and so on—that is nevertheless without any coarse substantiality. Their appearance is luminous and vivid but insubstantial, like that of a rainbow. The fundamental meaning of this third point is that the deities are the embodiment in form of wisdom, and therefore their form is not samsaric in any way—it is not produced in any way by samsaric causes and conditions.

The Mantra and Blessings

Next we come to the visualization that accompanies the repetition of the mantra. In the text it says to visualize in the center of the heart of oneself as the Medicine Buddha, and in the heart of the front visualization of the Medicine Buddha, the seed syllable HUM surrounded by the garland of the mantra. In detail, one visualizes a moon disc—a disc of white light that represents the moon—lying flat in the very center of one's body at the level of the heart. Standing upright upon this disk is visualized the seed syllable of the deity, a blue HUM, which represents the deity's mind or wisdom. Surrounding the HUM is visualized the garland of the mantra from which rays of light will emanate and so forth.[31]

The HUNG *in the heart of the self and front visualizations is surrounded by the mantra garland.*
TAYATA OM BEKENDZE BEKENDZE MAHA
BEKENDZE RADZA SAMUDGATE SO HA

Having visualized the moon disc, the HUM syllable, and the mantra garland in the heart of both the self and front visualizations, you then think that from the syllable HUM and the mantra garland in the heart of the self-visualization rays of multicolored light shoot out towards the front visualization. These rays of light strike the heart of the front visualization, arousing its nonconceptual compassion and causing rays of multicolored light to emerge from the mantra garland and syllable HUM in its heart, which proceed to the eastern pure realm of the Medicine Buddha, called the Light of Vaidurya. On the tips of each of these multicolored rays of light are offering goddesses who make innumerable offerings to the Medicine Buddha, the seven other Medicine Buddhas, the sixteen bodhisattvas, and so on. These offerings serve to arouse their compassion; to remind them of their promises, vows, and aspirations to benefit beings; and to cause them to release their blessings.

The blessings of their body take the form of innumerable forms of the Medicine Buddha and his retinue—huge ones, tiny ones, and every size in between. These innumerable forms of the principal Medicine Buddha, the other Medicine Buddhas, and the bodhisattvas, rain down and dissolve into you as the self-visualization and into the front visualization, granting you the blessings of the body of the Medicine Buddha and his retinue.

At the same time, the blessing of their speech is emitted in the form of the mantra garlands, which in this case are multicolored. Mantra garlands of various colors rain down from the pure realms of the Medicine Buddha and dissolve into you as the Medicine Buddha and into the front visualization, granting you the blessings of their speech.

Finally, the blessing of their mind, which strictly speaking has no form, is for the purpose of this visualization embodied in the form of what is held in the Medicine Buddha's hands—the arura and the begging bowls filled with ambrosia. These are emitted and rain down and dissolve into you as the Medicine Buddha and into the front visualization, granting you the blessing of their mind.

If you can visualize clearly, it is best to do all of this very slowly and gradually. While you continue to say the mantra, you think that rays of light emerge from the self-visualization, go to the front visualization, and then from the front visualization outwards to the pure realms, proceeding gradually and slowly. Especially when the blessings of body, speech, and mind rain down upon and dissolve into you, you can do the visualizations in sequence: first, visualizing the blessings of body raining down, without being in any kind of a hurry and so quite distinctly; and then visualizing the blessings of speech and then the blessings of mind. If you find that the visualization is extremely unclear, if you wish, you can do it all at once. But if you do it gradually and slowly, you will find that you will get a much stronger sense of the blessings actually entering into you. By taking your time with the visualization, you will develop real confidence, a real feeling of the blessings entering into you.

When you receive the blessing of the Medicine Buddha, and of Buddhas and bodhisattvas in general, various unpleasant things—obstacles, sickness, demonic disturbances—will be pacified, and compassion, faith, devotion, insight, and so on will flourish and increase. In order to practice the descent of blessing most effectively, it is a good idea to focus the blessings on whatever is afflicting you most at that time. For example, if you are having a particular physical problem—an illness or some other physical problem—or a particular mental problem—a particular klesha, a particular type of stress, or particular worries—you can focus the absorption of the blessings of the Buddhas and bodhisattvas on that. You can focus it on the removal of wrongdoing and obscurations in general, but focus it especially on what you regard as your greatest concern at the moment. For example, you may feel that you lack a specific quality: If you feel that you lack insight or you lack compassion or you lack faith, then think that the blessing serves to promote that quality that you feel you are most lacking. And feel that through the absorption of these blessings you actually become filled with that quality as though it were a substance that were actually filling your whole body.

Those visualizations are for the usual, formal practice of the Medicine Buddha. In his book *Mountain Dharma: Instructions for Retreat*, Karma Chagmey Rinpoche recommends the following visualization for the actual alleviation of sickness. You can visualize yourself as the Medicine Buddha, if you wish, but the main focus is to actually visualize a small form of the Medicine Buddha, no larger than four finger-widths in height, in the actual part of your body that is afflicted. So if it is an illness or pain in the head, visualize a small Medicine Buddha in the head; if it is in the hand, visualize a small Medicine Buddha in the hand; if it is in the foot, then visualize a small Medicine Buddha in the foot. Visualize the Medicine Buddha in that place, and think that from this small but vivid form of the Medicine Buddha rays of light are emitted. These rays of light are not simply light, which is dry, but liquid light having a quality of ambrosia. This luminous ambrosia or liquid light actually cleanses and removes the sickness and pain—whatever it is. You can do this not only for yourself, by visualizing the Medicine Buddha in the appropriate part of your own body, but you can do it for others as well by visualizing the Medicine Buddha in the appropriate part of their body or bodies. The radiation of rays of light of ambrosia and so on is the same.

This can be applied not only to physical sickness but to mental problems as well. If you want to get rid of a particular type of anxiety or stress or depression or fear or any other kind of unpleasant mental experience, you can visualize the Medicine Buddha seated above the top of your head and think in the same way as before that luminous ambrosia or liquid light emerges from his body, filling your body and cleansing you of any problem, whatever it is.

You might think that all of this sounds a bit childish, but in fact it actually works, and you will find that out if you try it.

Conclusion of the Practice

Following the repetition of the mantra comes the conclusion of the practice.

I confess all wrongs and downfalls and dedicate all
virtue to awakening.
May there be the auspiciousness of freedom from sickness,
harmful spirits, and suffering.

First is the admission of defects. With an attitude of regret for anything that you have done that is wrong or inappropriate, you simply say, "I confess all wrongs and downfalls." Immediately after that you dedicate the merit or virtue of the practice to the awakening of all beings saying, "And dedicate all virtue to awakening." Then you make an auspicious aspiration which focuses your dedication, saying, "Through this dedication of merit, may there be freedom from sickness, harmful spirits, and suffering for all beings."

Next comes the dissolution of the mandala:

> *The worldly ones return to their own places.* BENZA MU.
> *The jnana and samaya sattvas dissolve into me,*
> *And I dissolve into primordial purity, the expanse of*
> *Samantabhadra.* E MA HO.

First a request to depart is addressed to the mundane deities, which is followed by the dissolution of the front and self-visualizations of the wisdom deities. When you say, "Worldly ones return to your own places, *vajramu,*" you think that the ten protectors of the ten directions, the twelve yaksha chieftains, and the four great kings—all mundane deities visualized in the entourage of the front visualization—return to where they would normally reside.[32] That leaves the eight Medicine Buddhas and the sixteen bodhisattvas in the front visualization. These deities, who are the wisdom deities embodying the visualized images of them,[33] dissolve into your heart as the self visualization. Then the self-visualization gradually dissolves into light and then into the expanse of emptiness, at which point you say, "And I dissolve into the expanse of the all-good primordial purity." At that point you rest your mind in the experience of emptiness.

All yidam practices include two stages: the generation stage and the completion stage. Everything up to this point—the visualization of the forms of the deities, the presentation of offerings and so on, the repetition of the mantra with the accompanying visualizations—are all aspects of the practice of the generation stage. When, subsequent to the dissolution of the visualization, you rest your mind in emptiness, this is the practice of the completion stage. It is through the practice of these two stages that you actually come to realize dharmata, the nature of things. Visualization and other generation stage practices function to weaken the kleshas, while completion stage practices, which include the practices of shamatha and vipashyana, serve to eradicate them.

I mentioned earlier that there are three Medicine Buddha practices that are used in our tradition—a long one, a medium one, and a short one—and that this is the short one. While this is the shortest, it is nevertheless considered the most effective. The long and medium forms of the Medicine Buddha are entirely sutra-oriented in style and content. This practice is a blend of the sutra tradition and the tantric or Vajrayana tradition. So while it is the shortest liturgically, it is the most complete because it has the most elaborate visualizations.

In the long and intermediate forms of the Medicine Buddha practice, because they are entirely sutric in approach, there is a preliminary meditation on emptiness, after which you imagine a palace as a residence for the front visualization and then you invite the deities to abide within that. There is not the precise development of the form of the deities, as in this case, nor is there any self-visualization, because it is entirely sutric. This practice which we are using includes the Vajrayana practice of self-visualization and the precise details of the visualization. Therefore, it is considered to be more effective, to have more power.

Now we have finished going through the practice of the Medicine Buddha—how to do it, what to meditate on, and what its meaning is. If you can do this full form of the practice regularly, that will be extremely beneficial, because it bears great blessing. But even if you can do it only occasionally, there will still be great benefit from your involvement in it. There is also a shorter form[34] of the practice that you can use when you do not have time to do the long form. It is a short supplication of the Medicine Buddha by name, which serves as a vehicle for cultivating faith in and devotion to the Medicine Buddha. As is taught in the sutra of Amitabha and in the sutra of the Medicine Buddha, recollecting and reciting the name of the Medicine Buddha is of incalculable benefit. Most of the benefits associated with the Medicine Buddha are connected with the twelve aspirations he made at the time of his initial generation of bodhicitta,[35] and most of these aspirations are connected in one way or another with his name. Therefore, most of the benefits connected with the Medicine Buddha can be gained by recollecting and reciting his name.

Questions & Answers

Question: Rinpoche, I was interested in hearing your different elaborations on the "seven articles" of the mandala offering. I have done the mandala offering in my ngöndro practice and there the offerings seem so much more concrete than the descriptions of the same articles we heard from you earlier today. Your descriptions of the "seven articles" of the chakravartin presented them much more as symbolic representations. Are they more concrete in some practices? Are there different practices? Are these different views? Do they come from the sutras, from the commentaries, from the Vajrayana? Or do they vary for certain people?

And then I have a particular question about the person of the chakravartin, the universal monarch. We in the West, wrongly or rightly, have the notion that democracy is the best way. I'm just wondering— this chakravartin seems like a wonderful being, yet he or she—you didn't mention any gender—this person seems to need help with faith, stability, exertion, with many different qualities. We in the West have found that a universal sort of monarch or ruler usually eventually goes wrong. Could you tell me what is different about this chakravartin that is going to make their rule so very successful, because we haven't had that experience?

Rinpoche: With regard to your first question, the correspondence between the "seven articles" of royalty, which are the characteristic possessions of a chakravartin, and the "seven limbs of awakening"— which are necessary resources on the path for bodhisattvas—is a standard one. In cases where the symbolic meaning of offering the "seven articles" of royalty is not explained, it simply means that it is a briefer explanation of the significance of that offering. This correspondence definitely does function in all uses of those things as offering substances or items.

With regard to your second question, the chakravartin only arises in certain periods of history, which are called the best times or the best ages. What distinguishes a chakravartin from some kind of cosmic dictator is the arising of the chakravartin in human society at that point as a solution to problems rather than the beginning of them. A chakravartin arises at a time when there is disputation as to who should lead the society. The chakravartin him or herself, is not particularly [eager or] anxious to do so, but is altruistic, capable, and acclaimed by the society at large, which places them in their position of authority. Now, it is entirely possible that after the reign of a chakravartin, if a dynasty is established, things could degenerate, as your question indicates. But then they would no longer be chakravartins.

Question: So, are you saying there could be a female universal monarch, a chakravartini?

Rinpoche: Of course.

Question: What is the Sanskrit name of Sangye Menla?

Translator: The most common name found in the sutras is *Bhaishajyai Guru,* which means the teacher of medicine. That is translated into Tibetan as *Mengyi Lama,* or *Menla* for short. That's why we call it Sangye Menla or the Medicine Buddha. Menla literally means Medicine Guru.

Question: Rinpoche, over and over again you talk about how in a way almost all of these practices are a backdrop for what the real practice is, which is faith and devotion that the practice will actually work. It seems that all practices in a way should be aimed at intensifying that. You say, "intense supplication," and there have been times in my practice when that just came, and I felt a fervour of faith. Then other times I really wished I had it, because I really felt like I needed it. You talk about generating bodhicitta or generating faith. What is the process of generating? I can put the thought in my mind, but if there is also pervasive doubt and pervasive cynicism . . . I come from a kind of culture of doubt and of questioning and of philosophical bullshit, so it's very difficult to talk about these concepts with absolute faith. What is the method of generating intense faith?

Rinpoche: The approach is to try to develop informed faith. Informed faith comes about through investigation. Through investigating the meaning of dharma you discover valid reasons why it is appropriate to have faith in it. That will naturally make faith a matter of common sense.

Question: Rinpoche, what is the translation of the mantra? And when does the visualization of the blessings' coming down in the form of small Medicine Buddhas and the begging bowl and the fruit and the mantra stop? And when it stops, it's not yet the dissolution, is it? What are we resting in at that point?

Translator: You mean after the descent of blessings ends, and before you dissolve the visualization?

Question: Right.

Rinpoche: The mantra that you recite is basically an elaboration of the name of the Medicine Buddha. It is more or less reciting the name of the Medicine Buddha in Sanskrit. The point at which you stop visualizing the blessings of body, speech, and mind being absorbed into you again and again is up to you. You can continue that visualization for the entire duration of your recitation of the mantra, in which case there is not much in-between that and the dissolution of the mandala. Or from time to time, you can stop visualizing and just rest in devotion. It is not the case that you need to spend absolutely every instant of your mantra recitation dissolving these things into you. As long as there is faith and devotion, then it does not have to be constant.

Question: Is this mantra best used for animals that are dying, and what about animals that might have just recently died, perhaps quickly?

Rinpoche: It will also benefit an animal that has recently died; it is going to be most effective, of course, if it is used just before the animal dies. But it will still benefit them afterwards.

Question: Rinpoche, thank you for the teaching. Given the aspirations of the Medicine Buddha, would it be appropriate to have a representation of the Medicine Buddha in the heart of the house, the family room, and particularly if the rest of one's family thinks the mother is completely strange. [laughter] And I've been told to recite *om mani peme hung* around dying and dead animals. Would it be more appropriate to recite the Medicine Buddha mantra?

Rinpoche: Reciting *om mani peme hung* or the Medicine Buddha's name or mantra to a dying animal will have pretty much equal benefit, so it is up to you. Both Avalokiteshvara and the Medicine Buddha have made specific aspirations to be of benefit to beings in that way. It does not matter, either one. With regard to your first question: While placing a large and prominent image of the Medicine Buddha in the very center of your home would ultimately have long-term benefits for the members of your family, it might, as your question indicates, create more problems in the short-term. Specifically, it might create more resistance. It would probably be better to allow your family to encounter the Medicine Buddha sort of incidentally, rather than having it thrust in their face.

Question: A small thangka on the wall, would that be better?

Rinpoche: If it does not cause disharmony within the home, then of course that would be fine. If it does, then it would be better that they encounter it somewhere outside the home.

Question: Could you explain the visualization for the short or condensed practice of the Medicine Buddha?

Rinpoche: There are two ways you can do this. One way is to make the supplication, paying homage to the Medicine Buddha and thinking that he is actually present in front of you and to visualize him by recollecting his appearance, his color, what he is holding, what he is wearing, and so on. Another equally valid way is to think that you are paying homage to him wherever he is, in which case you do not specifically have to visualize him at all.

Question: Rinpoche, I have a problem that keeps recurring in my visualization. The deity—Dorje Chang or the Medicine Buddha—is in front and I can see one side of it very clearly in detail and color, and the other side is practically in the dark. It is muddy, in the shade; the color is very indistinct, and when I get tired I can hardly see anything at all on that side.

Rinpoche: Is it always the same side?

Question: It is pretty much the same side. It is my left side, the deity's right side, that is clear; the other side is not. Also, if I'm sitting, facing straight ahead, and visualizing the deity right in front of me, and if my eyes are partially closed, it feels like the deity is off at an angle. I keep shifting my body to get it in, but it is already straight, but it feels like I'm sitting diagonally and looking over there.

Rinpoche: This is happening spontaneously to you; it is not something you are causing, so if you just leave it alone, if you just continue with the practice, it will take care of itself.

Question: Rinpoche, three questions. In the descent of the body, speech, and mind blessings, do they enter respectively into the three centers specifically, or do they enter generally into the body? Secondly, could you give us a little more detail about the sequence of the practice in terms of the small Medicine Buddha in a certain part of your body, or in others' bodies? And can that be done outside the formal practice?

And lastly, is there a connection between the Medicine Buddha and Jambhala? If there is, what is the connection? And if there is a difference, what is the difference? Is there a benefit to relating more to one or to the other?

Rinpoche: As to your first question, in the case of sadhana practice and the recitation of mantra, when you have the blessings of the three gates of the deity dissolving into yourself, you can think that they dissolve generally into your whole body, throughout your whole body without specifying that they dissolve into your head and so on. In the case of an abhisheka [empowerment], then they would dissolve into the specific parts of your body. As to your second question, you can do the application practice of visualizing a small Medicine Buddha in a specific part of your body or someone else's body, either during the formal practice of the sadhana, while reciting the mantra, or in post-meditation at anytime you want. As to the third question, there is a connection between the Medicine Buddha and Jambhala. The connection is basically that the twelve yaksha chieftains, who are guardians of the *Sutra of the Medicine Buddha* and his teaching, are of the same class or clan as the Jambhalas. Therefore, in a sense Jambhala is also a guardian of the Medicine Buddha's teaching. I had an indication of this when I was practicing the Medicine Buddha sadhana extensively at a Taiwanese monastery called Shi Lung Si. Monastics at the monastery and the other participants were also engaged in practicing the Medicine Buddha intensively. One of the reasons they were doing so, they said, was that whenever they engage in the Medicine Buddha practice communally, things go well at the monastery, which they felt had something to do with the activity of Jambhala coming along automatically with the supplication and practice of the Medicine Buddha. Therefore, I would say that if you have to choose just one of them to supplicate, the choice should be the Medicine Buddha, since it seems that if you supplicate the Medicine Buddha you get Jambhala's assistance automatically.

Question: Rinpoche, this practice seems so wonderful and complete that I'm having a hard time understanding why we haven't heard much about it until recently. I realize I haven't been practicing that long, but I'm wondering what the place of Medicine Buddha practice is. Is it something that was done a lot in monasteries? Why has it been so long in coming?

Rinpoche: As for the place that the Medicine Buddha practice is given in the monastic tradition in Tibet, it varies quite a bit. In some monasteries a great deal of it is done, and in other monasteries very little of it is done. And just about everything in between. There is no hard and fast rule. As for why you have not heard much about it until now, do not forget that Vajrayana is very new in the West. Basically we could say that Vajrayana has only been present in this country for thirty years. We have to look at how the Buddha taught. When the Buddha taught dharma, he started with what we call the common vehicle. And then he gradually, gradually deepened his presentation as people became prepared for it by their practice. In the same way, teachers have had to introduce and teach the dharma gradually in this country, simply because, as your practice progresses, your confidence and faith and understanding increase accordingly. For example, most of the teachers who began teaching in the West started by teaching shamatha practice, which was something that did not involve a great deal of faith, because you were working directly with what you could immediately experience in your own mind. The validity of it was obvious from the start. If they had begun by saying this is the fundamental practice of our tradition, you are to visualize the Medicine Buddha and believe me he exists, he has tremendous blessing, and if you pray to him, his blessing will enter you, you probably would not have believed it.

Question: Is this practice directly connected to Tibetan medical practice?

Rinpoche: Yes, it is connected. Medicine Buddha practices are used to consecrate the medicines while they are being prepared. Also the lineage of the medicine comes from a rishi called Rigpe Yeshe—"awareness wisdom"—who was an emanation of the Medicine Buddha. And when we look at the history of Tibetan medicine, we see that the foremost physicians of Tibet, including the great siddha Yönten Gonpo and others, subsequent to having visions of the Medicine Buddha or receiving his blessing, were able to discover new modes of diagnosis, new preparations of medicine, and would compose medicinal textbooks.

Question: Thank you, Rinpoche, for your transmission and your teaching. I have been taught up to this point that there are basically three ways to assist beings across the ocean of samsara to the shore of enlightenment: like a king, who would lead everyone to liberation; like a ferryman, who would put everyone in the same boat with him and cross over together with everyone, so to speak. Or like a shepherd, who would make sure everyone is there safely before he goes himself. I have confusion about being a shepherd on the one hand and healing and enlightening myself first before allowing everyone else to go in before me. Could you speak to that please?

Rinpoche: There are, as you indicated in your question, three ways that bodhicitta can be generated, according to the sutra tradition. These three different generations of bodhicitta, all of which are acceptable, correspond to how selfish you are. When someone is utterly unselfish, completely and absolutely altruistic, then when they generate bodhicitta, the attitude they will have is, "I will not attain Buddhahood, I refuse to attain Buddhahood, until each and every other being already has attained it." This is what is called shepherd-like bodhicitta, as you mentioned in your question. And that is considered the best style of bodhicitta generation from the point of view of the sutras; the best, because it is completely unselfish. The second best is the thought, "Well, I want to attain Buddhahood, they all want to attain Buddhahood, I hope we all attain Buddhahood together. I will bring myself and all beings to Buddhahood at the same time." This style, called the boatman-like or ferryer-like bodhicitta, is a little more selfish than the first, but it is still very unselfish. The third style, which really does have a little bit of selfishness in it, is the thought, "I really want to attain Buddhahood. I really want to attain full awakening. But after I have attained it, I will not abandon beings. I will also liberate all beings. But first of all, I definitely want to attain Buddhahood." That is king-like bodhicitta, which has some selfishness in it, but because it contains the aspiration to liberate all beings, it is still authentic bodhicitta.

The style of generation of bodhicitta in the Vajrayana sounds a lot like the king-like bodhicitta, but is not meant to be the king-like bodhicitta. The Vajrayana attitude is simply realistic. If you do not attain Buddhahood, you cannot liberate other beings. This attitude is not selfish; it is realistic. It could become selfish. You could turn it into king-like bodhicitta, or use it as an excuse for king-like bodhicitta. But it is not really meant to be generated in that spirit. The basic reasoning of Vajrayana bodhicitta is, "All I want is to liberate all beings. I obviously cannot do that right now. If I become a bodhisattva, with bodhisattva realization, I can do something, but I cannot liberate them completely, as a Buddha can. So, although what I want is to liberate beings and not myself, in order to do that effectively, I am going to have to attain Buddhahood myself first."

Question: Is there a Medicine Buddha practice that involves the laying on of hands?

Rinpoche: The laying on of hands could in some way be combined with the practice of visualizing a small form of the Medicine Buddha at the afflicted part of the ill person's body.

Question: Rinpoche, I have another question about choosing between practices. In considering tonglen practice, and Medicine Buddha, how would we decide when to use either one, given that you have both transmissions?

Rinpoche: Do you mean for your own development, or in order to benefit another person?

Question: Tonglen that we use for helping others, and it helps us as well. Also, Pema Chödron has talked about a way to use tonglen to help yourself.

Rinpoche: Both are equally beneficial in every way, in and of themselves. What you should emphasize in your practice is based upon what you have the greatest confidence in, what you have the greatest faith in, and what you have the greatest natural inclination for. So if you have greater confidence in tonglen, it will be more effective. If you have greater confidence in the Medicine Buddha practice, that will be more effective. Historically, we can see in the various lineages that some teachers have emphasized tonglen as their primary practice; other teachers have emphasized the Medicine Buddha or similar practices as their primary practice. It really depends upon your personal inclination.

Mudras

Ritual Gestures Help Clarify the Visualization

S*ome of you have inquired about the* mudras, ritual gestures, for this practice, so I will explain them. As you know, the main element in our practice is meditation, including visualization, which is mental in nature. But we use our other faculties, body and speech, to clarify and reinforce this mental process. We use speech, for example, to clarify visualizations by reciting the liturgical descriptions and so on, and we use the body to clarify visualizations through physical postures and gestures called mudras. The main point, of course, is the visualization practice itself. So it is acceptable, especially under certain conditions, to do the practice entirely mentally, without the additional use of mudras.

The first place in this practice where a specific mudra is used is in the invitation of the deity—when you have already visualized yourself as the Medicine Buddha and have visualized the Medicine Buddha in front of you, and are requesting the actual wisdom deity, the Medicine Buddha, to approach and finally dissolve into you as the self-visualization and into the front visualization.

This and other places in the practice are highlighted by the use of the Sanskrit language as part of the liturgy. The culmination of the invitation, the culmination of each section of offerings, as well as the essence mantra repeated during the main body of the practice are all said in Sanskrit. This is standard for all Vajrayana practices. The reason for this is that the Buddha taught in Sanskrit, and it is taught that all Buddhas of the future, as well, will teach in Sanskrit. So one uses Sanskrit for the highlights of the practice in order to cultivate a habit or form a connection with that language.

At the conclusion of the invitation in the liturgy you say the Sanskrit mantra, NAMO MAHA BEKENDZE SAPARIWARA BENZA SAMAYADZA DZA. What you are saying is, "Medicine Buddha, together with your retinue, please recollect your vajra samaya and approach." At that point you visualize that the Medicine Buddha and his retinue appear in the sky in front of you before dissolving into you and into the front visualization. The mudra that accompanies this mantra is called the mudra of assembly, and is made by crossing your arms at the wrists facing inward in front of your chest with the right one in front and the left one  closer to your body, and snapping your fingers.

Invitation mudra

The significance of crossing your arms at the wrists represents the cohesiveness of unimpaired samaya, which brings the wisdom deities. The snapping of your fingers signifies immediately, right now. This actually has the specific meaning of referring to a unit of time called an instant. An instant in this case refers to the smallest division of time measured in any given system. For example, in the general system used in India at the time of the Buddha, the day was divided into thirty periods, which in turn were divided into thirty periods, and so on, until you got down to a period of time so small it is difficult even to describe, and that was designated as an instant or a moment. In the *Kalachakra Tantra,* the day is divided into hours, which are divided into subsections, which are divided further and further and further until one gets a period of time so small that in our perception it has no duration, and therefore is something like timelessness or emptiness. In any case, an instant refers to the shortest possible unit of time imaginable.

The snapping of fingers in ritual use signifies or designates an instant. In the case of the invitation here, what you are saying by snapping your fingers is, "Please appear here and dissolve into me right now, without any delay whatsoever." During the offerings, what you are saying when you snap your fingers at the conclusion of the offering mudras is, "Please accept these offerings right now. May they be available to you and may you enjoy them right now, without having to wait." In the case of an ordination ceremony, such as the refuge ceremony, the snapping of fingers serves to designate the exact instant or moment in time at which you receive the vow.

Next one recites VAJRA SAMAYA TIKTRA LEN, which means, "Through the power of your recollection of your vajra samaya, please remain stable." During the previous mantra, when you invited the wisdom deities, you invited them and dissolved them into yourself. When you recite VAJRA SAMAYA TIKTRA LEN you dissolve them into the front visualization and request them to remain there stable as a field of offering for the accumulation of merit. The gesture here is that your hands are turned over so that they are palm up in front of your chest. It is very much like an elaborate or polite way of requesting someone to be seated.

Next, we come to the empowerment. The first five syllables of the empowerment mantra, OM HUM TRAM HRI AH ABHIKENTZA HUM, refer to the five male Buddhas of the five families. This is an empowerment both of yourself and of the front visualization. OM represents Vairochana, HUM Akshobhya, TRAM Ratnasambhava, HRI Amitabha, and AH Amoghasiddhi.

These five Buddhas of the five families are sometimes taught as Buddhas in five different pure realms external to you. And sometimes they are taught as the five aspects of your innate or intrinsic wisdom. qqIn the case of there being the five aspects of intrinsic wisdom, they correspond to the five wisdoms of a Buddha. So, for example, Vairochana, who is of the Buddha family, is the wisdom of the dharmadhatu. The wisdom of the dharmadhatu is the recognition of the unborn nature or emptiness of all things, which also pervades the other wisdoms, which is why it has that particular name.

These wisdoms are not really separate things. They are enumerated separately in order to show the qualities of wisdom. Generally speaking, one can say that the wisdom of a Buddha includes two aspects, two types of wisdom, which are also not really separate. One of them is the wisdom that knows how things are, and that refers to the recognition of absolute truth or the nature of things. This aspect of wisdom is equivalent to the wisdom of the dharmadhatu.[36] It is that wisdom that knows how things are, or knows the nature of all things.

The other wisdom of a Buddha is the wisdom that knows what there is. The wisdom that knows how things are knows the nature of all things, or absolute truth. But at the same time, a Buddha also knows what there is, which is to say, the distinct features of those relative truths or relative things, of which the absolute truth is the nature. This means that, while Buddhas recognize the unborn nature of each and every thing, the emptiness of each and every thing, they nevertheless see the manifestation or appearance of that thing clearly, without that clear seeing producing any kind of reification or illusion of solidity. Therefore, the way in which Buddhas see relative truth is like seeing something in a mirror. The image is seen extremely clearly and vividly, but there is nothing really there in the mirror [other than mere appearance], and that is also known. So the perception or wisdom of a Buddha, the recognition of relative truth, is called the mirror-like wisdom, which is seeing that, while things are unborn, they nevertheless have their distinct appearances. Mirror-like wisdom is the Buddha Akshobhya.

The third wisdom of a Buddha is called the wisdom of equality. This refers to the fact that, from the point of view of the mirror itself, regardless of what appears in it, while it appears distinctly and while the mirror has the capacity to display any image, there are no concepts on the part of the mirror about what it displays. There is no division of the display into self and other. There is no division of the display or image into good or bad, or into any other conceptual framework. This fact that Buddhas in their wisdom, which recognizes this display, are free of all of these deluded concepts, is the wisdom of equality, which is the Buddha Ratnasambhava.

The fourth Buddha is Amitabha, who embodies the wisdom of discrimination. A Buddha—we, when we have attained Buddhahood, or any other Buddha—possesses the three wisdoms, which have been explained: the dharmadhatu wisdom, the mirror-like wisdom, and the wisdom of equality. These being the characteristics of the wisdom of a Buddha, it is clear that they see or are aware without any kind of conceptualization. But because they are free of conceptualization, you might assume mistakenly that they are unable to distinguish between the characteristics of things. In other words, because Buddhas are free of the concepts of good and bad, does that mean that they are unable to distinguish good from bad in relative truth? Because they are free of the concepts of red and white, does that mean that they cannot distinguish a red thing from a white thing? In fact, it does not. Buddhas are perfectly able to distinguish the distinct characteristics of relative things or relative phenomena. That wisdom is called the wisdom of discrimination, which is an aspect of the wisdom that knows what there is—from the standpoint of distinguishing the aspects of wisdom according to that which knows how things are and that which knows what there is. This corresponds to the Buddha Amitabha.

The fifth wisdom is the wisdom of accomplishment, which is embodied by the Buddha Amoghasiddhi. This means that, because of the wisdom of a Buddha—because a Buddha possesses, for example, the wisdom of equality and the wisdom of discrimination—they are able spontaneously to accomplish their activity without conceptualization or effort. Such activity is unceasing, and uninterrupted. The activity of a Buddha never fails to accomplish its aim in a timely way. This is what is meant by the wisdom of accomplishment. So the empowerment that you receive at this point in the practice, while repeating the syllables OM HUM TRAM HRI AH, internally is the empowerment of the five wisdoms and externally is the empowerment of the five male Buddhas.

There is a mudra that goes with each of these syllables. The mudra of Vairochana, which accompanies the saying of OM, is to clasp your hands, intertwining the fingers tightly so that the two hands make a fist, and then extending the two middle fingers joined together. The mudra of Akshobhya, which accompanies the saying HUM, is to clasp your hands making a fist with the two forefingers extended. The mudra of Ratnasambhava, which accompanies the syllable TRAM, is to clasp your hands making a fist with the two ring fingers extended and joined. The mudra of Amitabha, which accompanies the syllable HRI, is to clasp your hands making a fist with the two thumbs extended and joined. And finally, the mudra of Amoghasiddhi, which accompanies the syllable AH, is to clasp your hands making a fist with the two little fingers extended and joined.

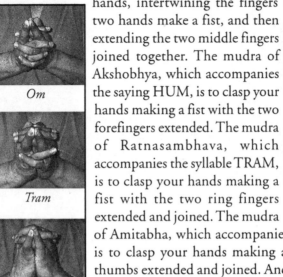

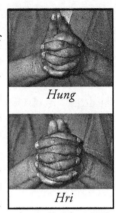

These mudras are connected with the way in which the five Buddhas are perceived—and this is common to all tantras—as being present in the external world. The Buddha Vairochana of the Buddha family is said to inhabit a realm in the center, called "densely arrayed." The Buddha Akshobhya of the vajra family is said to inhabit a realm in the east, called "manifestly joyous." The Buddha Ratnasambhava of the ratna or jewel family is said to inhabit a realm in the south, called "glorious." The Buddha Amitabha of the padma or lotus family is said to inhabit a realm in the west, called "blissful" or Sukhavati. And the Buddha Amoghasiddhi of the karma or action family is said to inhabit a realm in the north, called "perfect" or "perfectly complete activity." The central Buddha, Vairochana, is seen as pervasive, pervading all of the other Buddhas and pervading all of their activity.

Each of the other four Buddhas is also connected with a specific style of activity, a specific way of benefiting beings. Akshobhya embodies pacification. Ratnasambhava embodies enrichment and expansion. Amitabha embodies magnetizing. And Amoghasiddhi embodies forceful or direct activity.

When we talk of these five realms, we say that they are in the east, the south, the west, the north, and the middle, but obviously these directions are mere designations. They have no absolute reality or location. We cannot really say what east is, because a place that is east of one place is going to be west of another. It will be south of one and north of one. Is that place really east, or is it west? Maybe it is south, maybe it is north. You cannot say. So, the directions, of course, are empty. They are valid in relative truth. In a specific context that we have designated, we can meaningfully say that some place is east or west of another place. So they are valid in relative truth, but they are only valid relative to one another, and therefore have no absolute validity and are empty. So, we cannot really say where an eastern realm would be, except relative to our own body. Therefore, in the Buddhist tradition, we call wherever you are facing east.

So for that reason—and now these mudras are going to become a little more complicated—because east is identified as wherever you are facing, it is understood in invitation liturgies that a Buddha invited from the east—as, for example, Akshobhya—will approach you from the front. A Buddha invited from the south, like Ratnasambhava, will approach you from the direction of your right ear. A Buddha invited from the west, like Amitabha, will approach behind you towards the back of your head. And a Buddha invited from the north, like Amoghasiddhi, will approach you from your left. So therefore, when you receive the empowerment from these five Buddhas and then visualize that they dissolve into you, they dissolve into you from those directions. Therefore, the mudras that were previously demonstrated are touched to five points on your head. Because Vairochana, represented by the middle finger, is in the middle, you touch your clasped hands, making a fist with the middle finger extended, to the very center of the top of

Argham

Pandam

Pupe

Dupe

your head. Because Akshobhya, represented by the forefingers, is connected with the front, then you touch the clasped hands with the forefingers extended, to your forehead. Because Ratnasambhava, represented by the extended ring fingers, comes from the south, you touch the clasped hands with extended ring fingers, above your right ear. Because Amitabha, represented by the extended thumbs, approaches from the west, you touch your clasped hands with the thumbs extended to the back of your head or as close as you can get. Finally, because Amoghasiddhi, represented by the extended little fingers, approaches from the north, you touch the clasped hands with the extended little fingers, to the left side of your head above your left ear. The making and touching of these mudras is all coordinated with the recitation of the syllables.

When you are actually performing these mudras, the first three are obvious. But when you get to HRI, representing Amitabha, the thumbs at the back of your head, you do not go over the head. You go around from the right as far as you can get. Then you have AH on the left.

The performance of these five mudras while reciting OM HUM TRAM HRIH AH accompanies the receiving of empowerment from these five Buddhas, who then dissolve into you. When you say the rest of the mantra, ABHIKENTZA HUM, in order to acknowledge that the five Buddhas have dissolved into you, you extend your hands palm upward and then turn [or rotate] them in towards yourself until they are more or less palm downward, to represent the dissolution of the Buddhas into yourself.

Those are the mudras for the empowerment. Next we come to the mudras for the offerings. The first offering mudra here accompanies the mantra word ARGHAM. ARGHAM refers to the offering of drinking water. So the mudra is making the shape with your hands of a vessel or container that could contain drinking water, and it is done in the way that Rinpoche just demonstrated [by joining the fingers at their tips and the fingers and palms along the outside edge of the little fingers and the inner edge of the palms as they face upward, with the thumbs resting on the edge of the palms and forefingers].

The second offering, PANDAM, represents water for washing the feet. The custom during the time of the Buddha was that water would be poured from a conch shell over your feet. So the mudra done at this point is to grasp the end of your forefingers with the last joint of your thumbs and extend the other fingers forward palms upward, which is the mudra of the conch.

The third offering, PUPE, is the offering of flowers. The mudra depicts casting flower petals with your hands [the nails of the four fingers of both hands, held palms upward in a light fist restrained by the thumbs, suddenly released by the restraining thumbs and extended forward].

DUPE is the offering of incense, and therefore the gesture or mudra with the hands represents containers of finely scented incense powder [both hands held in fists, fingers arranged on top of each other grasping the thumb, which points downward].

The next offering, ALOKE, represents lamps or lights. The position of the hands with the thumbs extended upward represents a lamp and its burning

Aloke

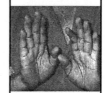

Gende

Newideh

Shapta

wick [same mudra as for incense, except that the thumbs, now pointing upward, are free of the fist-clenched fingers].

The next offering, GENDE, represents the rubbing of perfumed water onto the body, and so the gesture with the hands is like the gesture of anointing or rubbing perfumed water onto someone's body [both hands held, palms facing forward, perpendicular to the ground, fingers pointing upward, moving slightly].

The next offering, NAIVEDYE or NEWIDEH, is food, which is represented by the NAIVEDYE torma, which is found in the appropriate bowl on the shrine. The mudra here depicts that, with the hands held palms up and the ring fingers extended upward to depict that torma which is on the shrine.

SHAPTA, which means "sound" the first time it appears in this offering, is the offering of music. The gesture here is like the way that the clay drum would be beaten with the fingers [thumbs of each hand grasping the ring and little fingers, the middle finger and the pointing finger extended straight forward with the pointing finger on top, moving slightly up and down with a beating motion].

Following those eight offering are the remaining five offerings of this section, which as you will remember, are offerings of the objects of the five senses. The first of these, RUPA, means form, and here refers to beautiful form. The mudra that represents it is the mudra of the mirror, with your right hand extended palm outward, and your left hand in a fist with the thumb extended upward and touching the palm of the right hand at the base as though it were the handle of a mirror. This represents the fact that forms are perceived like images or reflections in a mirror.

The second mudra is SHAPTA, which here refers to all sounds. The mudra, however, is always something representing a musical instrument. Some people at this second SHAPTA do the lute mudra, or guitar mudra, however, my own tradition is simply to repeat the previous drumming mudra.

GENDE, which represents beautiful scents, gets the same mudra as it did before when it specifically represented perfume.

And RASA, which is the offering of tastes, gets the same mudra as ARGHAM, except in this case it is a container of food rather than a container of water.

And SAPARSHE, which represents tactile sensations, gets the mudra of holding aloft fine fabric, which is done by revolving the hands until the palms are facing outward and thumb and ring finger are touching.

When you say TRATITSA, which means individually, then you turn your hands so that the palms are up and snap your fingers.

During the next offering sections—offering the eight auspicious substances, the eight auspicious signs, and the seven articles of royalty— you continue to hold your hands joined in angeli, the mudra of supplication or prayer, as you do during all offerings sections. There is no specific mudra for these and no snapping of the fingers.

When we offer the mandala with the mantra, OM RATNA MANDALA HUM, there is the usual mandala mudra.

Translator: I guess there are a lot of people here who do not know this mudra. Put your hands more or less palm up. Interweave your fingers, with both sets of fingers visible above the palms, not with the fingers behind the backs of the hands. Then with your thumbs grab the ends of the little fingers of the opposite hands. And then with your forefingers, hook around the top joint of the middle fingers of the opposite hands. Then un-interweave your ring fingers so that they stick straight up back to back. That is the simplest way I know to describe it. And there's no finger snap.

Rinpoche: The remaining three sections of offering—ablution, drying, and dressing—have no mudras other than the palms being joined [in angeli, the mudra of supplication or prayer].

However, the way in which your palms are joined in these practices is quite specific. The hands are not pressed against one another so that the palms are flat against each other. There is space left between your palms, so that the shape of your hands is like a budding flower. It is therefore called the lotus mudra, and represents a lotus flower that is about to open. The lotus is a symbol of dharma in general. It is born in mud or in a swamp, but when the flower emerges, it is stainless and beautiful. So the lotus—and by extension the mudra—represents the practice of dharma, and therefore, in order to remind yourself of that, your palms are joined in these practices in that way.

Questions & Answers

Question: Rinpoche, you have said that in the future the dharma would be taught in Sanskrit by other Buddhas. Could you explain why that would be? Is there something about the Sanskrit language that connects us more closely with the enlightened state? Or will we in the future, as we practice dharma, as we come closer, hopefully, to the enlightened state, be able to understand and make these sounds more intelligibly? Or is this not a definitive teaching and thus to be interpreted from the standpoint of the time of the Buddha when this teaching was given?

Rinpoche: First of all, as to whether or not the statement that all Buddhas of the future will teach in Sanskrit is a definitive statement or a statement with a hidden intention—which is to say, one which does not mean what it literally says, but means something that is indicated by what it literally says—is something I cannot resolve. I cannot say to you, "It is a definitive statement to be taken literally," or, "It is a symbolic statement with a hidden meaning." I cannot resolve this question because the source of this idea is the *Badhrakalpa Sutra,* the *Sutra of the Fortunate Eon,* and in that sutra the Buddha gives the names of the parents, the style of teaching, the length of teaching, the number and qualities of the retinue attending the teachings, and so on, for each of the one thousand Buddhas of this particular kalpa. This includes the three Buddhas who preceded him, and the others who will succeed him. It is in this sutra that he states, for example, that Maitreya will be the fifth Buddha of this kalpa and the Lion's Roar will be the sixth Buddha. He discusses all of the thousand Buddhas up to the very last one, called Rochana. In the same place where the Buddha predicts their coming, he says that they will all teach in Sanskrit. It would be very difficult to try to ascertain exactly what his intention was in saying that.

The effect of using Sanskrit in liturgical practices is basically to establish the blessing [of the original words of the Buddha] in the most important places in the sadhana—in the mantras, which are repeated,[37] and in the areas of the practice that are highlighted, such as the culmination of the invitation, the culmination individually of the various offerings, and so on. For this reason, then, even when these practices were undertaken outside of the Sanskrit-speaking world, these sections were left in the original language and remain untranslated. Whether or not as an implication of this we can consider Sanskrit a fundamentally superior language depends not so much on the idea of its being superior as its being sacred because we believe the Buddha taught in Sanskrit. There are some Buddhist traditions that maintain the view that the Buddha's teachings were originally given in Pali. But the Vajrayana tradition maintains that his original teachings for the most part were given in Sanskrit. Because of that, by using Sanskrit in liturgical practice, we feel that we bring the Buddha's blessing, the blessing of the Buddha's speech, into our practice.

Question: So, does this prediction then still fall under the teaching of impermanence?

Rinpoche: What do you mean?

Question: What I mean is, is this set in stone or does this also fall under the heading, as we're always taught, that nothing is permanent?

Rinpoche: The impermanence aspect of this is a fluctuation in the use of Sanskrit in the world. In the Buddha's time, people in the society in which the Buddha was living actually spoke Sanskrit. Now nobody speaks Sanskrit; it is considered a dead language. But according to the sutra, it will come back, and in that way Sanskrit will return to use, and then become a dead language, and then return to use again, and then become a dead language again, and so on. That is an instance of impermanence.

Question: Rinpoche, I'd like to share the tapes of these teachings with KTC sangha, and I'd like to know if that is an appropriate thing to do, and also whether it would be appropriate to practice the Medicine Buddha in a group including individuals who have not received the empowerment. And would it be appropriate to do the short Mahakala practice in the chant book alone at home?

Rinpoche: As for your first question, anyone can practice the Medicine Buddha, whether they have the empowerment or not. As far as instituting its practice in a group, if it were part of a KTC activity, you would need first to receive permission from the appropriate teachers. Secondly, if you have faith in the short Mahakala practice, it is certainly okay to do it at home.

Question: Rinpoche, this question is not directly related to the topic at hand, but since it involves issues of faith and devotion, I thought it might be relevant and beneficial. This has to do with the nature and appearance of the Gyalwang Karmapas in general. As you know I have been praying to Karmapa as part of my practice, and it is said in the Kagyu tradition that Karmapa is a tenth-level bodhisattva. I've definitely come to believe that, even though I've never had any direct contact with Karmapa. But once, when I was having difficulty in my practice, I went to read the songs in the *Kagyu Gurtso* of the Eighth Gyalwang Karmapa, Mikyo Dorje. And there Mikyo Dorje refers to himself as an ordinary individual. My small mind cannot encompass how such a high-level bodhisattva can think of himself as an ordinary individual. Rinpoche, would you please dispel my confusion?

Translator: Can I abbreviate that a little bit?

Question: Oh, please.

Rinpoche: This type of statement, like the one you mentioned by Gyalwang Mikyo Dorje in the *Kagyu Gurtso*, is typical of great teachers, because their primary responsibility is to serve as a good example for their students, which means that they have to display a manner that is free of arrogance. So, although it is not literally true that they are ordinary beings, they will nevertheless say things like, "I am a completely ordinary person, full of kleshas, with no qualities whatsoever." By saying that, they display the importance of being free of arrogance. You should not take such statements literally.

Question: Rinpoche, is it still appropriate and beneficial to practice the Medicine Buddha sadhana if I have not practiced any ngöndro?

Rinpoche: It makes no difference.

Question: I was wondering if you could talk about what would be a proper mode of conduct if you found yourself being attacked by a sexual predator. If you were able to defend yourself, what would be the right thing to do?

Rinpoche: Basically, the dharmic answer to this would be prevention as much as possible, which would basically fall into two categories. First of all, through mindfulness avoid situations where you are likely to be a victim of that kind of attack. And the second approach is to discourage anyone who seems to be capable of that kind of attack or behaviour by being a little bit tough, so that they do not ever get the idea that they can get that close to you.

Question: Rinpoche, when I am here, it becomes very clear to me that the best thing to do would be to go home and organize my life so that I am practicing many hours per day. What happens when I actually go back home is that the connection to the teachings seems more distant, and what seems more immediate and real are the needs around me. I begin to have the thought that it is actually selfish or self-absorbed to practice a lot, and that it is more beneficial to help other people. I think this is a fault. Could you comment on that?

Rinpoche: Well actually both are correct. Neither is a fault. To wish to practice a great deal is correct, and to be attentive to the needs of those around you, and to put them first, is also correct. So you have to gauge the exact balance according to your particular situation, using your own insight. The only rule of thumb is not to be too extreme in either way. Not to be so extreme in the amount of practice that you pay no attention to those around you and their needs, or so extreme in limiting your practice for their benefit that you do not practice very much at all.

Question: He portrayed the front visualization as larger than the one that I am visualizing as myself. And I thought that somewhere it was also being said that we are the same. So why am I portraying the front one as larger? That would create some insecurity in me that I am never quite good enough.

Translator: Larger, do you mean that his body is bigger? You are not just talking about the retinue?

Question: No. It kind of makes me feel like he has got more power than I do.

Translator: He never said that the front visualization was larger.

Question: It is in the text, maybe.

Translator: Oh, that is where it is.

Rinpoche: Well, the author of the text must have had a specific reason for saying it at that time.

Question: I imagined it was to give me more confidence, but at some point I guess I could visualize him to be the same size as the self-visualization.

Rinpoche: You can visualize them as the same size.

Question: Is the front visualization a mirror image of the self-visualization or is it the other way around?

Rinpoche: It is not literally a mirror image. In other words, in both the self- and front visualizations the right hand of the Medicine Buddha is extended holding the arura and the left hand in both cases is holding a begging bowl on the lap.

Question: Rinpoche, there have been lots of instructions for sadhana practitioners about how to visualize, and I would just like to hear your instructions to us about how to do the self-visualization properly, given that we have all these attachments to our bodies and to ourselves and that it is difficult to work with that situation. I wanted to hear how you would instruct us to properly visualize the self as the deity.

Rinpoche: Well, here you are not trying to—and you do not have to—first get rid of the fixation on your body. The idea is that you replace the fixation on your ordinary body by adding to that the fixation on your body as the body of the Medicine Buddha.

Question: Rinpoche, is samaya primarily fulfilled by faith and devotion, overriding possibly completing a practice? Say, for instance, you are doing some practices and then you encounter a practice like this one and decide you want to do this one. Is it primarily the faith and devotion as opposed to the actual steps of completing any particular practice?

Rinpoche: Yes, basically samaya is maintained by your faith and devotion.

Medicine Buddha Sutra

The Buddha Shakyamuni Taught
This Sutra to Inspire Us to Practice

Twelve Extraordinary Aspirations
for the Benefit of Sentient Beings

There are three sutras primarily concerned with the Medicine Buddha.
One sets forth the twelve aspirations of the Medicine Buddha.
Another sets forth the aspirations of the seven other Medicine Buddhas.
The third, an extremely short sutra, sets forth the dharani or mantras of
the various Medicine Buddhas. I am now going to explain the main
one, the sutra that sets forth the twelve aspirations of the Medicine
Buddha. Before I begin, you should know something about the difference
between sutras and shastras. Sutras are the Buddha's teachings, and
shastras are commentaries on them. Shastras are constructed in order to
give a summary of the meaning; therefore, they get right to the point—
whereas sutras always begin with an introduction that gives the setting
for any particular teaching of the Buddha. A sutra will tell you where
the Buddha was living when he gave that particular teaching, why he
happened to give it, who asked him to give it, who and how many were
there when he gave it, and exactly what he said and what others said
that caused him to say what he said. The Buddha went just about

everywhere in India. The setting for this particular sutra was Vaisali, one of the six major cities in India at that time. The retinue in the midst of which the Buddha taught this sutra was extremely large. It consisted of a great many monks and nuns and a great many bodhisattvas, both male and female; it consisted of monarchs, the ministers of these monarchs, and the common people from the kingdoms of these monarchs. There were also innumerable spirits and local divinities in attendance, all of whom had assembled in order to hear this teaching.

The foremost disciple in this gathering—in fact, the person who specifically asked the Buddha to give this explanation, which later came to be known as the *Sutra of the Medicine Buddha*—was the bodhisattva Manjushri. The sutra begins with Manjushri taking a certain physical posture and making the request. The posture that Manjushri takes is the same physical posture we take when we formally take the vow of refuge, when we take other forms of pratimoksha ordination, and when we take the bodhisattva vow. Manjushri's left knee is raised, his right knee is on the ground,[38] and his palms are joined in a gesture of devotion in front of his heart. Manjushri takes this posture because it is the posture that the Buddha's disciples always took whenever they addressed him. And the reason we take this posture in formal ceremonies today is that they did it then. We do it in order to recollect the Buddha when we take refuge or any other ordination.

Facing the Buddha and taking that posture, Manjushri addresses the Buddha, asking him to teach about those Buddhas who had made extraordinary aspirations for the benefit of beings—what their aspirations were, and what the benefits of recollecting their names would be. He asks him to explain these things for the benefit of beings in the future.

The Buddha's first response to Manjushri's request is to praise him for making the request in the first place. Addressing Manjushri, the Buddha says, "It is excellent and fitting that you have made this request, because your motivation in doing so is compassion and a wish to bring about the means of purification of obscurations in general, and especially the means of eradicating the sickness of beings in the future."

While praising Manjushri for making this request, the Buddha enjoins him to listen well to the detailed explanation he was about to give. Commentators have explained that this injunction has three specific meanings. The Buddha says, "Manjushri, for that reason, listen well, listen fully, and hold this in your mind." Each of these three points—listen well, listen fully, and hold this in your mind—has a particular meaning with respect to how to listen to the teachings. The first injunction—"Listen well"—means, listen with an appropriate motivation. If you have a good motivation for listening, then the dharma you hear will be contained in a pure form in your mind. On the other hand, if you listen with an impure motivation—with attachment or aversion or the like—then your mind will become like a container or cup that holds poison, which then turns whatever is poured into it into poison.

The second injunction of the Buddha—"Listen fully"—means, listen attentively. You may have a good motivation for listening to the teachings, but if you are distracted—if you do not direct your mind to what is being said—then listening is of no use. Your mind will become like a cup that is turned upside-down; nothing can be poured into it.

The Buddha's third injunction is, "Hold it in your mind." Even if you have a good motivation and listen well, if you forget what is being taught, then it is lost from your mind. Your mind is then like a broken cup, which, no matter how much is poured into it, will allow it all to leak back out again.

Then the Buddha tells Manjushri that in the eastern direction, innumerable realms away—which means that if you pass beyond this particular realm, the realm of the Buddha Shakyamuni, and go in the eastern direction past a truly large number of other realms—you will reach the Buddha realm called the Light of Vaidhurya or the Light of Lapis Lazuli. In that realm there abides the Buddha Bhaishajyai Guru, the Medicine Buddha, also known as the Light of Lapis Lazuli or the Light of Vaidhurya, who teaches the dharma there. The Buddha tells Manjushri that because of the twelve extraordinary aspirations made by the Buddha Bhaishajyai Guru before he attained enlightenment, while he was still engaged in the practice or conduct of a bodhisattva, there is tremendous benefit in recollecting his name and tremendous blessing in supplicating him. In fact, the benefits that accrue from devotion to the Medicine Buddha are based primarily upon the aspirations he made while still a bodhisattva.[39] They are explained in the sutra so that we may understand how the blessings of the body, speech, and mind of the Medicine Buddha can enter into us and what the benefits of their doing so will be. The Buddha Shakyamuni taught this sutra in order to inspire us to practice. The idea being conveyed here is that meditation on the Medicine Buddha, supplication of the Medicine Buddha, and recollection of the name of the Medicine Buddha bring extraordinary benefits. By understanding that, you will feel enthusiastic about the Medicine Buddha practice. This enthusiasm will cause you to practice, which in turn will cause you to attain the result of practice.

The first of the twelve aspirations made by the Medicine Buddha while still a bodhisattva is, "In the future, when I attain perfect awakening and become a Buddha, may my utterly luminous body illuminate innumerable worlds, and may all the beings who see it come to possess a body just like that, adorned with the thirty-two marks and the eighty signs of the body of a Buddha." The essential aspiration here is to have, upon awakening, the extraordinarily luminous form of a Buddha, and on the basis of that, to bring about the liberation into Buddhahood of any being who sees him. This does not mean that, immediately upon seeing the Medicine Buddha's form, you become a Buddha just like the Medicine Buddha. It means that seeing the Medicine Buddha, even seeing a painted depiction of the Medicine Buddha, or even just hearing about the thirty-two marks and eighty signs and so forth of the Medicine Buddha, instills a habit within your mind. How much of a habit is instilled depends upon your attitude towards what you see or encounter. If you have great faith in and devotion to the Medicine Buddha, then a very strong habit is instilled. If you have some degree of devotion, then some degree of habit is instilled. If you have a little devotion a little habit is instilled. And if you have only the slightest amount of devotion only the slightest amount of habit is instilled. Regardless of how much or how little, eventually this habit will lead to your attainment of that same form as the Medicine Buddha, as well as to the perfect accomplishment of what he has aspired to.[40] If you have great faith in the Medicine Buddha, this will happen much more quickly, and if you have no faith whatsoever, it will happen very slowly. But it will definitely still happen. It is because of this first aspiration of the Medicine Buddha that there is so much benefit in seeing any depiction of him, whether you see it all the time, or whether you see it occasionally—it will do you great benefit.

The second aspiration of the Medicine Buddha, made as a bodhisattva, is also connected primarily with his appearance. It is as follows: "In the future, when I attain perfect awakening and become a Buddha, may my body be as brilliant and lustrous as the jewel of vaidhurya or lapis lazuli. May it be stainless and luminous, vast, pleasing, glorious, majestic in every way. And may all who see it be benefited by it." The apparent and obvious result of this aspiration is the form that the Medicine Buddha exhibits in his pure realm, which form literally has the qualities of being luminous and lustrous and majestic, and so on. But as an additional consequence of this aspiration the Medicine Buddha exhibits his form indirectly even in the midst of impure realms, such as our own, so that beings who are ignorant of what is to be accepted and what is to be rejected, of what is to be done and what is not to be done, can still be inspired by seeing an image of the Medicine Buddha or by hearing his name. As a consequence, although they may not be directly interested in hearing about what is to be done and what is not to be done, a devotion to correct action will gradually grow in their minds through having seen these things or having heard these things.

The third aspiration of the Medicine Buddha as a bodhisattva was that upon his awakening (upon becoming a Buddha) through prajna and upaya (knowledge and method) he be able to bring about prosperity for all beings. This aspiration is particularly concerned with alleviating a type of suffering that is very common in the human realm, which manifests in its most extreme form as poverty. But even when we human beings are not poor, we still think that we are poor. We have not only the suffering of poverty, but the suffering of unceasing ambition—and also the suffering of constant struggle to secure ourselves, and to secure greater and greater prosperity. The first two aspirations were connected with bringing beings to ultimate liberation. This aspiration is more connected with benefiting beings, and especially human beings, in the short term. It is very important because we may tend to think sometimes that the concerns and aspirations of Buddhas only do us good in the long run—that they are only concerned with our liberation and do us no immediate good in this life. This aspiration indicates that this is not true. This aspiration is designed to bring about immediate help. This means that, if you supplicate the Medicine Buddha, it can affect your prosperity in this life. This will not work as immediately as taking a pill, but it can actually make a difference.

The fourth aspiration of the Medicine Buddha is that he be able to extricate beings who have taken incorrect paths and place them on paths that lead to liberation. All of us want to be happy, and we select various ways to lead our lives that we think will make our lives happy. For each of us that is our path. Unfortunately, while some of us actually select ways to make ourselves happy, many of us—thinking to make ourselves happy—select ways that are in fact merely causes of more and more suffering. The primary focus of this aspiration is to be able to lead beings away from those counterproductive paths or lifestyles and into paths that lead to liberation. This is done through exhibiting the forms of Buddhas, through the presence of their speech in the form of sutras and so on, through the demonstrations of the activities of Buddhas, and so on. These things have occurred in our lives already. In one way or another, we have come into contact with some form of depiction of the form of the Buddha, we have heard the sutras or the teachings of the Buddha, or we have been inspired by places connected with the Buddha's life. In short, in whatever way, this activity of the Buddhas has already caused us to change our course of action.

The second part of this fourth aspiration is the wish also to establish those beings concerned only with their own liberation on a path that leads to the full liberation of all beings—in short, on the Mahayana path. This refers in part to something that is stated very clearly in texts such as *The Jewel Ornament of Liberation,* which states that, after someone attains the state of an arhat or arhati—either as a shravaka or as a pratyekabuddha—and has achieved full liberation for themselves from samsara, eventually—sometimes after a very long time—a Buddha will reveal his or her form to the arhat or arhati, inspiring that being to enter the path of Mahayana and attain full Buddhahood. The second part of this fourth aspiration is an aspiration to do just that—to exhibit his form in order to cause beings who are immersed in paths leading to personal liberation alone to engage in paths that will lead to the liberation of all beings, and by doing so, to inspire those beings to increase their love, compassion, and bodhicitta.

The fifth aspiration of the Medicine Buddha is that subsequent to his awakening or Buddhahood he be able to inspire morality in all beings. In the words of the sutra, what he suggests is the moral discipline of a monk or a nun. But by extension, this refers to the practice of morality in general, which is to say, conducting yourself physically, verbally, and mentally in a way that is beneficial to and not harmful to others. The idea here is that the inspiration of a Buddha inspires one to behave morally. Seeing the image of a Buddha or hearing the teachings of a Buddha has caused us to enter the door of the dharma to begin with, and to change our physical, verbal, and mental conduct somewhat. Whether upon beginning the practice of dharma you practice with extraordinary diligence, which is wonderful, or not, which is still okay, there will still be some kind of improvement in your conduct. The primary aspiration here of the Medicine Buddha is that, through his blessing, practitioners be able to maintain morality without impairment. The secondary aspiration is that—since ordinary beings will turn away from moral conduct from time to time, and thereby become confused— the Medicine Buddha be able to prevent those who turn away from morality from remaining in a state of inappropriate conduct, so that they will return to moral conduct and avoid lower rebirths.

Part of the fifth aspiration is that for beings who have mistaken the path, who have turned away from moral conduct, the positive habits that they created in the past when they first adopted moral conduct again become foremost in their minds, through the blessings of the Buddhas, thereby causing them to return to moral conduct.

The sixth aspiration concerns those who are born with congenital physical problems. It is an aspiration by the Medicine Buddha to be able by his blessing to heal anyone who is born with any congenital physical problem or defect, such as impaired senses, impaired limbs, or virulent disease. From the point of view of ordinary thinking, you might think it impossible that the condition of someone born with a congenital physical problem could be alleviated. Yet it is quite possible that such a person could benefit through intense supplication of the Medicine Buddha. And in the cases in which they are unable to ameliorate their condition immediately, the supplication and recollection of the name of the Medicine Buddha and the practice of the sadhana would still generate great lasting benefit.

The seventh aspiration of the Medicine Buddha is that merely hearing his name would alleviate the sufferings of sickness and poverty that afflict those who find themselves seriously ill with no help, no friends, and no resources; that merely by hearing or recollecting his name or by seeing an image of him, beings in that type of situation would be freed from both the sicknesses they suffer and the poverty that reinforces the sicknesses; and that furthermore, those beings, once having heard the Medicine Buddha's name, would never again become ill throughout all of their lifetimes until their attainment of Buddhahood. This sounds like an extremely vast and profound, even an extreme, aspiration. But it is by no means impossible that it could be fulfilled, especially for someone who has intense devotion to the Medicine Buddha, recollects his name, supplicates him, and so on. This aspiration is an instance of one of the particular benefits of the recollection of the Medicine Buddha's name.

Often we find ourselves witnessing the death of a small animal, an insect, a bird, or some other creature that is about to breathe its last breath. It is gasping away its last few moments of life. Because we have Buddha nature and because these beings also have Buddha nature, of course we feel empathy and compassion for them. But the compassion sometimes seems futile, because we simply do not know what to do. Because of the blessings of Buddhas and bodhisattvas, however, there are things that we can do. One, for example, is to recite the name of the Medicine Buddha in the hearing of that dying animal. This is probably not going to heal its sickness immediately. Dying birds will not likely suddenly wake up and fly off. But what it will do is ultimately in the long term better than that; it will establish the basis for that being's future liberation.

The eighth aspiration of the Medicine Buddha concerns freeing human beings in particular from situations of discrimination. It refers to situations like the caste system that was in place in India in the Buddha's time. It often happens in human society that a certain class or group of people will be isolated from the rest and considered to be so far inferior that even their humanity is disputed, as has happened at times to the class known as the "untouchables" in India. The idea here is that, if one of these beings sees an image of the Medicine Buddha or hears the name of the Medicine Buddha, they will generate enough confidence in their humanity, enough recognition of and confidence in the fact that they are just as much a fully fledged human being as whoever is discriminating against them, that they will be able to escape that situation. And it has happened many times that people born in the lowest caste in societies like India could escape their caste restrictions in various ways, which could be viewed as an instance of the blessings of Buddhas.

The ninth aspiration of the Medicine Buddha is to free all beings from the noose or lasso of mara. The lasso of mara refers to that which obstructs liberation. In this case it means any cultivated view that is sufficiently incorrect that it leads you down the wrong path, any view that is actually leading you away from liberation rather than towards it. Now any kind of view—which is to say, any kind of consciously cultivated or developed understanding of how things are—is produced through one's own investigation and analysis of phenomena, using one's own intellect or intelligence. This analysis can either be correct, thereby producing a correct view, or it can be incorrect or faulty, thereby producing an incorrect view. Given our native intelligence, we all have the capacity to engage in these kinds of analyses, and therefore we are capable of coming to either correct or incorrect conclusions. If the view you take of things is basically correct, then it will be a strong cause of your liberation. And by causing your liberation it will be an indirect cause of the liberation of others. In short, a correct view of how things are produces all manner of happiness. On the other hand, if your view is sufficiently incorrect and actually becomes a perverted or misguided use of your intelligence, then it will obstruct your path to liberation, thereby preventing you from liberating others and becoming an obstacle to happiness.

There are two types of misguided or malfunctioning intelligence. One is a strongly incorrect understanding of how things are, which actually leads you on the wrong path, and the other is an analysis that causes you to doubt what is actually true, and therefore causes you to be unable to accept the truth. In either case, the aspiration of the Medicine Buddha here is to free beings from those kinds of misconceptions or misunderstandings, and to establish them on the correct path to liberation.

The other part of this ninth aspiration is connected with the conduct of beings. If your view is correct, then that will cause you to engage in appropriate conduct, which is the conduct of a bodhisattva. And if your view is incorrect, your conduct will follow suit; it will also be incorrect. What is understood here by correct conduct is conduct that does not harm others or yourself, but benefits others and yourself. This conduct naturally ensues from having a correct understanding, a correct view, of how things are. The aspiration of the Medicine Buddha here while still a bodhisattva is that the blessing and the activity of his teaching that will ensue upon his attaining Buddhahood will lead beings to a correct understanding and, therefore, to correct conduct that will cause them to attain liberation.

The tenth aspiration of the Medicine Buddha is to free beings from persecution by their rulers. As literally stated, this means, through the Medicine Buddha's blessing, to free and protect beings from imprisonment, execution, and all the other hardships and cruelties that absolute monarchs impose upon their subjects. But by extension, this also refers to all analogous situations in which something in the external world interferes with your well being—to sickness, to any kind of abuse or persecution by others—regardless of who they may be—and to all the other sorts of dangers and disasters that constantly threaten us. Because the nature of our existence in the world is impermanence, we are constantly in some kind of danger and live in some kind of fear of one thing or another happening to us. The point of this aspiration is that through the blessing of the Medicine Buddha beings be protected from these dangers, and from the fear of the arising of these dangers.

A very commonly displayed image of samsara called the Wheel of Existence shows at the center the three poisons[41] and outside of that the six realms.[42] Outside the six realms, it shows that this [entire wheel of transmigratory existence], which represents samsara, is being held between the teeth and the lap by a very wrathful figure. This wrathful figure represents the basic danger and fear that characterizes samsaric existence. As is shown in the painting, sometimes one is happy, and sometimes one is miserable. But in either case, the basic nature of one's existence is change. Because it is change, it is uncertainty, and because it is uncertainty, it is danger. And because it is danger, it is fear. And all of this uncertainty, danger, and fear is represented by this wrathful figure. During the Buddha's lifetime, his senior students and the shravakas were frequently asked by many different people what his teachings were all about. They would be asked many different questions. And when they went to the Buddha and explained that they were not always able to answer all of these questions, he came up with the idea of painting this Wheel of Existence on the door of every Buddhist temple to serve as a representation, in one image, of the Buddhadharma.

The purpose of Buddhadharma, of course, is to free one from fear and danger. It is to that end that the Buddha taught the dharma, including this sutra of the Medicine Buddha. We all have fears and anxieties. And these fears and anxieties really stem from the fact that samsaric or cyclic existence is fundamentally full of impermanence, and therefore full of suffering. If you ask, is there no way to transcend these fears and anxieties, the answer is, "Yes, there is a way. If you practice dharma, and if, by so doing, you connect with the blessings, the compassion, and the aspirations of Buddhas such as the Medicine Buddha, fear and anxiety can be transcended," which is to say that, if you practice with great diligence, you can transcend all fear once and for all. But even if you do not practice with that much diligence, even if you only practice a little bit, or even if you merely have some contact with the dharma, there will be some benefit. It will help to some extent. And ultimately, you will be liberated into a state beyond all fear. So, in this tenth aspiration, the expressly stated aspiration to free beings from the persecution of unjust monarchs really refers to freeing beings from the sufferings of samsara altogether, which means freeing them from the grip of impermanence. And the point of this is that it is possible to transcend the fear and danger which impermanence otherwise imposes upon us.

The eleventh and twelfth aspirations have in common that they are connected with freeing beings from the suffering of poverty. Specifically the eleventh aspiration is to free beings from the suffering of lacking the necessities of life—from the sufferings of hunger and thirst, and the related suffering of constantly having to struggle to survive. This aspiration of the Medicine Buddha is to free beings from lack of food and drink and from the need to struggle to acquire them, and by extension, to extend to all beings the experience of what is referred to by the Buddha as the delightful taste of dharma. This means that the Medicine Buddha aspired not only to give beings the physical means of survival, physical nutrition, but also the spiritual nutrition of the dharma.

The delightful taste of dharma means hearing the dharma and tasting it in that way, and then practicing it and, through practicing it, becoming truly happy. When one has practiced dharma to the point where one has attained a true and stable state of happiness, one no longer needs to experience the sufferings of samsara, which means that there will no longer be physical suffering, nor will there be mental misery. The benefit of dharma, and the way in which one tastes its delightful taste, can occur to various degrees and in various ways. Sometimes one is benefited simply by hearing the dharma. Sometimes one is benefited by reflecting upon its meaning; sometimes, by meditating upon it. And in some cases the degree of benefit is limited to having a slight contact with it. But in any case, all of these are ways in which, through the aspiration of Buddhas, dharma benefits beings and frees them from suffering.

The twelfth aspiration of the Medicine Buddha focuses on actual poverty and specifically on the lack of things that give us comfort. First the Medicine Buddha aspires to be able to provide clothing for all those beings who lack sufficient clothing and are therefore subject to suffering from heat or cold, the elements, and so on. Beyond that, he aspires to provide ornamentation, which means things like jewellery and so forth, for those who lack them. In the same vein, he aspires to provide musical instruments and the sound and presence of music in one's life for those who lack them. This aspiration centers around fulfilling the wishes of beings and giving beings what they want and what will make them happy in the short run. From one point of view, you might think that this means that simply by praying to the Medicine Buddha you can produce a shower of designer clothing from the sky or whatever musical instruments you might happen to want. So you might actually try praying with those expectations, and you might be very disappointed when they are not fulfilled. This does not mean, however, that the Medicine Buddha's aspiration was pointless or ineffective. The way this aspiration takes effect, and indeed the way they all take effect, is that through the aspiration and power of the Medicine Buddha beings come into contact with dharma. Beings meet images, representations, or other expressions of the activity of the Medicine Buddha or of other Buddhas. As a result, they abandon the wrongdoing and wrong thinking that reinforce their obscurations, gradually weakening or getting rid of their obscurations altogether, and gradually gathering the accumulations of merit and wisdom through actions performed under the inspiration of the dharma and the inspiration of Buddhas. This changes their situation. Either in that life, or in a future life, they start to acquire the things that they want and have lacked to that point. So it is not the case that this twelfth aspiration does not work simply because clothes do not rain down upon you immediately. It works, but it works in a less direct and more gradual way.

So in the *Sutra of the Medicine Buddha,* the Buddha Shakyamuni set forth these twelve aspirations that were made by the Medicine Buddha upon his initial generation of bodhicitta. Then, continuing to address Manjushri, who had requested this explanation, the Buddha points out that as a result of the Medicine Buddha's aspirations, his qualities—both the qualities of his form and being, and the qualities of his realm, which have arisen from his aspirations—are unlimited. The Buddha Shakyamuni also mentions that in his realm the Medicine Buddha has two main disciples in his retinue, bodhisattvas referred to by the names Luminous Like The Sun and Luminous Like The Moon. And then, continuing to address Manjushri, the Buddha says that a man or woman who possesses faith, and therefore diligence and insight, should supplicate the Medicine Buddha, should meditate upon the Medicine Buddha, and should recollect the name of the Medicine Buddha.

The Benefits of Hearing and Recollecting the Medicine Buddha's Name

The *Sutra of the Medicine Buddha* first explains the twelve aspirations of the Medicine Buddha, after which the Buddha begins to talk about the benefits of supplicating, recollecting or even hearing the Medicine Buddha's name.

The first is that, if even those who are most avaricious hear the name of the Medicine Buddha, they will be freed from avarice and from its results. The Buddha mentions that there are people so avaricious they cannot stand to give anything away. He points out that when people cannot stand to give anything away, it is fundamentally because they do not realize there are benefits in doing so. This lack of realization is what keeps them so obsessed with holding onto their possessions. Such people never think of generosity. If they are forced by circumstances to give something away, it makes them extremely unhappy, even if they have to give it away to members of their own family. The problem with this is that if you have that degree of avariciousness, you are likely to have a somewhat unpleasant rebirth. The Buddha says at this point that if even such an extremely avaricious person hears the name of the Medicine Buddha and makes some kind of connection with him—which basically means knowing something about the Medicine Buddha's qualities— then this will inspire in them an understanding of the value of generosity. And as they come to understand the value of generosity, they will actually become generous. Becoming generous, they will not have an unpleasant rebirth. And throughout all their future lives, this momentum of generosity will be present, so that not only will they always be generous, but they will actually become a source of encouragement to others to be generous as well. That is the first benefit explained at this point in the sutra of recollecting the name of and supplicating the Medicine Buddha.

The second benefit is that, if those who behave immorally hear the name of the Medicine Buddha, they will come to behave morally and therefore will be freed from the karmic result of immorality. The Buddha again addresses Manjushri saying that, similarly, there are some people who simply cannot behave themselves. They have no interest whatsoever in morality. They think morality is pointless. The reason that they have no interest in morality is that they do not understand its value. They do not understand the benefit of behaving morally, and they do not understand the problems that behaving immorally leads to. At the same time they have no interest in dharma or spirituality of any kind, because they do not understand its value. Not knowing its value, of course, they have no interest in it. But when a person in even such an extreme state of mind as that hears the name of the Medicine Buddha, they will come to have respect for and gradual interest in both morality and the practice of dharma. As a result they will behave appropriately and they will study and practice dharma, which will cause them not only to be happy in this life, but to come to have better and better and happier and happier lives, life after life. The momentum of their conduct and of their study and practice will be maintained, and will increase as time goes on. We see this development in our own experience. Many of us start out knowing nothing about dharma and therefore not having much respect for or faith in it, simply because we do not know what it is. And we may have had so many questions and doubts about the notions of morality that we had heard about that we really did not respect that either. But at some point something inspired us. We saw something, such as an image of the Buddha, or we heard something, such as an explanation of dharma or the name of a Buddha. Something caught our attention, and caused us to entertain the idea of dharma practice, which caused us to change our way of life to some extent and to practice dharma. Whether you are new to the practice of dharma or are completely immersed in it, in either case something has happened. This something happening is exactly what is referred to in this benefit of the hearing of the Medicine Buddha's name. As it says in the sutras, a being such as ourselves comes in contact with some form of the activity and blessing of a Buddha—an image of a Buddha, the name of a Buddha, or teachings that come from a Buddha—and being inspired by that, eventually we develop some degree of faith and compassion for other beings [which leads to the development of other good qualities].

Of course, our faith in dharma and our devotion to dharma are not unfluctuating. There are times when we apparently have strong faith and devotion, and other times when doubts arise that seem to obstruct or impede our faith and devotion. In either situation, what is necessary is the same: to supplicate or pray with all available faith and devotion, based on a fundamental confidence in the Buddhas and in their teachings. If you supplicate in that way, when you have faith, your faith will increase. And if you supplicate in that way when you have doubts, your faith will increase and your doubts will lessen. So whether or not you are afflicted by hesitation or doubt about dharma, you have to do the same thing. As the Buddha points out at this point in the sutra, supplication of Buddhas, with all the faith and devotion one can muster, is always important.

The third benefit is for those who are so intensely jealous and competitive that they always praise themselves and try to maximize in appearance their own qualities and prestige and always deride others. Such persons devote themselves to defeating and deriding others, and to making others look bad. If they continue in this course of action, they will be reborn in one of the three lower states—the animal realm, the preta realm, or the hell realm—and will experience a great deal of suffering. But if they hear the name of the Medicine Buddha, through the blessing and inspiration of that hearing, they will become much less competitive, will cease deriding others, and will thereby be freed from the karmic results of such actions.

What will happen as a result of such persons' hearing the Medicine Buddha's name is that their attitude will change. They will become more insightful, and through the development of that insight, they will become more skilful and appropriate in their choices of actions. At the same time, their minds will start to calm down and become tranquil. They will eventually become diligent in virtue and will find themselves surrounded by virtuous friends—friends that have virtuous intentions and who also behave appropriately. Without the intervening blessing of the Medicine Buddha attendant upon hearing his name, given their previous course of action, they would be most unlikely to be surrounded by virtuous friends. The virtuous friends by whom they find themselves surrounded—including teachers, but also just friends in general—are one of the conditions that influence them and cause them to change their ways. When someone is intensely and ruthlessly competitive and jealous, they harm others and accumulate a great deal of negative karma. This intense competitiveness and its attendant lifestyle is referred to as the lasso or noose of mara [Tibetan: *shakpa*]. This noose is cut when the person hears the name of the Medicine Buddha. Up to that point, the limitation in their outlook, which reinforces their active and aggressive competitiveness, is an obscuration or ignorance that is like being stuck inside an eggshell. Unable to break out of the eggshell, they are unable to grow. Their innate capacity for insight and wisdom is prevented from developing. When they hear the name of the Medicine Buddha, they break out of the eggshell, and this causes their innate capacity for insight and wisdom to develop. This insight dries up their kleshas, especially the klesha of jealousy, which is like a wild river. This river gradually dries up. Of course, this does not happen automatically or without effort. Through the blessing of hearing the name of the Medicine Buddha, such people encounter teachers and other people who influence them in a virtuous direction, while at the same time their own insight is developing. As a result, they engage actively in methods that will eradicate or dry up the kleshas.

That is the short term benefit. In the long term, the person who hears the name of the Medicine Buddha will be freed from the sufferings of birth, aging, and death. Birth, of course, is the beginning of aging, which always culminates in death, so birth and death are all considered one process. While the sufferings of birth, aging, and death are normal events in our lives, through hearing the name of the Medicine Buddha, one is freed eventually or ultimately from the suffering associated with them. That is the third benefit.

The fourth benefit of hearing the name of the Medicine Buddha is that it pacifies the disputatious. There are some people who just like to fight. They dispute at any opportunity. They like to cause discord. They like to slander and harm other people any way they can. They harm people physically, verbally, and sometimes by cursing them magically. They are malevolent and can actually harm people. In this case, if either the malevolent person or the victim of that person's malevolence hears the name of the Medicine Buddha, the whole situation will calm down. If the malevolent person, the curser, hears the name of the Medicine Buddha, then their malevolence will decrease. They will lose their wish to go around fighting with people and cursing them. If the victim of their malevolence hears the name of the Medicine Buddha, the malevolent person will be unable to harm them. And if they have enlisted local [demonic] spirits in the service of their malevolent aims and ambitions, the spirits will be powerless to harm the intended object of their curse. This does not mean that through the power of the Medicine Buddha these spirits will be violently repelled. It means that the spirits will become benevolent, and eventually the person who hears the name of the Medicine Buddha and is the proposed object of the malevolence and the person acting malevolently—the magician or whatever—will also become benevolent.

To this point we have explained the alleviation of the defects, the negative conduct, and the negative results of avarice, immorality, jealousy, and malevolence. Next, the sutra states the direct benefits of the name itself, the qualities and various other benefits that the hearing and recollection of the name will bring. It says that any man or woman with faith who recollects the name of the Medicine Buddha, engages in the moral conduct of the eightfold renewal and purification commitments or vows for a month or a week or a few days—or otherwise behaves themselves properly with body and speech, and aspires to rebirth in the realm of Sukhavati, the realm of Amitabha, will be reborn there miraculously immediately after their death. Those who do not wish to be reborn in Sukhavati will be reborn in the realms of the gods and enjoy the splendours and enjoyments of those realms. And—although normally when one is born in a god realm, after the merit that has produced that rebirth is exhausted, one is then reborn in a more unpleasant form of samsara—[those who recollect the name of the Medicine Buddha and conduct themselves appropriately] will not suffer a lower rebirth. Their lifetimes will continue to be pleasant. If they wish in particular to be reborn human again, they will be reborn in the most fortunate and pleasant circumstances within the human realm. They will be healthy, courageous, intelligent, and benevolent, and because of their characteristics, they will continue to behave in a positive way and inspire others to do so as well.

To this point in the sutra the Buddha has stated five benefits of the recollection of the name—the alleviation of four defects and the direct benefits. Next, Manjushri addresses the Buddha and the assembly who are listening to the teaching and describes the importance of the sutra. He says that it is important to recollect this sutra, to read the sutra, to write the sutra, to keep a copy of the sutra around you, to venerate the sutra by offering flowers and incense and other offerings to it, and to proclaim the meaning of the sutra to others. If these things are done, he says, many benefits will accrue. The entire region in which these activities are occurring will be blessed and will be protected by the four great kings and other deities who are present in the mandala.

In response to what Manjushri has said, the Buddha adds that whoever venerates the Medicine Buddha should construct or acquire an image of the Medicine Buddha—a statue, a painting, or a depiction of some type—or should visualize the Medicine Buddha. Venerating that for a week or for whatever period, they should intensely supplicate the Medicine Buddha, eating pure food—which means food that is not gained through harming others—washing frequently, wearing clean clothes, and so on, and in that way venerate the sutra and the image by making physical offerings to them, including all sorts of things such as parasols and victory banners and so on.

For this veneration to be effective, the one who is venerating has to have a good intention. A good intention here is defined as having four characteristics. The first is that the venerating mind be stainless. Stainless here means free of the stain of selfishness or competitiveness. Your intention in doing the practice must be not merely to benefit yourself, but to benefit all beings, and your intention must be free of competitiveness. The second quality of a good intention is that it be unsullied. Unsullied here means that you have unsullied faith, faith without reservation, faith that is without a feeling of antipathy towards the object of the faith, faith that is without such crippling doubt that it does not function.

The third characteristic of a good intention is the absence of malevolence. Malevolence can take many different forms. There is manifest anger, anger that is evident and will be acted on right away. There is resentment. Resentment is still malevolence, but it is something that you carry under the surface and that waits for a future time to emerge. There is spitefulness, which makes you want to say or do something nasty. And then there is wanting to harm people in a more organized way than merely being spiteful. The absence of all of these forms of malevolence is an attitude that sincerely wishes that others be happy and that they be free from suffering, which means that if you see a being that is happy, you delight in that and want that being to be even more happy and to be free from whatever suffering they are still afflicted by. If you see a being that is suffering, you want that being to be free from all the suffering that they are undergoing and to be completely happy.

The fourth characteristic of a good intention is impartiality, an attitude that directs benevolence equally to all beings without exception. There is no preference for some beings, and less concern for others. The attitude is that all beings are more or less fellow travellers on the same road.

With this kind of good intention, if the practitioner physically circumambulates the image of the Medicine Buddha, mentally recollects the twelve aspirations of the Medicine Buddha, and either recites the sutra of the Medicine Buddha or at least recollects the benefits of the name of the Medicine Buddha as stated in the sutra, then they will accomplish their wishes.

The reason that it says that they will accomplish their wishes is that people have different wishes. Some people wish for longevity, and they can accomplish longevity through engaging in these activities— through supplicating the Medicine Buddha, through circumambulating the image, through having faith in and devotion for the Medicine Buddha, and so on. Some people do not care much how long they live; they are more interested in wealth, and so such a person would wish to achieve wealth and could do so by this method. Some people are not concerned about wealth either, but want to have children. And they can have children through this method, although obviously not through this method exclusively.[43] Some people wish for success in the secular world, in business and so on, and they can achieve such success through this method. The significance of this is that you can achieve what you wish through doing the same secular or business things, but with much less effort.

In the same way, if someone is afflicted with nightmares or bad dreams, experiences inauspicious signs, sees things that they think are unlucky, or experiences things that disturb them and produce anxiety, if they make offerings to the Medicine Buddha, pray to the Medicine Buddha, recollect the sutra and the Medicine Buddha's twelve aspirations, and so forth, then the inauspicious signs and bad dreams and so on will gradually disappear.

And not only will inauspicious signs disappear, but if you are in a situation where you are endangered by such things as fire, water, poison, or weapons, by falling off a cliff, or falling victim to any other sort of accident, or by elephants, lions, tigers, bears, poisonous snakes, scorpions, or centipedes—if you are endangered by any of those things—then if you supplicate the Medicine Buddha, those dangers will disappear.

And also supplication to the Medicine Buddha will protect you from the dangers of war—being caught in the middle of a war—of robbery, and of banditry.

If someone who has faith in the Buddhadharma, and especially in the Medicine Buddha, whether man or woman, takes some form of ordination—such as the refuge vow, the vow of an upasaka or upasika [the vows of a lay disciple], the bodhisattva vow, or monastic ordination—through the blessing of the Medicine Buddha they will be able in most cases to maintain them. But if such a person does not maintain them, then they will become depressed. They will think, "I undertook such and such a commitment and I was unable to keep it. I am obviously someone who cannot accomplish anything I set out to do. Things are not going very well, terrible things are going to happen to me in this life, and after I die I am definitely going to be reborn in the lower realms." If this happens to you, then if you supplicate the Medicine Buddha, make offerings to the Medicine Buddha, and have devotion to the Medicine Buddha, you will be freed from the danger of those disasters and inferior rebirths.

The next thing mentioned in the sutra is actually the answer to a question that was asked earlier. It says in the sutra, when a women is giving birth to a child, if she expects great difficulty—great agony and suffering in doing so—if she supplicates the Medicine Buddha with devotion, then the birth will occur free from extreme difficulty. The child will be born easily, without harm to the mother or the child, and the child will be healthy, intelligent, and will be strong from birth.

At this point the Buddha has stated a number of extraordinary benefits of supplicating and making offerings to the Medicine Buddha. Next the Buddha addresses not Manjushri, but Ananda. He addresses Ananda because Ananda is not at this point a great bodhisattva. He is a shravaka, a practitioner of the Hinayana path. The Buddha has taught the sutra and explained its benefits. He has talked about the extraordinary qualities of the Medicine Buddha, his twelve aspirations and their effects, the effects of the recollection of the name of the Medicine Buddha, and so on. So addressing Ananda, the Buddha says, "Ananda, do you believe what I have said? Do you have faith in this, or do you have doubt about it?"

In response to the Buddha's question, Ananda says, "I have no doubt of the truth of what you have said. I believe everything you have said. In fact, I believe everything you have ever said, because I have witnessed the qualities of your body, speech, and mind. I have witnessed your miracles, and I have witnessed your immersion in samadhi. So I know it is impossible for you to mislead beings, and I have no doubt of the validity of anything you say. But, there are some beings who will not believe this. There are some beings who, when they hear this, will want to think that all of this is impossible or untrue. Will they not incur tremendously negative karma through hearing about this Buddha and this sutra and having antipathy for them, or disbelief?" So he ends by asking the Buddha a question.

The reason that Ananda asks this question is that in theory there could be a problem in this situation. Theoretically, if someone thinks untrue what a Buddha has said about another Buddha and their benefits and blessings, that could become an obstacle to that being's progress towards awakening. But the Buddha answers as follows: "Ananda, there is in fact no such danger in this case. It is possible that a being might initially disbelieve these things, but since they have heard the name of the Medicine Buddha, then through the blessing of having heard that name, it will be impossible for their disbelief and antipathy to last very long, which is an instance of the qualities and power of this Buddha. This is something that is so profound only bodhisattvas can understand it."[44] But ultimately it means that one's initial disbelief will not become an obstacle to one's liberation, and will not cause one to accumulate such negative karma that one will be reborn in the lower realms and so on. If someone has doubts, disbelief, or even antipathy towards this sutra, it is not going to be a big problem because of the blessing imparted by the Buddha in the way he taught the sutra and because of the aspirations of the Medicine Buddha himself.

This is important to know, because from time to time, of course, we do have doubts. We read something in a sutra such as this and we think, "But that is just impossible." And then we think, "Oh no, I have wrong views about the sutra; something terrible is going to happen to me." In any case, this is not going to be a problem here.

The next event in the dialogue is that the great Bodhisattva Chagdrul, one of the sixteen bodhisattvas in the retinue of the Medicine Buddha and therefore present at this teaching by the Buddha Shakyamuni, arises from his seat, adopts the posture that Manjushri had adopted in order to request this teaching, and addresses the Buddha. In addressing the Buddha and the entire gathering here, Chagdrul is not actually asking a question. He is himself stating further benefits of the sutra. He begins by saying that it was most kind of the Buddha to teach the sutra, to explain the twelve aspirations of the Medicine Buddha and their effects, to explain the benefits of the sutra and of the name, and so on. Then he says that he has something to add, and says that through the power of the Medicine Buddha, if someone becomes extremely sick—so sick that they are in agony and are surrounded by their family and their friends, and the family also is agonized by the sickness of the person—and even if it gets to the point where the person appears to be dying—when their perception of this world is becoming more and more vague and they seem to be starting to perceive the next world, the intermediate state—if even at that time there is intense supplication to the Medicine Buddha, through the blessing of the Medicine Buddha that person may be revived.

Chagdrul continues, "Because such benefits as these are possible—benefits both for this and future lives—men and women with faith should venerate, worship, and supplicate the Medicine Buddha. This is extremely important."

At that point Ananda addresses the Bodhisattva Chagdrul, saying, "While you say it is important to make offerings to and to worship the Medicine Buddha, how should we do this?" In response Chagdrul says, "In order to free oneself and others from sickness and suffering, it is important to recollect the name of the Medicine Buddha seven times during the day and seven times during the night."

Now, when it says in the sutra that there will be such and such benefits from merely hearing, recollecting, or keeping in mind the name of the Medicine Buddha, this does literally mean that to some extent there will be some benefit from merely hearing, merely remembering, or merely keeping the name in mind. But mainly, when it says the recollection of the name, it means something more than the simple recollection of the name per se. It means the recollection of the qualities of the Medicine Buddha, the recollection of the name in appreciation of the Medicine Buddha's qualities, with an attitude of sincere faith and great enthusiasm. Furthermore, it means not simply the appreciation that there is a Buddha in a certain realm far away who has such and such qualities, but includes the actual wish to emulate the Medicine Buddha, the wish to achieve the same Buddhahood, to enact the same aspirations and benefits for beings, and therefore the wish to diligently engage in the path in order to attain that same state. To recollect the name really means to recollect and know the Medicine Buddha's qualities and to actually engage enthusiastically in the path leading to the attainment of those qualities. Now, it is not the case that there are no benefits whatsoever to simply hearing the name per se; there are. But ultimately the great benefits which arise from the blessing of the name of the Medicine Buddha arise from practice based upon devotion to the Medicine Buddha, and not merely from simply hearing his name.

Chagdrul continues to address Ananda, saying that if the practitioner venerates and prays to the Medicine Buddha, then "the monarch will be fully empowered." This literally means that the monarch of the country in which this veneration is occurring will be properly empowered as the monarch. But what it implies or is saying is that the whole country in which the practice occurs will become happy, which is symbolized as the proper empowerment of that country's monarch. This means that through the practitioner's practice, sickness, warfare, the action of malevolent spirit—such as the spirits connected with the various constellations, planets, and stars—disasters such as untimely wind, excessive rainfall, or drought, and epidemics and civil strife will all be averted. For these to be averted the practitioner must pray to and venerate the Medicine Buddha with great love and compassion.

In other words, through supplication of the Medicine Buddha disasters will be averted, sickness and the malevolent influence of spirits will diminish, and other problems or upheavals in the country in which the practice occurs will be pacified. This means that while we practice dharma and, therefore, supplicate the Medicine Buddha for the benefit of all beings, by doing so we also secure our own happiness and the benefit of the country and region in which we practice.

Ananda then asks the Bodhisattva Chagdrul another question. He asks, "How is it possible through the supplication and blessing of the Medicine Buddha for someone who is almost dead to be awakened in the manner that Chagdrul has described?" And Chagdrul says that this is possible because the person's life and vitality are not really exhausted. A condition exists that has almost caused their death, and that will cause their death if it is not removed. But it can be removed. He then lists nine different conditions of untimely death—untimely here meaning unnecessary—and says that through supplication of the Medicine Buddha it is sometimes possible to remove these conditions, thereby averting death and allowing the person to revive.

Then the twelve yaksha chieftains, who have been present throughout the Buddha's teaching and have heard everything that has passed up to this point, address the Buddha as a group. They express their appreciation for having heard the sutra. They say, "We are most fortunate in this way to have heard the name of the Medicine Buddha and to have heard of his qualities and benefits, because simply through having heard this teaching we are freed from the fear of falling into lower realms." They say this because they are mundane gods[45] at that point in time, and without having heard the sutra would be in the same danger as ourselves of falling into a lower rebirth. But they are confident that, having heard the name and the benefits of the Medicine Buddha, they are no longer in danger of being reborn in the three lower realms. Therefore, they say, "We are delighted by this and we all take refuge, therefore, in the Buddha, in the dharma, and in the sangha." Because they have been inspired by hearing the sutra, by hearing about the Medicine Buddha's name, and so forth, they take refuge and commit themselves to being beneficial to sentient beings and to never harming them. And so in a sense, they also generate bodhicitta and promise to protect beings.

In addition, the twelve yaksha chieftains say, "Especially, we will protect any place where there is the sutra of the Medicine Buddha and we will protect any persons and any place where there are persons who venerate the Medicine Buddha." In that way the twelve yaksha chieftains—and also the four great kings—vow to protect the sutra and its followers, and to free all of these beings from harm.

In response, the Buddha addresses the twelve yaksha chieftains and their followers, saying, "Excellent. As you say, having heard the name of the Medicine Buddha you are now free of the danger and fear of falling into lower states. Your delight and confidence in this, the gratitude you have expressed, and especially your commitment to the welfare of beings and of the teachings that this has inspired in you are excellent."

Now, for this reason, whether you regard it as the blessing of the Medicine Buddha himself and of his name, or as the protection of the twelve yaksha chieftains, if you regularly supplicate the Medicine Buddha, it will protect you. I can speak of this from my own experience. Once when I was living at Rumtek Monastery in Sikkim, I needed to go into town. There was a car that regularly went from the monastery into town, and I knew the driver and had expressed my need to go that day. But for some reason he didn't wait for me. He left without me. So I found another car to go to town in, and as a result I am still alive. The first car got into a terrible accident, and while the driver survived, the passengers were all killed. Especially because I am so fat, I would definitely have been squished for sure. So I regard it as the blessing of the three jewels that my life was saved, because there was no obvious reason why he should have left without me.

Now the reason that I connect this with the Medicine Buddha is that sometime before that I had gone into the presence of His Holiness Sakya Trizin Rinpoche[46] and had requested a divination from him as to whether or not I was facing any obstacles. He said, "If you will do the Medicine Buddha practice one hundred times, then you will be free from whatever obstacles might otherwise affect you." And so I did this very Medicine Buddha practice that we have been studying one hundred times, and I think that is why I was not killed in that accident. So when it says here that the Medicine Buddha practice will protect you from untimely death through poison and accidents, and so on, I believe it.

At this point, the Buddha has finished teaching the main body of the sutra. The Bodhisattva Chagdrul has made his remarks and the twelve yaksha chieftains have expressed their appreciation and commitment. At that point Ananda arises once again and addresses the Buddha, thanking him for teaching the sutra and saying, "Now that you have given this teaching, what should we call it in the future? This teaching will have to have a name."

And the Buddha says, "You can call it either *The Twelve Great Aspirations of the Medicine Buddha*, or you can call it *The Vow and Commitment of the Twelve Yaksha Chieftains*."

Finally, after the Buddha has given the name by which the sutra is to be known in the future, all of those receiving the teaching, foremost among them Manjushri, Vajrapani, and the other bodhisattvas, as well as the twelve yaksha chieftains and so on, express their delight and rejoicing in the sutra's having been taught and their having heard it and say, "Excellent," and so forth.

And then, at the very end of the sutra, it says, "That is the completion of the *Sutra of the Great Aspirations of the Medicine Buddha*." That line is present at the end to show that the sutra is complete. It is entirely possible that one could have in hand only part of a sutra without the end of it. To show that it is complete and goes all the way to the end, those words are added.

That completes our discussion of the *Medicine Buddha Sutra*. There is another sutra connected to this, called the *Sutra of the Aspirations of the Eight Medicine Buddhas*, which refers to the principal Medicine Buddha of the *Medicine Buddha Sutra* and the other seven Medicine Buddhas in his retinue. These are distinct Buddhas, but their aspirations are fundamentally the same, so I am not going to explain that sutra separately.

Questions *&* Answers

Question: Thank you Rinpoche. May I ask for a definition of a yaksha? Is it a human being? What is the Tibetan?

Translator: *Nöjin.*

Question: Is it a human being, is it other than a human being?

Rinpoche: Yakshas are not human. They are nonhuman beings who are most often perceived as gods of wealth.

Question: When they were attending this teaching of the Buddha Shakyamuni, would they have been seen by human beings who were there? I mean by ordinary human beings, not by great bodhisattvas and so forth?

Rinpoche: The way it is put in the sutra, it sounds as though everybody could see them.

Question: And do they have flesh bodies or do they have bodies of light?

Rinpoche: I do not know.

Question: And if they are worldly deities, have they gotten enlightened in the meantime? And if they have not, why are we prostrating to them?

Rinpoche: Well, I do not know if they have attained awakening, but because at that time they promised to protect the Buddha's teachings, they become dharmapalas, and we take refuge in them as mundane dharmapalas.

Question: I see, but if they show up, do we have to do what they tell us?

Rinpoche: You had probably better.

Question: Rinpoche, in the other Buddhist practices, which many of us have done—shamatha, vipashyana, the various sadhanas, and so forth—I have great confidence. Even though I may not be a good practitioner, I have great confidence that they lead to the ultimate goal. But I am wondering if they have any effect on health as we conventionally understand it, because many times it seems they do not. Or I do not know. Sometimes I feel very sick, so I am wondering if Rinpoche would comment on that.

Translator: Which practices? Are you talking about all of them as a group or the Vajrayana practices in particular?

Question: Tonglen, shamatha, vipashyana, and the various sadhanas and that sort of thing.

Rinpoche: Well, the main yidam sadhanas like Vajrayogini and Chakrasamvara are not particularly said to have much effect on sickness, but practices such as shamatha can be very helpful for sickness.

Question: As Rinpoche knows, in the Shambhala centers there has always been a great effort made to protect the teachings, especially the Vajrayana teachings, and so this is sort of a new situation for us in terms of the instruction that this can be made more available. And so there are still issues going on about how to do that properly. I am just wondering if Rinpoche could elaborate a little bit more on some other possibilities for presenting these teachings properly—so that people actually receive proper instruction and understand what is going on while at the same time making them more available.

Rinpoche: I think you can make it as freely available as possible, because there is no possibility of anyone getting into trouble with this. This is connected with the part of the sutra in which Ananda addresses the Buddha, saying, "Is there not a possibility that people hearing about this and disbelieving it might accumulate negative karma and be worse off than if they had not heard it in the first place?" And in answer to that the Buddha says, "No, even if they initially react with disbelief or even antipathy, the blessing of the Medicine Buddha itself will cause their minds to change."

Question: Forgive me, Rinpoche, I feel very much like the person that Ananda was talking about, though I want very much to believe. When I was a little girl in my convent in London in 1939, the nuns told me that if I prayed with great devotion and sincerity to Jesus to make Hitler a good man, the war would not happen; we would be able to prevent it and be protected from it. So, of course I felt I didn't have enough devotion, and I felt very bad about it. My heart really breaks to think of people in Tibet who are much more evolved than I was and have much more devotion, who are doing the Medicine Buddha practice and still they have war. Would you please shed some light on this?

Rinpoche: Well, first of all, as I said, the result of dharma practice is usually not immediate. It usually does not manifest as an immediate and dramatic or miraculous transformation of the circumstances. I mentioned for example that if you pray for wealth you are not immediately going to have a shower of gold come from the sky. But there is always a benefit. The benefit manifests as an effect that emerges gradually over a long term and maybe as a transformation of circumstances, as in the story that I told you. Now, for example, I would not say that your prayers as a child just before the outbreak of the Second World War were wasted. For example, you were not killed in the London Blitz, but many other people were.[47] And as for Tibet, of course as everybody knows Tibet was overcome by warfare. And we simply have to accept the fact that when a very large and populous country invades a small one, they are going to win. It is very hard to escape from that. If we look at it from a political point of view, we would have to say that Tibet was lost, but from a dharmic point of view, the dharma tradition of Tibet is far from lost. In fact it is doing better than it was before. It used to be that in Tibet, if someone actually travelled from Tibet as far as Kalimpong in northern India, that was a real journey. That was really expanding, bringing the teachings across the world. But now there is almost nowhere on this planet where there are not Tibetan Buddhist dharma centers, Tibetan stupas, retreats, and so on.

Question: Is there an end to experience once we attain Buddhahood?

Translator: From the point of view of that Buddha?

Question: Well yes, I suppose. But also, once everyone in the Mahayana view is liberated, is there a cessation of experience? Or what happens exactly?

Translator: So, are there two questions? When one person attains enlightenment, do they cease to experience, and when everybody attains enlightenment, is everything going to be over?

Question: Or what happens? Yes.

Rinpoche: When someone attains full awakening, Buddhahood, they do not cease to experience. What they experience is by our standards inconceivable, and all that can be said about it is that it is utterly pure.

All of the appearances they undergo are pure, the environment in which they experience themselves is a pure realm, and so on.

Implicit in your second question is the question, "Will there ever come a time when all beings will have attained Buddhahood?" This question has to be asked before you can ask what will happen then. And the answer is no. There will never come a specific time when samsara will be over for all beings. There will never come, it is taught, a time when all beings without a single exception will have attained Buddhahood, because beings are infinite in number. And when we say, "I resolve to do this and that until samsara is completely emptied," we do so in order to generate an open ended and unlimited aspiration and commitment. We say that, not because we think that there will come a specific time when samsara will be emptied and our contract terminated, but because we do not want to have a limited aspiration. We do not want to have an aspiration that says, "I will perform benefit for beings, but only for three years or only for this long."

Now, returning to your first question, there are contexts in which it is taught, for example in the common Middle Way School presentation of the awakening of a Buddha, that after awakening, that Buddha exists only in the perception of others, both pure and impure, and does not experience himself or herself. But in the Vajrayana that is not taught. In the Vajrayana it is definitely taught that the real sambhogakaya realm, the true or perfect sambhogakaya, is in fact self-experience; it is how a Buddha experiences himself or herself.

Question: Rinpoche, you have gone into great detail about the sutra tradition and about how the Medicine Buddha came to be known in this world. That knowledge of the Medicine Buddha actually originated with the Buddha Shakyamuni, and that gives me great confidence in terms of the origin of this practice, because I have confidence in the Buddha Shakyamuni himself. However, a large part of the practice that you have given us is also tantric in nature, and the very detailed visualizations clearly come from somewhere else. Can you give some details about their origins so that we can have similar confidence in and knowledge about their origins?

Rinpoche: This practice is a combination of sutra and tantra. I have explained its sutra origin. Basically it doesn't have a tantric origin going back to the Buddha Shakyamuni independent of its origin in the sutras. It is basically a sutra practice connected with tantra. In other words, it is a practice according to the sutras that adopts and adapts the methods of the tantras, specifically some of the methods of Anuttarayoga tantra. This became a tantric practice after the Buddha's time through the realization and teachings of the bodhisattvas who received it from the Buddha and the various mahasiddhas who received it from them. In that sense it is different from a primarily tantric practice like Chakrasamvara or Kalachakra, the origins of which are one or more specific tantras taught by the Buddha, belonging to a specific class of tantra such as some form of Anuttarayoga and so on. And in that sense it is also unlike the various lower tantras—the yoga, carya and kriya tantras—which also go back originally to the Buddha Shakyamuni. Here it is basically a sutra practice that makes use of the methods of Anuttarayoga tantra, and there is no specific tantra that is a scriptural basis for it as is the sutra.

Question: What about all of the detail, all of the richness of the visualization. Is that contained in the longer sutras? The palace and its various colors, etc. Is there a specific being even after the Buddha's time from whom this originates?

Rinpoche: Well, the palace is based upon the description in the sutra of the Medicine Buddha, which says that the Medicine Buddha's realm is called such and such, it is like this, and it has such and such a palace, and so on. The retinue is based also upon the sutra. In the sutra all eight Medicine Buddhas and the sixteen bodhisattvas are mentioned as being present at the teaching, and the twelve yaksha chieftains, the ten protectors of the directions, and the four great kings are also described as being present at the teaching. By visualizing them surrounding the Buddhas and bodhisattvas, you insure the receipt of their protection and blessing.

Question: For fear of totally beating a dead horse, you know all of the lights and the Medicine Buddhas raining down, are these based on other tantric practices?

Rinpoche: Yes.

Question: Rinpoche, when I go home and talk to my family and friends and say I have been at the Medicine Buddha retreat and they ask me who or what is the Medicine Buddha, I do not know what to tell them. I want to create a definition that is going to bring them benefit, and although I know that hearing about the Medicine Buddha will help them, I do not want to initially turn them away. So could you give sort of a short answer in layman's terms? I do not know if that is possible. And also, we have a new cat and I want to expose him to the Medicine Buddha, but he might not stay at the shrine with us when we are practicing. So, is it appropriate to put a picture of the Medicine Buddha near his food bowls or by his bed? Or is that not appropriate? Will simply living with dharma practitioners be helpful for an animal when he hears us just sort of talking dharma?

Rinpoche: To answer your first question, probably the most convenient thing to say to your family is that you were taught and practiced a form of meditation designed to lead to physical health and freedom from sickness, and leave it at that. As for putting an image of the Medicine Buddha near where your cat eats and sleeps, that is fine.

The Correct View Regarding
Both Deities and Maras

In the sutra that we have been studying there is a great deal of presentation of the idea of veneration, even worship of this deity, the Medicine Buddha, and through veneration and worship, achieving what is called cutting the noose of mara. So we have the idea of some sort of external mara that is somewhere down there and some sort of external deity that is somewhere up there. Given this type of presentation we may come to the conclusion that the deity being supplicated, such as the Medicine Buddha, has the omnipotence and the external existence of a creator, as though he or she actually causes us to experience the pleasant and unpleasant things that we undergo. It may seem that since, if you pray to the Medicine Buddha, you will somehow receive the two attainments—the common and supreme attainments—that if you do not pray to the Medicine Buddha, you will get into trouble. But the Vajrayana view of the effect or effectiveness of the supplication of deities is fundamentally different from this idea. The idea in the Vajrayana is that the blessing associated with the deity, the attainment you gain through this type of practice, is a result of your practice of the path.[48] Your accomplishment of the path leads to its result, which fundamentally is caused by your own meditative state or samadhi, cultivated by yourself within yourself. The capacity you have to cultivate such a samadhi and thereby attain these results is your own fundamental nature, which is referred to as Buddha nature. This potential is something that each and every being has. It is usually obscured by the presence of temporary stains or obscurations. These stains are removed by the practice of the path, by the practice of meditation, by the practice of the generation and completion stages. And when these obscurations have been removed and the innate qualities of this Buddha nature are revealed, that is the result. So this practice is not really the worship of an external deity. It is primarily a way of gaining access to your own inherent or innate wisdom.

Because this is the view of the Vajrayana with regard to the nature of deities, the uncommon method of the Vajrayana is to visualize oneself as the deity. Thus, in this practice you visualize yourself as the Medicine Buddha. But in the common vehicle, the basic teachings of the Buddha, [the Hinayana teachings], it appears as though it is taught that the ultimate result of the path is what is called arhat without remainder. There it is taught that when someone completes the path—which means that they remove or abandon all of the causes of samsara, all karma, and all kleshas—then they naturally attain the result of that removal, which is the cessation of the results of those causes, which means the total cessation of samsaric existence for that individual. Since they have abandoned the causes and therefore experience the cessation of the results, according to the common vehicle, there is nothing whatsoever left— which is called arhat without remainder. So from the point of view of the common vehicle, one's own liberation depends entirely, without any exception whatsoever, upon one's attainment through meditation, and there is no point whatsoever in supplication or prayer to anyone or anything outside oneself, because there is simply no one to pray to.

The Vajrayana view is different from that. According to the Vajrayana, as according to the Mahayana, there have appeared innumerable Buddhas and bodhisattvas. All of them have entered the path by generating bodhicitta, have traversed [or are in the process of traversing] the path by gathering the accumulations of merit and wisdom for three periods of innumerable kalpas [according to the Mahayana], and finally have completed [or will complete] the path by attaining full awakening or Buddhahood. Having attained Buddhahood, they actually have the capacity to grant their blessing, and it is for that reason that we make offerings, that we perform prostrations, that we supplicate, and so on. So in the Vajrayana we not only visualize ourselves as the yidam, but we also visualize the yidam, such as the Medicine Buddha, in front of us as well. Focusing on the front visualization, we make offerings and so forth in order to gather the accumulations, and we supplicate the deity and receive its blessing. So from the Vajrayana point of view, there is in fact something to pray to, and doing so does facilitate one's attainment of the result.

Connected with this is one's understanding of the aim of practice. Sometimes, in the way dharma is presented, it seems as though the only acceptable goal of doing dharma practice is the attainment of perfect awakening in order to liberate others, and it seems to be said that it is utterly inappropriate to think of any benefit for this life at all, which implies there exist no methods in dharma for benefiting oneself in this life. In fact, this is not the case. Especially in the Vajrayana tradition we talk about the attainment of the two siddhis or two attainments. One of them is the supreme siddhi or supreme attainment. Through the practice of meditation—through the practice of the generation and completion stages—you gradually remove the two obscurations—the mental/emotional afflictions and the cognitive obscurations—and you eventually attain Buddhahood. The attainment of Buddhahood is the supreme attainment. But if you think that this is the only benefit or only reason for practice, that is not entirely the case. In the Vajrayana we also speak of the common siddhis or common attainments. Through meditating upon a yidam you can also attain longevity, freedom from sickness, wealth and so on, and it is because of this emphasis in Vajrayana on the common attainments that there are so many different deities. For example, in order to attain wealth you would practice a wealth deity such as Jambhala. In order to attain physical well-being and freedom from sickness you might practice a deity such as the Medicine Buddha. In order to increase your insight into the meaning of the teachings you might practice Manjushri. Doing practices for these reasons is not regarded as inappropriate in any way. Since these practices exist, it is obviously not impossible to attain these things by doing them.

That is the view with regard to the deities that are meditated upon and supplicated. Then there is the other side of things, mara or the maras, which we might think of as being down there, in the same way that deities might be thought of as being up there somewhere. There are two ways in which we generally think of mara. One way is to think that mara refers to one's own mental afflictions, one's own kleshas alone, and not as any kind of external being that is trying to tempt one or interfere with one's spiritual progress. And sometimes we think that maras are completely external, and we think that everything that goes wrong is caused by some kind of external malevolent force that is attempting to victimize us. Both of these views are somewhat extreme.

Mara is most commonly presented in the Buddhist tradition as four different types of maras, called devaputramara, the mara that is the child of the gods; kleshamara, the mara that is the mental afflictions; skandhamara, the mara that is the aggregates; and finally mrtyumara, the mara that is the lord of death. These are primarily internal. The first of these, devaputramara, the mara that is the child of the gods, refers not to some kind of external demonic force but primarily to your own great attachment and great craving. Therefore, it is given the name of child of the gods, because when this mara is depicted iconographically—because it is craving or wanting something so much—it is not depicted as something ugly and threatening, but as something attractive, because that is the feeling-tone of attachment. It is liking things so much that it interferes with your dharma practice and your attainment of awakening. The second mara, kleshamara, the mara that is mental afflictions, is your mental afflictions themselves. These become a mara because, due to the beginningless habit of maintaining and cultivating them, they keep on popping up again and again. They are very hard to abandon or even to suppress, and when they are momentarily absent, they come up again, and in that way they interfere with your practice of dharma.

The third mara is skandamara, the mara of the aggregates. The aggregates here refer to the five aggregates that make up samsaric existence—forms, sensations, perceptions, thoughts,[49] and consciousness. Now, these aggregates are themselves mara, because being aggregates or composite, they are impermanent. Being impermanent they are constantly changing, and therefore they are always a cause, directly or indirectly, of suffering. In order to attain permanent happiness, in order to transcend the suffering of samsara, we must transcend the five aggregates. There is simply no way to attain a state of permanent happiness within the bondage of these aggregates.

The fourth of the four maras is death itself, which is depicted iconographically as wrathful or unpleasant. Death, of course, is what we are most afraid of. Death is what comes with great agony and fear and pain.

These four maras are fundamentally internal; they are not external beings. Victory over the four maras requires the practice of dharma, the practice of meditation. Specifically, it requires the realization of the selflessness of persons and the selflessness or emptiness of things in general. In order to realize these two aspects of selflessness or emptiness, one meditates on emptiness, and, especially according to the Vajrayana tradition, one meditates upon the nature of one's own mind, since this is an evident emptiness, an obvious or directly experienceable emptiness.[50] Therefore, the practice of shamatha and vipashyana, tranquillity and insight meditation, that takes as its basis the recognition of the nature of one's own mind, is a direct method that leads to the realization of the emptiness of one's own nature, and on the basis of that realization, one can gradually attain the ultimate fruition, final awakening, at which point one has conquered all four maras once and for all. And that is how one conquers the mara that is internal.

Vajrayana practice therefore includes the practices of both shamatha and vipashyana. But the typical practices of the Vajrayana are not limited to those practices; they also include the two broad and inclusive categories of the generation stage and the completion stage. According to the Vajrayana, the four maras are considered to be impure appearances, the projections of bewilderment and the presence in one's mind of those tendencies—the kleshas and the cognitive obscurations—that cause those projections. The four maras consist of impure appearances and the reification of them, and this includes impure or negative karma as well.[51] The attainment of victory over the four maras according to the Vajrayana tradition comes about from transcending these impure appearances and coming to experience pure appearances. One attains the experience of pure appearances by meditating upon appearances as pure, by meditating upon one's environment as a pure realm, one's body as a pure form, and so forth. Now if this were a meditation upon things as other than what they truly or fundamentally are, it would never work. But because our basic nature is Buddha nature, and because the temporary obscurations that cause us to perceive things as impure are secondary to that nature—and by temporary or secondary we mean that they can be removed, that they are empty, that they are not intrinsic to the nature—because our basic or true nature is Buddha nature and those obscurations that hide it are not intrinsic to it and can be removed, therefore, just as our true nature is pure, appearances are also fundamentally pure. It is in order to reveal this basic nature and reveal these pure appearances that we practice the generation stage.

Initially, generation stage practice is extremely difficult, because it goes directly against the grain or the current of our habit of impure projections, which causes the impure appearances we experience. But eventually [with effort] the habit of regarding things as pure is cultivated to the point where one generates a clear appearance or a clear perception of things as pure. From that point onward, gradually, the actual, pure nature of phenomena or appearances begins to be revealed, and it is for that reason that we practice the generation stage meditation upon yidams. It is also in order to reveal this pure nature of appearances that we regard things not as the ordinary solid things that they appear to be—ordinary earth, ordinary stones and so on—but as the embodiment of emptiness manifesting as vivid pure appearances. In this way, through practicing the generation and completion stages, we attain the ultimate result.[52]

Sometimes when we are practicing, we experience adverse conditions, obstacles of various kinds—such as physical illness or mental depression, or various external setbacks in whatever we are trying to do. These come from one of two causes—from previous actions or karmas, or from present, suddenly arising conditions. Although normally we regard the maturation of our previous actions as something that, once it arises, is very difficult to change, nevertheless, if you supplicate the Buddhas and bodhisattvas, make offerings, gather the accumulations, and so on, you can purify your karma. Purifying your karma also purifies some of your kleshas at the same time.[53] We all have kleshas for sure, but they can be defeated by the appropriate remedies, if the remedies are sincerely and consistently applied. With the application of the appropriate remedies—especially with the blessings of Buddhas and bodhisattvas—one can alter one's karma and reduce the power of one's kleshas, [thereby eliminating or reducing one's obstacles and adverse conditions].

The other cause of obstacles is what is called "sudden conditions." One type of sudden condition is a karmic debt, a situation in which what is happening is not the direct result of your immediately previous actions, but is being imposed upon you by another being because of a negative karmic connection you made with that being [in a previous life]—for example, a being whom in previous lives you have beaten up, killed, or stolen from, and so on. Sometimes this is a human being who for no apparent reason takes such dislike to you that they start persecuting you. Sometimes it is a nonhuman being, a spirit with no apparent physical form, who, because of your having harmed it in a previous life, takes every opportunity to cause you obstacles in this life. These things are quite possible; they happen to us. In such a situation, if you supplicate the Medicine Buddha, make offerings, make virtuous aspirations and so forth, this being's aggression will be pacified, and you can free yourself from the obstacle.

Questions & Answers

Question: Rinpoche, it seems as though in the West many of the teachings that have been provided to us have put a great amount of emphasis on our mental afflictions or kleshas, and there has not really been much teaching on physical afflictions, which is in a sense what we have been talking about, some of the ways of working with physical afflictions. I wonder if Rinpoche would comment a little bit more about the view to take—both from the relative and the absolute standpoint—when physical afflictions and physical difficulties and sicknesses occur, as well as ways of working with physical afflictions in the post-meditation experience. That is part one of the question.

Rinpoche: Well, of course, physical difficulties, physical suffering, and sickness are always happening in one way or another for us. These are relative truths, relative phenomena. As relative phenomena they are interdependent, which is to say, each and every aspect of these situations is in fact the coming together of many conditions that depend on one another in order to appear as what they appear to be, as for example sickness or physical pain. Therefore, because they are interdependent, because they are not true [immutable] units, there is always a remedy of one kind or another. For example, in the context of the Medicine Buddha practice, visualizing the body of the Medicine Buddha, reciting the mantra of the Medicine Buddha, requesting the blessing of the Medicine Buddha—all of which are primarily mental, primarily acts of meditation and visualization—initially pacify your mind, but by pacifying your mind, because of the interdependence of mind and body, these acts start also to pacify your physical illness. If you are ill, they will help to pacify the illness. And if you are not ill, they will help to prevent the advent of illness.

At the same time, we also make use of physical remedies, medicines, for sickness. But as we know from experience, sometimes a medicine will work and sometimes, for some reason that is not necessarily apparent, something interferes with the proper functioning of the medicine, and it does not effectively treat even an illness for which it is appropriately prescribed. Supplication of the Medicine Buddha will help prevent that interference with or ineffectiveness of medicine, and will help the medicine take its proper effect.

Question: There are here many health care practitioners and/or educators who often work with people who are not practitioners but who certainly have some quality of openness. Could Rinpoche comment a bit on how we, as medical practitioners and as educators in medical schools—as we begin to practice and study and understand the Medicine Buddha and what you have talked about—how we can apply all of this as we work with our patients and with our students in medical schools?

Rinpoche: Well, the most important thing to have in working with a patient and to communicate in teaching physicians is that the fundamental ground of the alleviation of sickness, which must be common to all health care practitioners, is the sincere and committed wish to help others, the sincere wish to remove suffering and at least the proximate causes of suffering. And so the four-fold unsullied and stainless attitude that was described earlier in the sutra is very important. Freedom from aggression and the wish to benefit the patient are the most important things, and these need to be communicated and to be present.

Question: I may just be asking Rinpoche to repeat himself, but I think I need to hear it. The first question is about faith and devotion. When we supplicate intensely, I am trying to understand better what exactly we're supplicating. What have we faith in and what do we have devotion to? Is it faith that the practice will actually work or that the deity actually exists, or a combination?

Rinpoche: It is both. The point is that faith and devotion bring the accomplishment of whatever you are trying to do. If you have faith, you will accomplish whatever it is, and if you do not have faith, you won't. This is simply how things work. If you have faith, then you will do it. You will do something properly, and doing it properly will cause it to work. You will achieve the result. And if you do not have that much faith in something, you will do it half-heartedly or not at all, and therefore you will not achieve the result. So having faith really means fundamentally trusting and believing in the process. With respect to the Medicine Buddha practice, it means believing first and foremost that it will work. Trusting in the process will automatically entail—and therefore produce—faith in and devotion to the deities involved, the lama who taught you the practice, and so on.

Question: And does devotion have to do with just the recognition of the superior qualities of whatever it is you are devoted to?

Rinpoche: In Tibetan, the word that gets translated as devotion is usually expressed in English in two words that have distinct meanings. The first word means enthusiasm, and of course enthusiasm is simply being really interested in something. But this specific type of enthusiasm, as is indicated by the second word, which literally means respect, is an enthusiasm founded upon, as you indicated, a recognition of the extraordinary qualities of someone or something.

Question: Could you talk about the relationship between purification and blessing?

Rinpoche: These two—purification and receiving blessings—are distinct. They are not exactly the same. Purification means that the obscurations—the cognitive obscuration, which is ignorance, and the afflictive obscurations, which are the mental afflictions and the karmic obscurations or the negative karma that you have accumulated—are gradually purified, which means removed from you. And receiving blessing means that through your supplication of the Buddha or of the dharma, you receive their blessing. For example, when you supplicate the Medicine Buddha, through the power of your own supplication combined with the power of the twelve aspirations made by the Medicine Buddha, something happens, and that is called blessing. On the other hand, while purification and blessing are distinct, either one can cause the other. The removal of obscurations allows you to receive the blessings [more fully] and receiving blessings brings about the removal of obscurations.

Question: Thank you very much Rinpoche.

Question: I have two questions, the first question is, can you explain the difference between our Buddha nature and a Buddha in particular with regard to the notions of omniscience and the inseparability of samsara and nirvana?

Translator: The question is, can you explain the difference between our Buddha nature and a Buddha, someone who has attained Buddhahood, and particularly in regard to the issue of omniscience and the inseparability of samsara and nirvana. Is that the question.

Question: Yes. There is an adjunct actually to that. How can one be realized without consciousness? I think they are connected, those two.

Translator: By consciousness what do you mean?

Question: The aggregate that is impure that you talked about before.

Rinpoche: The Buddha nature that is present in our nature as the ground of being is like a bird in its eggshell, a bird that has not yet emerged from the egg. And a Buddha is like that bird flying in the sky, having broken out of the eggshell. We each and everyone have the innate potential that manifests as the qualities of Buddhahood. But this potential, which is our essence, is hidden by our obscurations, and therefore, as long as it is hidden, we call it a seed. We use the term Buddha to refer to someone in whom this previously hidden essence has become revealed. So there are basically two situations: a being whose basic nature is still hidden and a being whose basic nature has been revealed. When that basic nature is hidden, we call it a potential, a kernel or seed, an essence, or Buddha nature. And when that basic nature has been revealed, then we call that being a Buddha.

Question: You didn't answer the question about how you can be realized without consciousness.

Translator: Oh yes, I am sorry.

Rinpoche: You do not "lose consciousness" when you attain Buddhahood. You transform consciousness. The function of consciousness is transformed into wisdom. In our present state, consciousness functions somewhat haphazardly and imperfectly. Sometimes our consciousnesses are so intense that they are overwhelming and sometimes they are so obscure or dim that they do not really function properly.

Question: This is quite quick. Is it within mara's ability to convince a person that they are a realized Buddha when they are not, or that they are a lineage holder or a bodhisattva when they are not? And if it is, how does a person protect himself or herself against that illusion, particularly given that to be a realized Buddha and/or lineage holder and/or a bodhisattva is what one aspires to be?

Rinpoche: It sounds possible.

Question: Well how do you protect yourself against it?

Rinpoche: Basically by preserving a good motivation and cultivating a lot of love and compassion.

Question: Thank you, Rinpoche, and thank you, Lama, for your translations. My question is regarding sangha. Most of us do not have any trouble taking refuge in the Buddha or taking refuge in the dharma, but when it comes to taking refuge in the sangha, we roll our eyes and nervously giggle. Here this whole week, we have been together as a sangha, all working cooperatively together, but when we leave here we'll go to our different cities and our different groups and get into situations where we have come from many different schools—Nyingma, Kagyu, Geluk, Sakya, and others—and many different teachers, many different ways of doing things. And what I have seen happen in Seattle is one group thinking that their way is the best, this teacher over here is said to have some shady past, some other teacher does not teach at all in Tibetan, with all their various differences, and even within individual groups, the various concepts: well, this person has taken refuge, so they are sangha, even though maybe they do not practice very often; this person practices all the time, but has not taken refuge; that person practices all the time but does not come to the center. So there are all these various ideas about what sangha is and how to behave towards sangha members, and I would like it if Rinpoche could address what sangha is, what a practitioner is, and what the correct view and behaviour towards those would be.

Rinpoche: Our attitude towards the sangha is indicated by the definition of taking refuge in the sangha. Taking refuge in the sangha is accepting the sangha or the community as companions on the path. So the basic view you have of other practitioners is that they are fellow travellers on the same path. That being the case, you do not particularly have to examine whether or not someone is what either you or someone else might consider a full-fledged bona fide member of the sangha. You do not need to worry about what the criteria are for making that appraisal. It does not matter whether someone is of the same particular lineage or not, whether their approach in practice is exactly the same as yours or not, whether they have taken the vow of refuge or not. They are on the same path, trying to reach the same goal. The fundamental function of the sangha is—by being on the same path and having the same goal— to encourage one another to practice dharma, to cause one another to remain involved and to become more involved in dharma and its practice, rather than to lead one another farther and farther away from the path.

Question: In that respect then, Rinpoche, would one expect sangha to get larger rather than to become more and more narrow?

Translator: As a community you mean?

Question: Yes.

Rinpoche: Well, it is good if it does, because the greater the number, then the greater the momentum of the practice of that specific sangha. And the greater the momentum, the more courage and the more deeply involved people tend to get.

Question: Thank you, Rinpoche. My question concerns care of people who are terminally ill, people who are dying of something like cancer, and the relief of pain. I have been told that it is better not to relieve pain too much because it is karma coming to fruition, that if you do not feel it now, you are going to feel it later, in the next life or whenever, which seems to me not the most compassionate view, particularly if the person who is dying in pain is not a dharma practitioner. Could you speak to that please?

Rinpoche: It is possible that the agony of a dying person is a result of their previous karma, but your giving them medicine that reduces that pain does not remove the working out of that karma. It affects how bad the pain is, but the karma itself is still ripening. So by alleviating the pain of a dying person, you are not dooming them to a worse fate later on. So by all means they should be given pain medication.

Question: Thank you.

Question: You have been talking a lot about impure and pure perceptions. I am having a hard time understanding or thinking what might constitute something that is pure in its perception. Is it bright or light? On the other hand what is an impure perception?

Rinpoche: It has more to do with the mind that is perceiving than it does with the actual physical characteristics of what is perceived. A simple example of this is that if the same person looks at the same thing in two different emotional states, they will see them differently. The effect of what they see will be very different. For example, if someone looks at something while they are very angry, while they are feeling really spiteful and mean, they will see it as irritating or as unpleasant, and if the same person looks at the same thing when their emotional state is one of love and compassion, something very positive, they will see the same thing as having a positive nature or quality. That basically is what is meant by impure perception or appearances and pure perception or appearances, but the difference between those two states—the same person in basically two different moods—is very slight. While that is the principle on which it operates, it can go much further than that. If you can imagine a mind that is completely pure of any kind of negativity whatsoever, what that person would experience is what we would call true, pure appearances. And a mind that is filled with various sorts of negativity experiences impure appearances.

Question: Thank you for the teachings, Rinpoche. I have a couple of questions. I am wondering, in the subtle level of the judging mind, when one is aware of judgments coming up—not when one is angry, but when these judgmental tendencies arise—how can one work to antidote these in the present moment?

Rinpoche: Are you talking about meditation or post-meditation?

Question: Post-meditation in interaction with others or even in simple observation in daily life.

Rinpoche: The first step is to recognize the tendency. If you are in the habit of recognizing these sorts of subtle judgmental thoughts as what they are, then the habit of recognizing them and not wishing to invest in them will accrue, and they will occur less and less often.

Question: So how is that really happening?

Rinpoche: If you are not interested in cultivating those thoughts and you apply mindfulness and alertness, they will automatically happen less and less and disappear.

Question: You mentioned the two main bodhisattvas of the Medicine Buddha, Luminous Like The Sun and Luminous Like The Moon. I was wondering if you could expand on that some.

Rinpoche: I think that they are other names for Manjushri and Chagdrul. Luminous Like The Sun would be Manjushri, and Luminous Like The Moon would be Chagdrul.

Question: You spoke a little bit about spirits and not wanting to get them angry or to offend them. I am increasing my faith in the Medicine Buddha and I am sure that its practice is great, but I wonder if you have more guidance for one who does healing work where actual spirit possession may happen, and what perhaps to do or to focus on after doing such a session?

Translator: Do you mean, if you are trying to heal someone who is possessed by a spirit, or if you the healer get attacked by the spirit?

Question: Well, both perhaps. You are working with somebody, and a spirit depossession happens, and they kind of reclaim their body. Generally what I have experienced is just staying really strong and clear, but sometimes there is fatigue or other things that may happen afterwards. So both.

Rinpoche: The most important thing in that situation is that the practitioner have compassion not only for the possessed person but for the possessing spirit as well. Of course, we normally have compassion for the possessed, but we may not have that much compassion for the possessor. The possessed person deserves our compassion, because they are suffering. But the possessor—equally or perhaps even more so—

deserves our compassion, because they are doing what will become the cause of great suffering for themselves in the future. If you have that attitude of compassion for the spirit, it will facilitate the extrication of the spirit, and also will not leave that sort of staleness, and so forth, that will otherwise ensue.

Somehow Our Buddha Nature
Has Been Awakened,
We Are Very Fortunate Indeed

All of you are no doubt extremely busy, but in spite of that, you all decided to come here, and for that, in and of itself, I thank you. Beyond that, having come here, you have all practiced and listened to the teachings with great diligence and attentiveness, and I thank you especially for that as well. As it says in the *Jewel Ornament of Liberation,* "While all sentient beings without exception possess Buddha nature, this Buddha nature is hidden by our obscurations," as in the analogy I gave of a bird in an egg shell. There are different ways that Buddha nature can be present in a person. While it is equally present per se in everyone, it can either emerge and be somehow awakened, or not. When Buddha nature is dormant, when there is no evidence in the person's life of the presence of it, that person has no immediate opportunity for liberation. On the other hand, when the qualities of Buddha nature emerge, when it becomes awakened or aroused, then its qualities are revealed and the person can begin to attain liberation. Now in the case of all of you, your having decided to come here, your having done so, and your having practiced diligently is ample evidence of the awakening or emergence of your Buddha nature, and I consider this evidence further that your practice of dharma will continue to progress until you attain liberation. So that is why I thank you for coming here and practicing.

While you have been here, you have been listening to and practicing specifically the dharma connected with the Medicine Buddha, which in the long term will be a cause of your complete liberation and in the short term a cause of physical and mental well-being. So you are extremely fortunate, because this practice is extremely beneficial. Now as you go on with your lives and attempt to integrate practice into your daily life, you will find that sometimes you will have what will seem like a more or less perfect opportunity. It will fit right into your life without any contradiction or problem, and there will not seem to be any impediments or obstacles that interfere with your practice. And sometimes you will find that there will seem to be any number of obstacles impeding or obstructing your practice, time constraints and so forth, and it may get to the point that you feel you have no opportunity to practice, at least not as much as you would like. In such situations, do not be discouraged. Do not think, "I have obstacles, I have real problems, I am never going to be able to practice. No matter what I do, things always go wrong," and so on. Do not allow yourself to become depressed by the temporary obstruction of your practice, and always remember that even merely encountering such dharma, even hearing it, is something that is extremely fortunate, extremely beneficial in and of itself. Whatever contact you have made and whatever practice of dharma you have done will never be lost. The benefits of it can never be destroyed or removed and will lead you sooner or later to complete liberation.

It says in the *Jewel Ornament of Liberation* that in one of the sutras the Buddha discusses the benefit of having less than complete faith. Now obviously there are some people who have intense and complete, unquestioning faith in the three jewels, and especially in the dharma, and of course that is wonderful. But there are other people who have less faith in the dharma, which is to say that they have some faith in it, but they also have some questions and doubts. The image that the Buddha uses to describe these situations is that if someone has complete faith, they are going to join both palms together in front of their heart in a gesture of utter devotion and trust. But someone with less faith might just put one hand up in front of their chest. So what the Buddha is describing is a situation in which someone has what we could call "half faith." They have faith but they also have a lot of doubt. And the Buddha poses the question, "Is there going to be any benefit, is there going to be any result to putting one hand up in a gesture of half faith or half devotion?" And his answer is, "Yes, there will definitely be a great result; there will be great benefit, and the benefit of this will never be lost." It will eventually lead to that being's perfect awakening. So in that way the Buddha praises an attitude of faith even if it is what we might consider half-hearted.

A second analogy the Buddha gives begins with imagining a place of practice such as this one. Initially, in order to come here, one generates the intention to do so. So someone might think, "I need to go to such and such place and practice intensively." Now obviously, if you actually get there and practice, there will be great benefit, but suppose someone, having decided, "I want to go there and practice," takes a few steps in order to get there, and after merely few steps something gets in their way, a situation comes up that prevents them from actually ever reaching the place and practicing. And the Buddha asks, "In such a situation would there be a result?" And the answer is yes, there would be a tremendous result, great benefit; even having taken a few steps towards a place of practice with the intention of practicing, even though you never get there and never practice, will ultimately still be a cause of perfect happiness. So as you go on with your lives and you go on with the process that has included listening to dharma and practicing dharma, sometimes you will find that you are free of impediments and obstacles that interfere with your practice, and other times you will find that things just get in the way of your practice. But when things get in the way, do not be too discouraged; remember that all of this is always beneficial, and that it is not an abnormal situation for sometimes there to be the freedom to practice and other times not. So never think ill of yourself when you experience impediments.

That is the way this is explained in the teachings of the Buddha, as quoted and expounded by Lord Gampopa. And if we simply think about it ourselves, we can arrive at the same conclusion. If we consider appearances, this world as we experience it, we normally experience things as being very lustrous and colorful and powerful and distracting, even seductive. And our minds are very easily pulled around, fooled, and seduced. Our minds are very naive. Especially because we have lots of thoughts about what we experience. We think that things are going to stay the same. We think that things are stable and so on. And we usually fool ourselves with all of these thoughts based on appearances. But somehow we have all generated the idea, the thought, that practicing dharma and specifically coming here and participating in this retreat would be worthwhile, that it would be important enough to make room for it in our lives. Most beings simply do not come up with this idea. Most beings would not choose to come here. The reason we did is that somehow our Buddha nature has become awakened a little bit, and the blessings of Buddhas and bodhisattvas have somehow entered into us and affected us. So while obstacles will arise from time to time, these are not as important as they may seem at the time. They are ultimately temporary and really unimportant. The process that has begun with the awakening of our Buddha nature and our making the choices we have already made is unstoppable. Ultimately it will lead to our liberation. So we are really very fortunate indeed. When you can, when you have the necessary conditions or resources to do so, by all means practice. And when you cannot, when things just get in the way of practice and make it impossible, then do not feel too sad, and recognize how extremely fortunate you are.

Now please conclude with the dedication of merit. When performing the dedication of merit, think that you dedicate the merit of this to the awakening of all beings in general and especially in the short term to the freedom of this world from all forms of sickness.

A Sadhana of Menla,
Compiled from the Clear Expanse of Mind,
A Mind Treasure Found within the Sky of Dharma Texts
and Called

A STREAM OF LAPIS LAZULI

A STREAM OF LAPIS LAZULI

Namo. Maha Bekandzeya. If they are available, arrange in front of a Menla thangka as many peaceful offerings as you can, such as a mandala and so forth; in this way the accumulations are completed. If these are not available, it is enough to make mental offerings while imagining the front visualization in the sky—nothing else is needed. Since this is the anuttara, the practitioner need not refrain from meat and alcohol nor perform the rituals of purification, such as taking the blessing of pure water. It is definitely necessary, however, to receive the empowerment and reading transmission for this practice, as it belongs to the anuttara tradition. Since it belongs to the nyingma tradition, the self and frontal visualizations are simultaneously generated; it is not necessary to create them separately. As it is a chanted meditation of the nyingma, your mind should meditate on the meaning of the words.

The supplication:

NAMO BEKENDZE MAHA RADZAYE

SÖ NAM YÖN TEN GYA TSHÖ TER NGA ZHING
You are endowed with an oceanic treasury of qualities and merit;

SAM GYI MI KHYAB THUK JEY JIN LAP KYI
By the blessing of your inconceivable compassion

DRO WAY DUK NGEL DUNG WA SHI DZE PA
You calm the suffering and torment of sentient beings.

BEN DUR YA YI Ö LA SOL WA DEB
I supplicate you, Light of Lapis Lazuli.

SHIN TU SER NA DRAK PÖ RAB CHING PE
Those bound by very intense greed

YI DAK NE SU KYE WAY KYE WO YI
Are born in the hungry ghost realm.

KHYÖ TSHEN THÖ NA MIR KYE JIN PA GA
If they hear your name, they are said to be born human and take
   delight in generosity.

CHOM DEN MEN GYI LA LA SOL WA DEB
I supplicate you, victorious Menla.

TSHÜL THRIM CHAL DANG ZHEN LA SHE TSÖN PE
Violating morality and abusing others,

NYAL WAR KYE WAY DRO WA DI DAK GI
Beings are born in the hell realms.

KHYÖ TSHEN THÖ NA THO RI KYE WAR SUNG
Hearing your name, they'll be born in the higher realms, it's said.

MEN GYI GYEL PO DE LA SOL WA DEB
I supplicate you, King of Medicine.

GANG DAK YEN DANG THRA MA DU MA YI
Whoever by repeated dissension and slander

RAB TU JE CHING LÜ SOK THRAL WA DAK
Creates deep schisms and takes life,

KHYÖ TSHEN THÖ NA DE DAK TSHE MI NÜ
Hearing your name, they cannot harm others.

MEN GYI GYEL PO DE LA SOL WA DEB
I supplicate you, King of Medicine

TSHEN LEK SER ZANG DRI ME NANG WA DANG
Excellent Name, Appearance of Stainless Fine Gold,

NYA NGEN ME CHOK PEL DANG CHÖ DRAK YANG
Glorious Supreme One Free of Misery, Resounding Dharma Melody,

NGÖN KHYEN GYEL PO DRA YANG GYEL PO DANG
King of Direct Knowledge, King of Melody,

SHAKYAY GYEL PO NAM LA SOL WA DEB
And King of Shakyas, I supplicate you all.

JAM PEL KHYAB DRÖL CHAK NA DOR JE DZIN
Manjushri, Kyabdröl, Vajrapani,

TSHANG WANG GYA JIN CHOK ZHI GYEL PO ZHI
Brahma, Indra, the four Kings of the four directions,

NÖ JIN DE PÖN CHEN PO CHU NYI SOK
The twelve great Yaksha chiefs, and others,

KYIL KHOR YONG SU DZOK LA SOL WA DEB
I supplicate you, entire and perfect mandala.

DE ZHIN SHEK PA DÜN GYI MÖN LAM DO
The Sutra of the Seven Tathagatas' Aspirations,

MEN GYI LHA YI DO DE NYI DANG NI
And the Sutra of the Medicine Buddha,

KHEN CHEN ZHI WA TSHÖ DZE ZHUNG LA SOK
The treatise by the great abbot Santarakshita, and so forth,

DAM CHÖ LEK WAM TSHOK LA SOL WA DEB
I supplicate all the volumes of the genuine Dharma,

BO DHI SA TO THRI SONG DEU TSEN SOK
Bodhisattva Santarakshita, Trisong Deutsen, and others,

LO PEN GYEL LÖN JANG CHUP SEM PA DANG
Translators, scholars, kings, ministers, bodhisattvas,

GYÜ PAY LA MA DAM PA THAM CHE DANG
And all genuine lamas of the lineage,

CHÖ KYI WANG CHUK SOK LA SOL WA DEB
Powerful One of the Dharma, and others, I supplicate you.

DE TAR SOL WA TAB PAY JIN LAP KYI
Through the blessing of this supplication,

NE KAP NE DANG JIK PA NA TSHOK ZHI
May all variety of disease and dangers of this life be pacified.

CHI TSE NGEN SONG JIK PA KÜN ZHI NE
At death, may all fear of the lower realms be allayed.

DE WA CHEN DU KYE WAR JIN GYI LOP
Grant your blessing that we are then born in Sukhavati.

NAMO KÖN CHOK SUM DANG TSA WA SUM
To the sources of refuge, the three jewels

KYAB NE NAM LA KYAB SU CHI
And the three roots, I go for refuge.

DRO KÜN SANG GYE LA GÖ CHIR
To establish all beings in Buddhahood,

JANG CHUB CHOK TU SEM KYE DO
I awaken the mind of supreme enlightenment.

KA DAK LONG NE TRÜL PA YI
From the expanse of primordial purity emanate

NAM SA GANG WAY CHÖ PAY TRIN
Clouds of offerings filling the earth and sky

MEN DEL GYEL SI LHA MOR CHE
With mandalas, articles of possessions, and goddesses.

ZE ME GYUR CHIK PUD DZA HO
May they never be exhausted. PUD DZA HO.

DRO KÜN DE DEN DUK NGEL DREL
May all beings be happy and free of suffering.

DE LE NYAM ME TANG NYOM SHOK
May their happiness not diminish. May they abide in equanimity.

OM SOBHAWA SHUDDHA SARWA DHARMA SOBHAWA
   SHUDDHO HAM

TONG PA NYI DU GYUR
Everything becomes emptiness.

TONG PAY NGANG LE TONG SUM DI
From its depth, this triple universe becomes

TA NA DUK GYI PHO DRANG DU GYUR PAY NANG DU
the exquisite palace, where

SENG GEY THRI PE DA SO SÖ TENG DU
On lion thrones, each with a lotus and moon disk on top

RANG NYI DANG DÜN KYE KYI TSO WÖ SA BÖN
   HUNG THING KHA LE
Appear deep blue HUNGs, the seed syllable of myself and the main
   figure visualized in the front,

MEN LA KU DOK BE DUR YA TA BU Ö ZER THRO
   WAY KU CHEN
From which, arises Menla, his body the color of lapis lazuli and
   radiating light.

CHÖ GÖ SUM GI LUP PA
He is clothed in the three dharma robes.

CHAK YE CHOK JIN A RU RA DANG
His right hand in the mudra of supreme generosity holds an arura.

YÖN NYAM ZHAG LHUNG ZE DZIN PA
His left hand in the meditation mudra holds a begging bowl.

TSEN PE DZOK SHING DOR JE KYIL TRUNG GI ZHUK
PA
With the major and minor marks complete, he sits in the vajra posture.

KHYE PAR DU DÜN KYE KYI DAB MA NAM LA
In particular, on the lotus petals of the front visualization

THUB WANG LA SOK PAY SANG GYE DÜN DANG CHÖ
PU TI
Are the seven Buddhas, Shakyamuni and the others, and dharma texts.

DE GYAB SEM PA CHU DRUK
Surrounding them are the sixteen bodhisattvas,

DE GYAB JIK TEN KYONG WA CHU DANG
Surrounding them are the ten protectors of the world,

DE PÖN CHEN PO CHU NYI SO SÖ KHOR DANG CHE
PA
And the twelve great chiefs with their respective retinues.

GO ZHI LA GYEL PO CHEN PO ZHI
The four great kings are at the four gates.

DANG CHE PAY NE SUM YI GE SUM DANG THUK KAY
HUNG LE Ö ZER
From the three syllables in their three places and the HUNG in their
hearts,

THRÖ PE SHAR CHOK KYI SANG GYE SO SÖ ZHING
KHAM NE YE SHE PA
Lights radiate, invoking from the eastern Buddha realms, countless

PAK TU ME PA CHEN DRANG NE DAK DÜN NAM LA
    THIM PAR GYUR
Wisdom deities which dissolve into myself and the one visualized in
    front.

HUNG MEN LA CHE GYE LHA TSOK MA LÜ NAM
HUNG. The eight Menla brothers and all deities without exception

NE DIR CHEN DREN JIN CHEN WAB TU SOL
I invite here to this place. Please rain upon us your great blessings.

KAL DEN DE DEN DAK LA WANG CHOK KUR
Bestow the supreme empowerment on those who are worthy and
    faithful.

LOK DREN TSHE YI BAR CHE SEL DU SOL
Dispel false guides and obstacles to long life.

NAMO MAHA BEKENDZE SAPARIWARA BENZA
    SAMAYADZA DZA BENZE SAMAYA TIKTRA LEN
    OM HUNG TRAM HRI AH ABHIKENTSA HUNG

HUNG ME TOK DUK PÖ MAR ME DRI
HUNG. Flowers, incense, lights, scents,

ZHEL ZE RÖL MO LA SOK DANG
Food, music and so forth;

ZUG DRA DRI RO REK JA CHÖ
Forms, sounds, smells, tastes, touch, and all dharmas,

DAK GI LHA LA CHÖ PA BUL
I offer to the deities.

DAK CHAK TSHOK NYI DZOK PAR SHOK
May we perfect the two accumulations.

OM BENZA ARGHAM PANDAM PUPE DUPE ALOKE
GENDE NEWIDEH SHABTA RUPA SHABTA
GENDE RASA SAPARSHE TRATITSA HUNG

HUNG TRA SHI TSO WO DZE GYE DE
HUNG. The eight foremost auspicious substances,

TSO CHOK GYEL PO YUNG KAR SOK
The best royal white mustard seed, and the others,

DAK GI LHA LA CHÖ PA BUL
I offer to the deity.

TSHOK NYI YONG SU DZOK PAR SHOK
May the two accumulations be perfected.

MANGALAM ARTHA SIDDHI HUNG

HUNG TRA SHI TSO WO TAK GYE DE
HUNG. The eight foremost auspicious symbols,

TSO CHOK GYEL PO BUM PA SOK
The peerless royal vase and all others,

DAK GI LHA LA CHÖ PA BUL
I offer to the deity.

SEM CHEN TSOK NYI DZOK PAR SHOK
May sentient beings perfect the two accumulations.

MANGALAM KUMBHA HUNG

HUNG DÖ YÖN TSO WO RIN CHEN DÜN
HUNG. The sources of pleasure, the seven precious articles,

TSO CHOK GYEL PO NOR BU SOK
The most excellent royal one, the jewel, and the others,

DAK GI LHA LA CHÖ PA BUL
I offer to the deity.

DAK NI TSHOK NYI DZOK PAR SHOK
May I perfect the two accumulations.

OM MANI RATNA HUNG

HUNG KÜN GYI TSO WO RI RAB LING
HUNG. The foremost of all, Mount Meru

RI RAB LING ZHI LING TREN CHE
With its four continents and subcontinents

DAK GI LHA LA CHÖ PA BUL
I offer to the deity.

TSHOK NYI YONG SU DZOK PAR SHOK
May the two accumulations be perfected.

OM RATNA MANDALA HUNG

HUNG DAK GI DRI DEN DRI CHAB KYI
HUNG. With scented water

DE SHEK KU LA KU THRÜ SOL
I bathe the sugata's body.

LHA LA DRI MA MI NGA YANG
Although you, the deity, are flawless,

DIK DRIB DAK PAY TEN DREL GYI
This creates the auspicious connection for purifying all wrongs and
obscurations.

OM SARWA TATHAGATA ABIKEKATE SAMAYA SHRIYE
HUNG

HUNG   RE KAR JAM DRI DEN PA YI
HUNG. With a scented, soft white cloth

GYEL WAY KU NYI CHI WAR GYI
I dry the victor's body.

KU LA DRI MA MI NGA YANG
Though your body is flawless,

DUK NGEL DREL WAY TEN DREL GYI
This creates the auspicious connection for freedom from suffering.

OM KAYA BISHODHANI HUNG

HUNG   NA ZA DZE DEN NGUR MIK DI
HUNG. With these beautiful saffron robes

GYEL WAY KU LA SOL WAR GYI
I clothe the victor's body.

KU LA SIL WA MI NGA YANG
Although your body is never cold,

TRAK DANG PHEL WAY TEN DREL GYI
This creates the auspicious connection for vitality to flourish.

A Stream of Lapis Lazuli

OM BENZA WAYTRA AH HUNG

HUNG KU DOK BE DUR YA YI RI WO DRA
HUNG. Your body is like a mountain, the color of lapis lazuli.

DRO WA SEM CHEN NE KYI DUK NGEL SEL
You dispel the suffering of illness in sentient beings.

JANG CHUB SEM PA GYE KYI KHOR GYI KHOR
Surrounded by a retinue of eight bodhisattvas,

RIN CHEN MEN DZIN LHA LA CHAK TSHAL TÖ
Holder of Medicine, precious deity, I praise and prostrate to you.

TSHEN LEK RIN DA SER ZANG NYA NGEN ME
Excellent Name, Precious Moon, Fine Gold, Free of Misery,

CHÖ DRAK GYA TSHO CHÖ LO SHA KYA THUB
Resounding Dharma Ocean, Dharma Mind, Shakyamuni,

DAM PAY CHÖ DANG SEM PA CHU DRUK SOK
The genuine dharma, the sixteen bodhisattvas, and others,

KÖN CHOK RIN CHEN SUM LA CHAK TSHAL TÖ
To the precious three jewels, I offer praise and prostrate.

TSHANG DANG GYA JIN GYEL CHEN CHOK KYONG
    CHU
To Brahma, Indra, the Great Kings, the Protectors of the Ten
    Directions,

NÖ JIN DE PÖN CHU NYI YOK DANG CHE
The twelve Yaksha chiefs and all their assistants,

LHA MIN MEN GYI RIK DZIN DRANG SONG CHE
Vidyadharas and rishis of medicine, divine and human,

DÜ TSI MEN GYI LHA LA CHAK TSAL TÖ
To the deities of ambrosial medicine, I offer praise and prostrate.

DAK DÜN THUK KAY HUNG LA NGAK TRENG KOR
    WAR MIG LA
The HUNG in the heart of the self and front visualizations is
    surrounded by the mantra garland.

*Through radiating many-colored light rays, offerings are made to Menla in
the pure realm appearing in the east as the color of lapis lazuli. These lights
invoke his mind stream, whence Menla's bodies, large and small, his speech
as the mantra garland, his mind as the hand symbols of the arura and the
begging bowl filled with amrita, all falling like rain, dissolve into myself
and the front visualization.*

TAYATA OM BEKENDZE BEKENDZE MAHA BEKENDZE
    RADZA SAMUDGATE SO HA

Repeat as much as possible and then at the end:

DIK THUNG KÜN SHAK GE WA JANG CHUB NGO
I confess all wrongs and downfalls and dedicate all virtue to awakening.

NE DÖN DUK NGEL DREL WAY TA SHI SHOK
May there be the auspiciousness of freedom from sickness, harmful
    spirits, and suffering.

The fulfillment prayer:

JIK TEN PA NAM RANG NE BENZA MU
The worldly ones return to their own places. BENZA MU.

YE SHE DAM TSHIK LHA NAM DAK LA THIM
The jnana and samaya sattvas dissolve into me,

KA DAK KÜN ZANG LONG DU E MA HO
And I dissolve into primordial purity, the expanse of Samantabhadra.
E MA HO.

This was compiled from a mind treasure found within the Sky-Dharma texts and was arranged by Raga Asya. If there are contradictions, I confess them before the deity. Through this virtue, may all sentient beings, once freed from sickness, swiftly attain the level of Menla. Though the sutra rituals have the practice of washing [which is not done here], as this is a higher practice, found at the end of the [supreme] yoga tantra, there is no contradiction.

If you take this as your regular practice, the benefits are the following. If you are ordained, your discipline will be maintained; though there might be an occasion when it is not, having purified this obscuration, you will not fall into the lower realms. Having purified the negative karma of being born as a hell being, a hungry ghost, or an animal, you will not take such a birth. Even if you do, immediately liberated, you will take a felicitous rebirth in a higher realm, and gradually attain awakening. In this life as well, you will easily obtain food and clothing and not be harmed by disease, negative spirits, sorcery, or the punishments of rulers. You will be protected and guarded by Vajrapani, Brahma, the Great Kings of the four directions, and the twelve great Yaksha chiefs each with their 700,000 assistants. You will be freed from all harm: from the eighteen kinds of untimely death, the harm of enemies, carnivorous beasts, and so forth. All your wishes will be fully realized, and so forth. In the two more extensive sutras of Menla, the benefits are said to be inconceivable.

In the great monastic centers, such as Jang Damring Pelkhor Chöde, and their philosophical colleges, where the scholars find fault with most dharma and are difficult to satisfy, only this Menla ritual for prolonging life and clearing away the obscurations of death has spread widely. The ritual to be performed before the Jowo in Lhasa, Tibet's Bodhgaya, and before the Great

Awakened One at Samye is this ritual of Menla. You should trust that within any of the new and the ancient transmissions, the sutras and the tantras, nothing is more beneficial than Menla. There are many extensive and concise versions; this one has few words and the full meaning. Since it belongs to anuttara yoga, rituals of purification are not needed. Since the offerings are mental, it is all right not to offer tormas. Everyone should practice this. SHUBHAM DZAYENTU.

Translated under the guidance of Thrangu Rinpoche and Khenpo Karthar Rinpoche by Michele Martin with assistance from Ngodrup Burkhar and reference to translations by Lama Yeshe Gyamtso and Sarah Harding, Woodstock, N.Y., 1984, 1999, Kathmandu, 1999.

SHORT MENLA PRACTICE

HUNG KUN DOK BEN DUR YA YI RI WO DRA
HUNG. Your body the color of a mountain of lapis lazuli,

DRO WA SEM CHEN NAY CHI DU NGAL SEL
You dispel suffering of disease and death from all sentient beings.

CHANG CHUB SEM PA JAY CHI KOR JI KOR
Your retinue of eight bodhisattvas surrounds you—

RIN CHEN MEN DZIN LHA LA CHA TSAL TÖ
I praise and pay homage to the Deity Who Holds the Precious
    Medicine.

TAYATA OM BEKENDZE BEKENDZE MAHA BEKENDZE
    RADZA SAMUDGATE SO HA

SEM CHEN NAY PA JI NYAY PA
May the many sentient beings who are sick

NYUR TU NAY LAY TAR JUR CHIK
Quickly be freed from sickness

DRO WAY NAY NI MA LÜ PA
And may all the sicknesses of beings

TAK TU JUNG WA MAY PAR SHOK
Never arise again.

SHORTER MENLA PRACTICE

CHOM DEN DAY DE SHIN SHEK PA DRA CHOM PA
    YANG DAK PAR DZOK PAY
To you, Bhagavan, Tathagata, arhat, perfect and fully

SANG GYE MEN GYI LA BE DUR YA Ö KYI GYEL PO
    LA CHAK TSEL LO
Awakened Menla, King of Lapis Lazuli light, I offer prostrations.

CONCLUDING PRAYERS
FOR ALL MENLA PRACTICES

Bhagavat, who is compassionate equally to all beings,
The very hearing of whose name pacifies the three lower states,
Medicine Buddha, who eliminates the illnesses of the three poisons,
May there be the goodness of the Vaidurya Light.

May sentient beings, whatever illnesses they suffer,
Be liberated quickly from those illnesses.
May all the illnesses of beings, without exception,
Forever not arise.

May medicines be effective,
And may the intentions of the recitations of the secret mantra path be
    accomplished.
May demonesses, cannibal demons, and so forth
Attain compassionate mind.

The Twelve Great Aspirations of The Medicine Buddha

Excerpted from the Mahayana Sutra:
*The Vast Attributes of the Previous Aspiration Prayers of the Noble
Victor,
The Deity of Medicine, Light of Lapis Lazuli*

The first great aspiration:
"At a future time when I have attained unsurpassable, ultimate, and
perfectly complete enlightenment, having come to full awakening, then
may the light of my body make brilliant, stable, and especially radiant
the realms of this universe that are numberless, immeasurable, and
beyond any count. May all sentient beings be adorned with the thirty-
two marks and the eighty characteristics of a great, noble being. Thus,
may all sentient beings become just as I am." So he prayed.

The second great aspiration:
"At a future time when I have attained unsurpassable, ultimate, and
perfectly complete enlightenment, having come to full awakening, may
my body resemble precious lapis lazuli, and be fully adorned with
utter purity within and without, a radiant clarity free of stains, a great
agility in all things, blazing glory and brilliance, physical symmetry,
and a filigree of light rays brighter than the sun and moon. For those
born within this world and for those who have gone their separate
ways into the dark of the dead of night, may my light come in all
directions bringing happiness and contentment. May it also bring about
virtuous activity." So he prayed.

The third great aspiration:
"At a future time when I have attained unsurpassable, ultimate, and

perfectly complete enlightenment, having come to full awakening, through my wisdom and immeasurable skilful means, may countless realms of sentient beings have inexhaustible wealth. May no one be deprived of anything." So he prayed.

The fourth great aspiration:
"At a future time when I have attained unsurpassable, ultimate, and perfectly complete enlightenment, having come to full awakening, I will place on the path to awakening any sentient being who has entered a negative path. All those who have entered the shravaka path or the pratyekabuddha path, I will guide into the Mahayana." So he prayed.

The fifth great aspiration:
"At a future time when I have attained unsurpassable, ultimate, and perfectly complete enlightenment, having come to full awakening, may any sentient being near to me maintain celibacy.[54] Likewise, through my power, may other innumerable sentient beings beyond measure, having heard my name, hold their three vows and may their discipline not deteriorate. May those whose discipline has been corrupted, not enter into the lower realms." So he prayed.

The sixth great aspiration:
"At a future time when I have attained unsurpassable, ultimate, and perfectly complete enlightenment, having come to full awakening, may any sentient being who has an inferior body, incomplete faculties, an unpleasant color, a virulent, epidemic disease, impaired limbs, a hunchback, splotchy skin, may any being who is lame, blind, deaf, insane, or struck by illness, upon hearing my name, for each one, may their faculties become whole and their limbs be made perfect." So he prayed.

The seventh great aspiration:
"At a future time when I have attained unsurpassable, ultimate, and perfectly complete enlightenment, having come to full awakening, for any sentient being whose body is riddled with the pain of various illnesses,

who has no refuge nor protector, no material goods nor medicine, no throng of relatives, and who is poor and suffering, when my name comes to their ears, may all their diseases be pacified. Until awakening, may they be free of illness and remain unharmed." So he prayed.

The eighth great aspiration:
"At a future time when I have attained unsurpassable, ultimate, and perfectly complete enlightenment, having come to full awakening, if some people are intensely afflicted by the faults of a negative birth, despised for having it, and wish to be free of that place of birth, may they be liberated from taking this negative birth again. Until they attain ultimate awakening, may a positive rebirth always arise for them." So he prayed.

The ninth great aspiration:
"At a future time when I have attained unsurpassable, ultimate, and perfectly complete enlightenment, having come to full awakening, I will free all sentient beings from the maras' noose. I will establish in the correct view all those in disharmony due to various views and the problems of discord. Ultimately, I will teach them the practice of bodhisattvas." So he prayed.

The tenth great aspiration:
"At a future time when I have attained unsurpassable, ultimate, and perfectly complete enlightenment, having come to full awakening, may the power of my merit completely liberate [beings] from all harm: those who are terrorized by the fear of a ruler, who are in bondage and beaten, who have fallen into a trap, who are sentenced to death, who are under the heel of deception, who are not successful, and whose body, speech, and mind are afflicted by suffering." So he prayed.

The eleventh great aspiration:
"At a future time when I have attained unsurpassable, ultimate, and perfectly complete enlightenment, having come to full awakening, for

those who are burning with hunger and thirst, and who commit negative actions in their continuous efforts to search for food, may I satisfy them physically with food that has [a pleasing] color, smell, and taste. Later, I will bring them to the most blissful taste of the dharma." So he prayed.

The twelfth great aspiration:
"At a future time when I have attained unsurpassable, ultimate, and perfectly complete enlightenment, having come to full awakening, for those who experience suffering day and night, being naked with no clothes to wear, poor and miserable, [too] cold or hot, afflicted by flies and maggots, I will give generously whatever they can enjoy, [such as] clothes that have been dyed many colors. I will fulfil all their wishes just as they desire with a variety of precious ornaments and decorations, necklaces, incense, ointments, the sound of music, musical instruments, and hand cymbals." So he prayed.

Manjushri, these are the twelve aspirations made by the Victor, the Tathagata, the arhat, the Perfect Buddha, the Lapis Lazuli Light of Medicine, when he was practicing the conduct of a bodhisattva.

Translated by Michele Martin © March 2000.

Notes

1: The meditation on selflessness is traditionally divided into realizing the lack of true existence of a personal self, what we usually think of as the self, and realizing the lack of true existence of phenomena.

2: "The common tradition" is a way of referring to those teachings held in common by all traditions of Buddhism, which are the teachings on personal liberation of the Hinayana or lesser vehicle.

3: The Medicine Buddha, when understood as an individual Buddha who once was a sentient being, predates the Buddha Shakyamuni. Therefore, our knowledge of him is based, at least initially, on the teachings that arose spontaneously out of the supersensible cognition of the Buddha Shakyamuni.

4: The reader will notice that most of the deities in this particular mandala are male. One should not conclude therefore that this is typical of tantric mandalas. There are some mandalas—such at Arya Tara, Vajrayogini, and Chöd—in which the deities are virtually all female, others that are balanced, and others that vary slightly more one way than the other.

5: Shastras are commentaries on the original teachings of the Buddha.

6: Common to all traditions of Buddhism.

7: The practice of any yidam deity will result in the attainment of both the ultimate and relative siddhis. The ultimate siddhi is the stable realization of the radiant clarity or clear light nature of mind and all reality which we know as complete and perfect enlightenment or Buddhahood. The relative siddhis are such qualities as loving kindness, compassion, intelligence, the wisdom of insight, spiritual power, protection and the removal of obstacles, good health, longevity, wealth, magnetism, etc. The practice of a deity yields first the relative siddhis. If we pray to Chenrezig, the first result beyond the simple development of concentration will be an increase in loving kindness and compassion in our experience. If we pray to Manjushri-Sarasvati, we will gradually experience greater perspicacity, strength of intellect, and facility with music and language. If we practice Mahakala, we will experience protection and the removal of obstacles, if we practice White Tara we will develop greater insight and longevity, if we practice Green Tara we will experience liberation from fear, the quick removal of obstacles, joy, compassion and upliftedness. If we practice Vajrayogini we will begin to develop Mahamudra siddhi and increased warmth and magnetism. If one practices both the development and completion stages of any deity with sufficient devotion and application, one will eventually attain full realization, at which point all of the siddhis of all of the yidams will be spontaneously present.

8: It is important to note that these impure perceptions and attitudes are not stable, but are constantly changing moment by moment according to changing causes and conditions. Thus, in one moment one might think quite highly of oneself and actually see oneself as attractive, intelligent, and charming, and in a subsequent moment feel quite depressed about oneself and see oneself as tiresome and dreary. These perceptions and attitudes go through myriad changes, but they are all impure in the sense that we are always seeing *projections* of ourselves, others, and the environment, and not things as they truly are.

9: Buddhism, of course, does not assert any sort of cosmological beginning, so the use of "beginning here" has the same meaning as "from beginningless time."

10: This superimposition of impurity onto appearances is the same as referred to by Nagarjuna, in *In Praise of the Dharmadhatu:* "The phenomena that appear to the mental consciousness, the chief of them all, are conceptualized and then superimposed. When this activity is abandoned, phenomena's lack of self-essence is known. Knowing this, meditate on the dharmadhatu." The *sobhawa* mantra and the ensuing sadhana, as well as all other sadhanas and completion stage practices are methods for training the mind to abandon this activity of superimposition.

11: These syllables are to be visualized in Tibetan script.

12: The true nature, the ultimate nature

13: This color blue is generally described as deep blue, the color of an autumn sky high in the mountains.

14: Which thereby brings about the cessation of suffering.

15: Expressed variously as the nonconceptual wisdom of emptiness, the nonconceptual wisdom of clear light, radiant clarity, primordial awareness, the empty, clear, and unimpeded nature of mind, etc.

16: Unlike Amitaba's realm of Sukhavati or Dewachen, which is thought of as being in the western direction, these Buddha realms of the Medicine Buddhas are thought of as being in the eastern direction. However, it is important to understand how these directions are understood in the practice of Vajrayana. All deities are thought of as facing east. If you are visualizing yourself as the Medicine Buddha or as Chenrezig or as Vajrayogini, regardless of the direction in which you would find their individual Buddha realms, you are facing east. And the same is true of the deities of the front visualization , who are also thought of as facing east. Therefore, if in "real space" you happen to be facing south or north, as far as the visualization is concerned, you are still facing east. You would not think that the deities resided in their Buddha realms somewhere far off over your left or right shoulder. "To a yogi or yogini," as Kalu Rinpoche once said, "all directions are east."

17: Sanskrit, like Latin, is no longer a spoken language. Here the translator is reading the mantra in what scholars suspect was the original Sanskrit pronunciation. The mantras, as they appear in this text, are our English versions of the Tibetan versions of the original Sanskrit mantras. In this case *Vajra samaya ja ja* reads *Benza samaya dza dza.*

18: In connection with this process it is helpful to be familiar with two terms: *samayasattva* and *jnanasattva,* which could be roughly translated as "commitment being" and "primordial awareness being." The samayasattva is one's own personal visualization which one performs in order to maintain one's commitment to one's lama and to the practice of one's yidam. The jnanasattva is sometimes thought of as the "actual" deity which is a manifestation of the clear light nature of mind or the radiant clarity of mind and reality, which for the purposes of the visualization is thought of as residing off somewhere in its own particular Buddha realm. When the jnanasattva finally dissolves into the samayasattva, the jnanasattva and the samayasattva are thought to have become one and indivisible. In the ati yana, the samayasattva and the jnanasattva are considered from the beginning to be simultaneously present.

In *The Heart of the Buddha,* Chögyam Trungpa describes this process from a psychological perspective as it relates to the practice of Vajrayogini: "The visualization of oneself as Vajrayogini is called the *samayasattva:* the 'sacred bondage of one's being.' The samayasattva is basically the expression of the samayas of body, speech, and mind. It expresses one's commitment to the teacher and the teachings and one's trust in one's fundamental state of mind.

"Having visualized the samayasattvas of basic being, one invites what is known as *jnanasattva.* The jnanasattva is another level of being or experience. Jnana is a state of wakefulness or openness, whereas samaya is an experience of bondage, in being solidly grounded in one's experience. *Jnana* literally means 'wisdom' or, more accurately, 'being wise.' One invites this state of wisdom, this level of wakefulness, into one's own imperfect visualization, so that the visualization comes alive with a feeling of openness and humor."

19: Vases made of precious jewels and metals.

20: When represented in a seated posture and at rest, Vairochana is white with his hands in the teaching mudra; Akshobhya is blue with his left hand in the mudra of meditation and his right hand in the earth touching mudra; Ratnasambhava is yellow with his left hand in the mudra of meditation and the right hand in the mudra of generosity; Amitabha is red with both hands in the meditation mudra; and Amogasiddhi is green with his left hand in the mudra of meditation and his right hand in the mudra of fearlessness.

21: i.e. extreme asceticism

22: This is very interesting story, for the Buddha actually accepted and then postponed this event many times, before finally accepting the challenge. For a further description of this event, see Thich Nhat Hanh's *Old Path White Clouds.*

23: Generally referred to as the eight auspicious symbols.

24: Sometimes called the endless knot or the knot of eternity.

25: The takeoff point for this description is the Buddha Shakyamuni, but it should be understood that these attributes are present in male and female Buddhas alike.

26: Though these seven "articles of royalty" or seven "possessions" may appear as such—as articles or possessions—to an observer lost in dualistic perception who sees everything as "my and mine," "her and hers," "him and his," etc., they are better understood by adhering more closely to the actual meaning of the Tibetan words used here, *död yön*. *Död* means desirable, and *yön* means quality, skill or attribute. Thus, if one understands these seven "whatevers" as seven qualities or attributes of a chakravartin's mind—whether the chakravartin is thought of as male or female—it will be easier to understand that these "articles" or "possessions," to the extent that they appear to be external phenomena, appear naturally and effortlessly and totally without coercion in his or her mandala or world. Without this understanding, the notion of precious queen might appear as nothing more than another aspect of an androcentric universe. This misunderstanding is further undermined by understanding them as aspects of the path, as Rinpoche explains.

27: It is important to understand that the term prajna includes in one term the notions of knowledge, wisdom, and primordial awareness or transcendental awareness, which is the highest form of prajna. Worldly knowledge—medicine, literature, business management, economics or anthropology—is one form of prajna. Knowledge of the teachings of the Buddha and other enlightened beings is spiritual prajna. Both worldly and spiritual prajna are based on the acquisition of information, and though they may have a great deal of practical benefit, they will not by themselves liberate one from the root causes of suffering. Only the highest form of prajna, jnana—primordial awareness, which is liberated from the superimposition on experience of perceiver and perceived—will free one from the root causes of suffering.

28: And, by extension, for the benefit of all beings. In the view of the practice of Vajrayana, which is rooted in the Mahayana aspiration to attain budhahood in order to liberate all sentient beings, the mandala of the yogin or yogini's body, speech, and mind is the entirety of animate and inanimate existence, and whatever affects the one beneficially affects the other beneficially as well. Specifically, offerings are made as an antidote to desire and attachment and the self-clinging that underlies them. As one continues to make these offerings to enlightened sources of refuge, there begins to develop the understanding and then the direct experience of the emptiness or lack of inherent existence of all that to which one has been clinging, and one's desire and attachment and self-clinging begin to dissolve and give rise to the wisdom of discriminating awareness, to the transparent self-liberating kaleidoscopic vision of what is as the mere interdependent appearances of the clear light nature of mind, and to a palpable blessing that benefits beings. It is not in order to become a good person that one makes offerings; at root, one is already a good person. One makes offerings in order to discover the truth of reality or the truth of things, and in order to access the profound effectiveness in helping others that arises from that discovery.

29: These are usually represented as concentric squares.

30: The other five are Kshitigarbha, Sarvanivaranavishkambhi, Akashagarbha, Maitreya, and Samantabhadra.

31: The syllable HUM standing in the center of the deity's heart in both the self and front visualization faces forward, in the same direction as the deity. The mantra garland, visualized in Tibetan, faces outward—which means that one could read it standing outside the Medicine Buddha but not from the perspective of the HUM in the heart, beginning with TAYATA directly in front of the central seed syllable HUM and arranged in a circle surrounding the seed syllable.

32: What the translator is here calling mundane deities—in fact, if we met one of them, one suspects that one would think of them as anything but mundane, just as if we met Flash Gordon or Darth Vader we would hardly regard either of them as mundane—are what are oftentimes referred to as worldly deities, which means that, although they are said to reside somewhere in the gods' realms and are said to be very powerful, they are not said to be enlightened. Buddhists recognize the relative reality of such deities, make offerings to them in order to please them, ask them politely not to bother dharma practitioners, ask for their protection, even ask them sometimes to help out with the weather, but never take refuge in them, for they themselves are not thought to be liberated from samsara.

33: i.e. the jnanasattvas and the samayasattvas.

34: See page 173

35: The generation of bodhicitta is based on the altruistic wish to bring about the welfare, and ultimately the total liberation, of all sentient beings from all forms of suffering. What distinguishes bodhicitta from the ordinary compassionate aspirations to benefit others shared by all people of good will is the recognition that one cannot ultimately fulfil these aspirations until one has attained the state of mental purification and liberation of Buddhahood, which is the source of all positive qualities, including the omniscience that can see, individual by individual, the causes of suffering and the causes and path of liberation from suffering. This understanding gives rise at some point to the initial generation of the aspiration to attain the state of Buddhahood in order to liberate all sentient beings from suffering and to establish them all in states of happiness. This is called aspiration bodhicitta, which must be followed by what is called the bodhicitta of entering or perseverance bodhicitta, which is the training in loving-kindness, compassion, the six paramitas or transcendent perfections, etc. which lead to the attainment of Buddhahood. Aspiration bodhicitta and perseverance bodhicitta are both included in the term relative bodhicitta. Absolute bodhicitta is direct insight into the ultimate nature. This state of primordial awareness *is* compassion and loving-kindness and gives rise spontaneously and without preconception to compassionate activity.

36: Sometimes translated as the wisdom of all-encompassing space or the wisdom of all-pervasive space.

37: The repetition of the main mantra or mantras of a sadhana while performing various visualizations usually comprises the main body of any sadhana practice.

38: The supplicant is generally also sitting on his or her right heel.

39: It is sometimes said that Buddhas have no desire to benefit or liberate sentient beings in the ordinary dualistic sense of an "I" helping or liberating an "other". This is not of course to suggest that a Buddha does not care, rather that the natural and spontaneous activity of the totally purified clear light nature of mind is to work spontaneously for the benefit of sentient beings without preconceived ideas, without any sort of forced effort, and without habit-forming thoughts. This activity is conditioned, however, by the aspirations the Buddha makes before he or she attains Buddhahood, and particularly by those aspirations that the future Buddha makes after he or she enters the bodhisattva path of the Mahayana. Thus the great emphasis placed on the aspirations of the Medicine Buddha made when he was a bodhisattva. The activity of a Buddha is also conditioned by the merit and aspirations of sentient beings.

40: One should not, of course, prevent oneself from generating great faith in the Medicine Buddha simply because, looking at the deep blue, male, monastic form of the Medicine Buddha, one feels disinclined towards a male monastic lifestyle and feels that one would rather end up looking like Vajrayogini, White Tara, or Guru Rinpoche. The ultimate state of Buddhahood involves unlimited freedom of mind, which means that a Buddha can manifest at will in whatever form he or she chooses.

41: The three poisons are the three basic mental afflictions—passion, aggression, and ignorance—represented by a cock, a snake, and a pig, from which all of samsara arises.

42: The six basic categories of samsaric existence: the hell realms, the hungry ghost realms, the animal realms, the human realms, the asura or jealous god realms, and the god realms.

43: i.e. they can remove obstacles to having children.

44: One of the characteristics of having reached the first bodhisattva bhumi or level is that, due to the bodhisattva's understanding of emptiness and interdependence, he or she begins to have and to develop the kind of vision that enables them to understand all the various approaches to spiritual development, both Buddhist and non-Buddhist, and to understand the various methods or various sorts of spiritual technologies taught by the Buddha.

45: Worldly deities who are unenlightened and thus still bound in samsara.

46: The head of the Sakya lineage, one of the four principal lineages of Vajrayana Buddhism.

47: Implicit in this answer is an understanding of what we might call the developmental aspect of karma. If one commits a negative act such as killing, and does not regret it, but in fact becomes first defensive about it and then rationalizes it, then one is likely gradually to come to rejoice in it, saying, "I was right in this case to kill, and faced with similar circumstances, I would do it again." Which leads of course to the notion that who it was that was killed deserved to be killed, which can lead in turn to the notion that they ought to be killed, which can in turn lead to the notion that we ought to organize a movement to kill such people. This leads to the hardening of one's attitude, and leads to an increasing small-mindedness that becomes more and more attached to a mistaken notion of what one ought to do and thus to an increasing stupidity. As this kind of development becomes widespread, it leads to hatred between groups and to warfare.

On the other hand, if instantly upon killing, or at any later time along the way in the aforesaid type of development, one recognizes the error of one's ways, regrets it deeply, vows not to engage in such action again, and engages in some sort of activity to compensate for one's negative actions, this process of the development of the negative effects of a negative action is arrested. And if one continues to engage in compensatory virtuous actions, the negative karma will gradually be purified. And though it is inescapable that a result of that negative karma will ultimately have to be experienced, the way in which it ripens can be mitigated so completely it will hardly even be experienced. Thus it is said that the Buddha Shakyamuni in a previous life as a bodhisattva killed the being who later was reborn as Ananda because that being was planning to kill 500 arhats and rob them. The bodhisattva, realizing that he could not talk this person out of his planned mass murder, killed him, thus preventing the deaths of the 500 arhats, and preventing the prospective murderer from being born in a succession of hellish existences from which it would be extremely difficult to extricate himself. Of course, the bodhisattva continued to be reborn again and again as a bodhisattva, engaged in ever increasingly effective virtuous action, and continued to develop love and compassion for sentient beings until, according to tradition, he was finally reborn as the Buddha Shakyamuni. The prospective murderer was also reborn at that time and became Ananda, a devoted disciple of the Buddha and his personal attendant during much of his life. According to the Pali Canon, the Buddha once stepped on a stick, and realized that that was the karmic consequence of having killed the man who later became Ananda. As a Buddha, of course, he would not have suffered from the experience.

Here Rinpoche is implying that the young girl's prayers to God on behalf of Hitler were a form of compensatory action that may have been responsible for changing the way her own personal karma ripened to the extent that they actually protected her, while others, who may have had the very same type of karma, who did not pray or prayed too little too late, were killed in the bombing.

48: i.e., not a reward arbitrarily bestowed by a deity pleased by one's praises, promises, obedience, or other means of currying favour.

49: Usually referred to as samskaras or mental formations.

50: It is not difficult to establish through the use of reason the lack of true— i.e., singular, uncompounded, permanent—existence of external physical things, but it is very difficult to "see" or experience such lack of true existence of things directly.

51: To reify is to regard something abstract as being material or concrete. This is another way of referring to the phenomenon of solidification that Chögyam Trungpa introduced into our vocabulary. To think of ourselves as being small, insignificant, fundamentally flawed beings who are fundamentally angry, needy, or dim-witted is to reify or take as real and solid and unchangeable that which is in fact merely the ever-changing ripening and exhaustion of causes and conditions. And though this karmic process exists as mere appearance, it is empty in its essential nature. The manifestations of the ripening of karma appear, but are not truly real or solid. They have no true existence, and recognizing their emptiness or lack of true existence liberates one from the suffering associated with them. If one's recognition of the essential empty nature of the ripening of karma is profound and continuous enough, impure appearances cease, and the appearance of oneself as deity and one's environment as Buddha realm spontaneously arises. This process is jump-started and fast-forwarded through the profound methods of the generation and completion stages, as Rinpoche continues to explain.

52: In the end, the vision of everything that arises as vivid pure appearance is the generation stage, and the recognition of its emptiness is the completion stage.

53: The results of any particular action include not simply the "payback," but also the perpetuation and reinforcement in the mind of the klesha or kleshas that existed as the motivation for the action.

54: The idea of praying to be reborn in a realm where everyone is celibate is inimical to most Westerners, indeed, probably to most people, and these people will be happy to know that celibacy does not figure in as a necessary feature in a great many of the realms of tantric deities. But the opportunity to be reborn in a realm where celibacy is the norm is important to those whose obsession with sex is so great that it always involves them in perpetual emotional conflict and mental and social degeneration. Living and practicing in such a safe environment gives them the much-needed chance to break through the cycle of emotional, physical, and social degeneration.

In addition, for individuals who have *no other aim in life* but the attainment of liberation or Buddhahood, the pratimoksha vows of a monk or a nun, including the vow of celibacy, are considered the best—though not the only—foundation for the path until one has reached at least the first bodhisattva bhumi. (A commitment to moral living that includes sexual fidelity is also considered a good foundation.) Under ordinary circumstances, killing, stealing, lying, sexual intercourse, the use of intoxicants, etc., grow out of the kleshas of passion, aggression, and ignorance, which in turn are based on the very dualistic clinging that one is seeking to undermine through one's practice. Thus these actions reinforce the kleshas and the confusion in one's mind. In addition, sexual intercourse generally leads to families, which then drastically reduce the amount of time and energy that one can devote to formal meditation, which is the backbone of the path. Under such circumstances, it is more difficult, if not impossible, for beginners on the path to develop the profound vipashyana insight—the view of emptiness—which is the path to liberation and Buddhahood.

Glossary of Terms

Abhidharma. (Tib. *chö ngön pa*) The Buddhist teachings are often divided into the tripitaka: the sutras (teachings of the Buddha), the vinaya (teachings on conduct,) and the Abhidharma which are the analyses of phenomena that exist primarily as a commentarial tradition to the Buddhist teachings.

Abhisheka. (see *empowerment*)

Absolute truth. (Tib. *dondam*) There are two truths or views of reality—relative truth which is seeing things as ordinary beings do with the dualism of "I" and "other" and absolute or ultimate truth, which transcends duality and sees things as they are.

Afflictive obscuration. There are two types of obscurations that cover one's Buddha nature. The obscuration of the afflictive or disturbing emotions and the obscuration of dualistic perception, or sometimes called the intellectual obscurations or cognitive obscurations.

Aggregates, five. (Skt. *skandha*, Tib. *phung po nga*) Literally, "heaps." These are the five basic transformations that perceptions undergo when an object is perceived. First is form, which includes all sounds, smells, etc., everything that is not thought. The second and third are sensations (pleasant and unpleasant, etc.) and their identification. Fourth are mental events, which actually include the second and third aggregates. The fifth is ordinary consciousness, such as the sensory and mental consciousnesses.

Akshobhya. (Tib. *mi bskyod pa*) The sambhogakaya Buddha of the vajra family.

All-basis. (Tib. *kün shi nam she*) According to the Cittamatra school this is the eighth consciousness and is often called the ground consciousness or storehouse consciousness.

Amitabha One of the five Buddha family deities known as "Buddha of boundless light." Usually depicted as red.

Amoghasiddhi One of the five Buddha families and means "all-accomplishing one." Usually depicted as green.

Anuttarayoga tantra. (Tib. *nal jor la na me pay ju*) There are four levels of the Vajrayana and Anuttarayoga tantra is the highest of these. It contains the Guhyasamaja, the Chakrasamvara, the Hevajra and the Kalachakra tantras.

Arhat. "Free from four maras." The mara of conflicting emotions, the mara of the deva, the mara of death and the mara of the skandhas. The highest level of the Hinayana path. Arhat is male and arhati is female.

Arura. The myroblan fruit/plant held by the Medicine Buddha which represents all the best medicines.

Avalokiteshvara. (Tib. *Chenrezig*) The bodhisattva embodying the compassion of all the Buddhas. Depicted holding the wish-fulfilling gem between folded hands. One of the eight main bodhisattvas. The mantra associated with this bodhisattva is known as the king of mantras, OM MANI PEME HUNG.

Ayatanas. These are the six sensory objects of sight, sound, smell, taste, and body sensation; the six sense faculties, the visual sensory faculty, the auditory sensory faculty, etc., and the six sensory consciousnesses, the visual consciousness, the auditory consciousness, etc. They make up the eighteen constituents for perception.

Bardo. (Tib.) The intermediate state between the end of one life and rebirth into another. Bardo can also be divided into six different levels; the bardo of birth, dreams, meditation, the moment before death, the bardo of dharmata and the bardo of becoming.

Bindu. (Tib. *tigle*) Vital essence drops or spheres of psychic energy that are often visualized in Vajrayana practices.

Bodhicitta. (Tib. *chang chup chi sem*) Literally, the mind of enlightenment. There are two kinds of bodhicitta: absolute bodhicitta, which is completely awakened mind that sees the emptiness of phenomena, and relative bodhicitta which is the aspiration to practice the six paramitas and free all beings from the suffering of samsara. In regard to relative bodhicitta there is also two kinds: aspiration bodhicitta and perseverance bodhicitta.

Bodhisattva. (Tib. *chang chup sem pa*) "Heroic mind" *Bodhi* means blossomed or enlightened, and *sattva* means heroic mind. Literally, one who exhibits the mind of enlightenment. Also an individual who has committed him or herself to the Mahayana path of compassion and the practice of the six paramitas to achieve Buddhahood to free all beings from samsara. These are the heart or mind disciples of the Buddha.

Bodhisattva levels. (Skt. *bhumi,* Tib. *sa*) The levels or stages a bodhisattva goes through to reach enlightenment. These consist of ten levels in the sutra tradition and thirteen in the tantra tradition.

Bodhisattva Vow. The vow to attain Buddhahood for the sake of all beings.

Buddha. (Tib. *sang gye*) An individual who attains, or the attainment of, complete enlightenment, such as the historical Shakyamuni Buddha.

Buddha Shakyamuni. (Tib. *shakya tubpa*) The Shakyamuni Buddha, often called the Gautama Buddha, refers to the fourth Buddha of this age, who lived between 563 and 483 BCE.

Buddhafield. (Tib. *sang gye kyi zhing*) 1) One of the realms of the five Buddha families, either as sambhogakaya or nirmanakaya. 2) Pure personal experience.

Buddhahood. (Tib. *sang gyas*) The perfect and complete enlightenment of dwelling in neither samsara nor nirvana. Expression of the realization of perfect enlightenment, which characterizes a Buddha. The attainment of Buddhahood is the birthright of all beings. According to the teachings of Buddha, every sentient being has, or better is already, Buddha nature; thus Buddhahood cannot be "attained." It is much more a matter of experiencing the primordial perfection and realizing it in everyday life.

Buddha nature. (Tib. *de shegs nying po*) The essential nature of all sentient beings. The potential for enlightenment.

Chakrasamvara. (Tib. *korlo dompa*) A meditational deity which belongs to the Anuttarayoga tantra set of teachings. A main yidam or tantra of the New Schools.

Chakravartin. (Tib. *koro gyur wa*) Literally, the turner of the wheel and also called a universal monarch. This is a king who propagates the dharma and starts a new era.

Chakra. A complex systematic description of physical and psychological energy channels.

Channels, winds and essences. Nadi, prana and bindu; the constituents of the vajra body. These channels are not anatomical structures, but more like meridians in acupuncture. There are thousands of channels, but the three main channels that carry the subtle energy are the right, left and central channel. The central channel runs roughly along the spinal column while the right and left are on the sides of the central channel.

Cognitive obscuration. The subtle obscuration of holding onto the concepts of subject, object and action.

Common vehicle. The Hinayana.

Completion stage. (Tib. *dzo rim)* In the Vajrayana there are two stages of meditation: the creation/generation stage and the completion stage. Completion stage with marks is the six doctrines. Completion stage without marks is the practice of essence Mahamudra, resting in the unfabricated nature of mind.

Consciousnesses, sensory. These are the five sensory consciousnesses of sight, hearing, smell, taste, touch, and body sensation.

Consciousnesses, eight. (Skt. *vijñana,* Tib. *nam she tsog gye)* These are the five sensory consciousnesses of sight, hearing, smell, taste, touch, and body sensation. Sixth is mental consciousness, seventh is afflicted consciousness, and eighth is ground consciousness.

Daka. (Tib. *khandro)* A male counterpart to a dakini.

Dakini. (Tib. *khandroma)* A yogini who has attained high realizations of the fully enlightened mind. She may be a human being who has achieved such attainments or a non-human manifestation of the enlightened mind of a meditational deity. A female aspect of the protectors. It is feminine energy which has inner, outer and secret meanings.

Definitive meaning. The Buddha's teachings that state the direct meaning of dharma. They are not changed or simplified for the capacity of the listener, in contrast to the provisional meaning.

Desire realm. Comprises the six realms of gods, demi-gods, humans, animals, hungry spirits and hell-beings.

Dharani. A particular type of mantra, usually quite long.

Dharma. (Tib. *chö)* This has two main meanings: first, any truth, such as that the sky is blue; and secondly, the teachings of the Buddha (also called "Buddhadharma").

Dharmadhatu. (Tib. *chö ying)* The all-encompassing space, unoriginated and without beginning, out of which all phenomena arises. The Sanskrit means "the essence of phenomena" and the Tibetan means "the expanse of phenomena," but it usually refers to the emptiness that is the essence of phenomena.

Dharmakaya. (Tib. *chö ku)* One of the three bodies of Buddhahood. It is enlightenment itself, that is, wisdom beyond any point of reference. (see *kayas, three.)*

Dharmapala. (Tib. *cho kyong)* Dharma protector. A Buddha, bodhisattva or powerful but ordinary being whose job is to remove all interferences and bestow all necessary conditions for the practice of pure dharma.

Dharmata. (Tib. *chö nyi)* Dharmata is often translated as "suchness" or "the true nature of things" or "things as they are." It is phenomena as it really is or as seen by a completely enlightened being without any distortion or obscuration, so one can say it is "reality."

Dorje Chang. (see *Vajradhara)*

Dzogchen. (Tib.) Literally "The Great Perfection." The teachings beyond the vehicles of causation, first taught in the human world by the great Vidyadhara Garab Dorje.

Eight auspicious signs. Precious parasol, victory banner, conch shell, vase of treasures, golden fish, wheel, lotus flower and the eternal knot.

Eight auspicious substances. Conch shell, yoghurt, durva grass, vermilion, bilva fruit, mirror, givam, mustard seed.

Eight bodhisattvas. Manjushri, Avalokiteshvara, Vajrapani, Kshitigarbha, Sarvanivaranishkambhi, Akasharbha, Maitreya, and Samantabhadra.

Eight consciousnesses. The all-ground consciousness, mind-consciousness, afflicted consciousness, and the five sense-consciousnesses. The Hinayana sutras generally discuss mind in terms of six consciousnesses, namely, the five sensory consciousnesses and the sixth mental consciousness. The Mahayana Cittamatra school (Mind-only) school talks about the eight consciousness in which the first six are the same but has the seventh and eighth consciousnesses added. In the Hinayana tradition the functions of the seventh and eighth consciousness are subsumed in the sixth mental consciousness.

Eight fold noble path. Right view, right thought, right speech, right action, right livelihood, right effort, right mindfulness and right concentration.

Eight Medicine Buddhas. This refers to the principle Medicine Buddha and his retinue of seven other Medicine Buddhas: Excellent Name, Appearance of Stainless Fine Gold, Glorious Supreme One Free of Misery, Resounding Dharma Melody, King of Direct Knowledge, King of Melody and King of Shakyas.

Eight offerings. Drinking water, water for washing the feet, flowers, incense, lamps, perfume, food, and music.

Empowerment. (Skt. *abhisheka.* Tib. *wang)* The conferring of power or authorization to practice the Vajrayana teachings, the indispensable entrance door to tantric practice.

Emptiness. (Tib. *tong pa nyi* Skt. *shunyata*) A central theme in Buddhism. It should not lead one to views of nihilism or the like, but is a term indicating the lack of any truly existing independent nature of any and all phenomena. Positively stated, phenomena do exist, but as mere appearances, interdependent manifestations of mind with no limitation. It is not that it is just your mind. As mind is also free of any true existence. This frees one from a solipsist view. This is interpreted differently by the individual schools.

Enlightenment. (Tib. *jang chub*) The definition varies according to the Buddhist tradition, usually the same as Buddhahood. The Hinayana tradition defines liberation as the freedom from rebirth in samsara, with mind free of ignorance and emotional conflict. The Mahayana tradition holds that enlightenment is not complete without development of compassion and commitment to use skilful means to liberate all sentient beings. In the Vajrayana teachings, the foregoing stages of enlightenment are necessary, but ultimate enlightenment is a thorough purification of ego and concepts. The final fruition of complete liberation transcends all duality and conceptualization.

Five Buddha families. (Tib. *rig nga*) These are the Buddha, vajra, ratna, padma and karma families.

Five male Buddhas. Vairochana, Akshobhya, Ratnasambhava, Amitabha and Amoghasiddhi

Five female Buddhas. Dhatvishvari, Mamaki, Locana, Pandaravasini and Samayatara.

Five dhyani Buddhas. Vairochana, Akshobhya, Ratnasambhava, Amitabha and Amoghasiddhi. They are the pure aspects of the five elements and five emotions.

Five aggregates. (see *aggregates, five.*)

Five paths. (Tib. *lam nga*) According to the sutras there are five paths; the path of accumulation, the path of integration/junction, the path of seeing/insight, (attainment of the first bodhisattva level), the path of meditation, and the path of no more learning (Buddhahood). The five paths cover the entire process from beginning dharma practice to complete enlightenment.

Five poisons. (Tib. *ldug nga*) Temporary mental states that inhibit understanding: ignorance, pride, anger, desire, and jealousy. The three root poisons are ignorance, desire and anger.

Five wisdoms. The dharmadhatu wisdom, mirror-like wisdom, wisdom of equality, discriminating wisdom and all-accomplishing wisdom. They should not be understood as separate entities but rather as different functions of one's enlightened essence.

Form realm. God realms of subtle form.

Formless realm. (Tib. *zug med kyi kham*) The abode of an unenlightened being who has practiced the four absorptions of: infinite space, infinite consciousness, nothing whatsoever, and neither presence nor absence (of conception).

Four empowerments. (Tib. *wang shi*) The empowerments of vase, secret, wisdom-knowledge and precious word.

Four immeasurables. Love, compassion, emphatic joy, and impartiality.

Four reminders. The four ordinary foundations: the difficulty in obtaining the precious human body, impermanence and death, karma; cause and effect, the shortcomings of samsara. Reflection on these four reminders causes the mind to change and become directed toward the dharma.

Four seals. The four main principles of Buddhism: all compounded phenomena are impermanent, everything defiled (with ego-clinging) is suffering, all phenomena are empty and devoid of a self-entity, and nirvana is perfect peace.

Four noble truths. The Buddha's first teachings. 1) All conditioned life is suffering. 2) All suffering is caused by ignorance. 3) Suffering can cease. 4) The eight-fold path leads to the end of suffering: right understanding, thought, speech, action, livelihood, effort, mindfulness and meditation.

Generation stage. (Skt. *utpattikrama*, Tib. *che rim*) In the Vajrayana there are two stages of meditation: the generation and the completion stage. The generation stage is a method of tantric meditation that involves the visualization and contemplation of deities for the purpose of purifying habitual tendencies and realizing the purity of all phenomena. In this stage visualization of the deity is established and maintained.

Guru. (Tib. *lama*) A teacher in the Tibetan tradition who has reached realization.

Guru Rinpoche. (Tib.) (Skt. *Padmasambhava*) Or the "Lotus Born." The great 8th century Indian mahasiddha who came to Tibet taming all the negative elemental forces and spreading the Buddhadharma. In particular he taught many tantras and Vajrayana practices, and concealed many texts to be later revealed by his disciples.

Higher realms. The three higher realms are birth as a human, demi-god and god.

Hinayana. (Tib. *tek pa chung wa*) Literally, the "lesser vehicle." The first of the three *yanas*, or vehicles. The term refers to the first teachings of the Buddha, which emphasized the careful examination of mind and its confusion. It is the foundation of Buddha's teachings focusing mainly on the four truths and the twelve interdependent links. The fruit is liberation for oneself.

Interdependent origination. The twelve links of causal connections which binds beings to samsaric existence and thus perpetuate suffering: ignorance, karmic formation, consciousness, name and form, the six sense bases, contact, sensation, craving, grasping, becoming, rebirth, old age, and death. These twelve links are like an uninterrupted vicious circle, a wheel that spins all sentient beings around and around through the realms of samsara.

Jnana. (Tib. *yeshe*) Enlightened wisdom that is beyond dualistic thought.

Jnanasattva. *Jnana* is awareness and *sattva* means mind.

Kanjur. The preserved collection of the direct teaching of the Buddha.

Kagyu (Tib.) *Ka* means oral and *gyu* means lineage; The lineage of oral transmission. One of the four major schools of Buddhism in Tibet. It was founded in Tibet by Marpa and is headed by His Holiness Karmapa. The other three are the Nyingma, the Sakya and the Gelugpa schools.

Kalachakra. A tantra and a Vajrayana system taught by Buddha Shakyamuni.

Kalpa (Tib. *kal pa*, Skt. *yuga*) An eon that lasts on the order of millions of years.

Karma. (Tib. *lay*) Literally "action." The unerring law of cause and effect, eg. Positive actions bring happiness and negative actions bring suffering. The actions of each sentient being are the causes that create the conditions for rebirth and the circumstances in that lifetime.

Karmapa. The name means Buddha activities. The Karmapas are the head of the Kagyu school of Buddhism and were the first to implement the tradition of incarnate lamas. Karmapas are thought to be an emanation of the bodhisattva Avalokiteshvara.

Karmic latencies or imprints. (Skt. *vasana*, Tib. *pakchak*) Every action and that a person does has an imprint which is stored in the eighth consciousness. These latencies express themselves later by leaving the eighth consciousness and entering the sixth consciousness upon being stimulated by external experience.

Kayas, three. (Tib. *ku sum*) There are three bodies of the Buddha: the nirmanakaya, sambhogakaya and dharmakaya. The dharmakaya, also called the "truth body," is the complete enlightenment or the complete wisdom of the Buddha that is unoriginated wisdom beyond form and manifests in the sambhogakaya and the nirmanakaya. The sambhogakaya, also called the "enjoyment body," manifests only to bodhisattvas. The nirmanakaya, also called the "emanation body," manifests in the world and in this context manifests as the Shakyamuni Buddha.

Key instructions–a text's key instruction rests upon establishing the line of reasoning in a teaching. Seeing this line of reasoning, we can distinguish between the form and the content of the teachings. What key instructions do are wake a person up to the true nature of the experience that the teachings generate, such as the dissolving of the objective form of the experience, which can be seen as it truly is, appreciated as having no independent reality and hence no power, as would be the case if it existed independently. The key instruction that, if acted upon, generates a liberating personality transformation, is repeated at each level of the teachings.

King Trisong Deutsen. He was a dharma king of Tibet (790 - 858 CE) who invited Guru Rinpoche and Padmasambhava to Tibet to establish the dharma there.

Klesha. (Tib. *nyön mong*) Also called the "afflictive emotions," these are the emotional afflictions or obscurations (in contrast to intellectual obscurations) that disturb the clarity of perception. These are also translated as "poisons." They include any emotion that disturbs or distorts consciousness. The three main kleshas are desire, anger and ignorance. The five kleshas are the three above plus pride and envy/jealousy.

Lama. (Skt. *guru*) *La* nobody above himself or herself in spiritual experience and *ma* expressing compassion like a mother. Thus the union of wisdom and compassion, feminine and masculine qualities. Lama is also a title given to a practitioner who has completed some extended training.

Liberation. (see *enlightenment*)

Lojong. Mind Training. The Mahayana meditation system of the early Kadampa school, brought to Tibet by Atisha.

Lower realms. The three lower realms are birth as a hell being, hungry ghost and animal.

Mahakala. Dharmapala. A protector of the dharma and dharma practitioners.

Mahamudra. (Tib. *cha ja chen po*) Literally means "great seal" or "great symbol."

This meditative transmission emphasizes perceiving mind directly rather than through skilful means. It is especially emphasized in the Kagyu school. It refers to the experience of the practitioner where one attains the union of emptiness and luminosity and also perceives the non-duality of the phenomenal world and emptiness; also the name of Kagyupa lineage.

Mahapandita. (Tib. *pan di ta chen po*) *Maha* means great and *pandita* Buddhist scholar.

Mahasiddha. (Tib. *drup thop chen po*) A practitioner who has a great deal of realization. *Maha* means great and *siddha* refers to an accomplished practitioner.

Mahayana. (Tib. *tek pa chen po*) Literally, the "Great Vehicle." These are the teachings of the second turning of the wheel of dharma, which emphasize shunyata (see *shunyata*), compassion and universal Buddha nature. The purpose of enlightenment is to liberate all sentient beings from suffering as well as oneself. Mahayana schools of philosophy appeared several hundred years after the Buddha's death, although the tradition is traced to a teaching he is said to have given at Rajgriha, or Vulture Peak Mountain.

Maitreya. The Loving One. The bodhisattva regent of Buddha Shakyamuni, presently residing in the Tushita heaven until becoming the fifth Buddha of this kalpa.

Mandala. (Tib. *chil kor*) Literally "centre and surrounding" but has different contexts. A diagram used in various Vajrayana practices that usually has a central deity and four directions.

Manjushri. One of the eight bodhisattvas. He is the personification of transcendent knowledge.

Mantra. (Tib. *ngags*) 1) A synonym for Vajrayana. 2) A particular combination of sounds symbolizing the nature of a deity, for example OM MANI PEME HUNG

Mara. (Tib. *du*) Difficulties encountered by the practitioner. The Tibetan word means heavy or thick. In Buddhism mara symbolizes the passions that overwhelm human beings as well as everything that hinders the arising of wholesome roots and progress on the path to enlightenment. There are four kinds: *skandha-mara*, which is incorrect view of self; *klesha-mara*, which is being overpowered by negative emotions; *matyu-mara*, which is death and interrupts spiritual practice; and *devaputra-mara*, which is becoming stuck in the bliss that comes from meditation.

Middle Way School. (Skt. *Madhyamaka*) The highest of the four Buddhist schools of philosophy. The middle way means not holding any extreme views, especially those of eternalism or nihilism.

Mudra. (Tib. *chak gya*) In this book it is a "hand seal" or gesture that is performed in specific tantric rituals to symbolize certain aspects of the practice being done. Also can mean spiritual consort, or the "bodily form" of a deity.

Nadi. The channels in the vajra body through which the winds flow.

Ngöndro. (Tib.) One usually begins the Vajrayana path by doing the four preliminary practices which involve 111,000 refuge prayers and prostrations, 111,000 Vajrasattva mantras, 111,000 mandala offerings, and 111,000 guru yoga practices.

Nirmanakaya. (Tib. *tulku*) There are three bodies of the Buddha and the nirmanakaya or "emanation body" manifests in the world and in this context manifests as the Shakyamuni Buddha. (see *kayas, three.*)

Nirvana. (Tib. *nyangde*) Literally, "extinguished." Individuals live in samsara and with spiritual practice can attain a state of enlightenment in which all false ideas and conflicting emotions have been extinguished. This is called nirvana. The nirvana of a Hinayana practitioner is freedom from cyclic existence, an arhat. The nirvana of a Mahayana practitioner is Buddhahood, free from extremes of dwelling in either samsara or the perfect peace of an arhat.

Pandita. A great scholar.

Paranirvana. After the Buddha Shakyamuni passed from this realm: Buddha's are not said to have died, since they have reached the stage of deathlessness, or deathless awareness.

Prana. Life supporting energy. The "winds" or energy-currents of the vajra body.

Prajna. (Tib. *she rab*) In Sanskrit it means "perfect knowledge" and can mean wisdom, understanding or discrimination. Usually it means the wisdom of seeing things from a high (e.g. non-dualistic) point of view.

Pratimoksha ordination. "Individual liberation." The seven sets of precepts for ordained and lay people according to the vinaya.

Pratyekabuddha. "Solitary Awakened One." These are the body disciples of the Buddha. One who has attained awakening for himself, and on his own, with no teacher in that life. Generally placed on a level between arhat and Buddha. It is the fruition of the second level of the Hinayana path through contemplation on the twelve interdependent links in reverse order.

Protectors. (see *dharmapalas*)

Provisional meaning. The teachings of the Buddha which have been simplified or modified to the capabilities of the audience. This contrasts with the definitive meaning.

Ratna (Tib. *kern cho*) Literally "a jewel" but in this context refers to the three jewels which are the Buddha, the dharma, and the sangha.

Ratnasambhava (Tib. *rinchen jungnè*) The sambhogakaya Buddha of the ratna family.

Rebirth. Continuous, cyclic rebirth into the realm of samsara. Consciousness of an individual enters form according to his or her karma, the causes and conditions created by previous actions.

Relative truth. (Tib. *kunsop*) There are two truths: relative and absolute or ultimate truth. Relative truth is the perception of an ordinary (unenlightened) being who sees the world with all his or her projections based on the false belief in "I" and "other."

Root guru. (Tib. *tsa way lama*) A practitioner of Vajrayana can have several types of root guru: the vajra master who confers empowerment, who bestows reading transmission, or who explains the meaning of the tantras. The ultimate root guru is the master who gives the "pointing out instructions" so that one recognizes the nature of mind.

Rupakaya. (Tib. *zuk kyi ku*) The form bodies that encompass the sambhogakaya and the nirmanakaya.

Sacred outlook. (Tib. *Dag snang*) Awareness and compassion lead the practitioner to experience emptiness (*sunyata*). From that comes luminosity manifesting as the purity and sacredness of the phenomenal world. Since the sacredness comes out of the experience of emptiness, the absence of preconceptions, it is neither a religious nor a secular vision: that is, spiritual and secular vision could meet. Moreover, sacred outlook is not conferred by any god. Seen clearly, the world is self-existingly sacred.

Sadhana. (Tib. *drup tap*) Tantric liturgy and procedure for practice, usually emphasizing the generation stage.

Samadhi. (Tib. *tin ne zin*) A state of meditation that is non-dualistic. There is an absence of discrimination between self and other. Also called meditative absorption or one-pointed meditation; this is the highest form of meditation.

Samantabhadra. *Samanta* means all and *bhadra* means excellent. "He who is All-pervadingly Good" or "He who's Beneficence is Everywhere." There are two Samantabhadras, one is the dharmakaya and the other is one of the eight main bodhisattvas, embodiment of all Buddhas aspirations. In the Vajrayana tradition Samantabhadra is the primordial Buddha and representative of the experiential content of the dharmakaya.

Samaya. (Tib. *dam sig*) The vows or commitments made in the Vajrayana to a teacher or to a practice. Many details exist but essentially it consists of outwardly, maintaining a harmonious relationship with the vajra master and one's dharma friends and inwardly, not straying from the continuity of the practice.

Sambhogakaya. (Tib. *long chö dzok ku*) There are three bodies of the Buddha and the sambhogakaya, also called the "enjoyment body," is a realm of the dharmakaya that only manifests to bodhisattvas (see *kayas, three*).

Samsara. (Tib. *kor wa*) "Cyclic existence." The conditioned existence of ordinary life in which suffering occurs because one still possesses attachment, aggression and ignorance. It is contrasted to nirvana. Through the force of karma motivated by ignorance, desire and anger one is forced to take on the impure aggregates and circle the wheel of existence until liberation.

Sangha. (Tib. *gen dun*) "Virtuous One." *Sang* means intention or motivation and *gha* means virtuous. One with virtuous motivation. One of the three jewels. Generally refers to the followers of Buddhism, and more specifically to the community of monks and nuns. The exalted sangha is those who have attained a certain level of realization of the Buddha's teachings.

Santarakshita. Indian master who was an abbot of Nalanda University. He was invited by king Trisong Deutsen to Tibet in the eighth century and thus helped establish Buddhism there.

Sentient beings. With consciousness, an animated being as opposed to an inanimate object. All beings with consciousness or mind who have not attained the liberation of Buddhahood. This includes those individuals caught in the sufferings of samsara as well as those who have attained the levels of a bodhisattva.

Seven articles of royalty. Seven distinguishing articles of a chakravartin: precious jewel, precious wheel, consort, precious minister, precious excellent horse, precious elephant, and the precious general. Inwardly they represent the seven limbs of awakening.

Seven limbs of awakening. The virtue of faith, insight, samadhi, joy, diligence, mindfulness, and equanimity. Externally they are represented by the seven articles of royalty.

Shamatha. (Tib. *shinay*) Tranquillity meditation. One of the two main types of meditation, calm abiding, the meditative practice of calming the mind in order to rest free from the disturbance of thought activity, the other is insight.

Shravaka. "Hearer" corresponds to the level of arhat, those that seek and attain liberation for oneself through listening to the Buddhas teaching and gaining insight into selflessness and the four truths. These are the Buddhas speech disciples.

Siddha. (Tib. *drup top*) An accomplished Buddhist practitioner.

Siddhi. (Tib. *ngodrup*) The spiritual accomplishments of accomplished practitioners. "Accomplishment." Usually refers to the "supreme siddhi" of complete enlightenment, but can also mean the "common siddhis," eight mundane accomplishments.

Six paramita. Paramita means "transcendental" or "perfection." Pure actions free from dualistic concepts that liberate sentient beings from samsara. The six paramitas are: diligence, patience, morality, generosity, contemplation, and transcendental knowledge or insight.

Six realms. The realms of the six classes of beings: gods, demigods, humans, animals, hungry ghosts and hell beings.

Skilful means. Ingenuity in application.

Stupa. (Tib. *chorten*) Objects of offering, or objects for accumulating. A stupa is a monument symbolic of the dharmakaya and contains the relics of Buddhas or other enlightened beings. These, like your Guru, are focal points for veneration and our path to Buddhahood. Any disrespectful act toward them is disrespect for enlightenment itself.

Sukhavati. (Tib. *Dewachen*) The pure realm of Buddha Amitabha, "The Land of Great Bliss."

Sutra. (Tib. *do*) Literally "Junction." The combination of the Hinayana and Mahayana, or the combination of wisdom and compassion. Texts in the Buddhist cannon attributed to the Buddha. They are viewed as his recorded words, although they were not actually written down until many years after his *paranirvana.* They are usually in the form of dialogues between the Buddha and his disciples. These are often contrasted with the tantras which are the Buddha's Vajrayana teachings and the shastras which are commentaries on the words of the Buddha.

Tantra. (Tib. *gyu.*) Literally, tantra means "continuity," and in Buddhism it refers to two specific things: the texts (resultant texts, or those that take the result as the path) that describe the practices leading from ignorance to enlightenment, including commentaries by tantric masters; and the way to enlightenment itself, encompassing the ground, path, and fruition. One can divide Buddhism into the sutra tradition and the tantra tradition. The sutra tradition primarily involves the academic study of the Mahayana sutras and the tantric path primarily involves practicing the Vajrayana practices. The tantras are primarily the texts of the Vajrayana practices.

Tara. (Tib. *drol ma*) An emanation of Avalokiteshvara, she is said to have arisen from one of his tears. She embodies the female aspect of compassion and is a very popular deity in Tibet. Her two common iconographic forms are white and green.

Tathagatagharba. The same as Buddhanature. The inherently present potential for enlightenment in all sentient beings.

Ten directions. These are the four cardinal directions, their mid-directions (i.e. NE, SE, etc.) plus up and down. Basically it means "everywhere."

Tenjur. Commentary on the Kanjur; also tantras of meditation, healing, scientific and technical instructions etc.

Thangka. Religious cloth scroll painting, depicting various aspects of enlightenment.

Therevada. A school of Buddhism mainly practicing the Hinayana.

Three jewels. (Tib. *kön chok sum*) Literally "three precious ones." The three essential components of Buddhism: Buddha, dharma, sangha, i.e., the Awakened One, the truth expounded by him, and the followers living in accordance with this truth. Firm faith in the three precious ones is the stage of "stream entry." The three precious ones are objects of veneration and are considered "places of refuge." The Buddhist takes refuge by pronouncing the threefold refuge formula, thus acknowledging formally to be a Buddhist.

Three realms. These are three categories of samsara. The desire realm includes existences where beings are reborn with solid bodies due to their karma ranging from the deva paradises to the hell realms. The form realm is where beings are reborn due to the power of meditation; and their bodies are of subtle form in this realm. These are the meditation paradises. The formless realm is where beings due to their meditation (*samadhi*), have entered a state of meditation after death and the processes of thought and perception have ceased.

Three roots. Guru, yidam and dakini. Guru is the root of blessings, yidam of accomplishment and dakini of activity.

Three vehicles. Hinayana, Mahayana, and Vajrayana.

Tonglen. Giving and taking. A bodhichitta practice of giving one's virtue and happiness to others and taking their suffering and misdeeds upon oneself.

Torma. (Tib.) A sculpture made out of tsampa and moulded butter, used as a shrine offering, a feast offering substance, or as a representation of deities. There are traditional designs for each of the many types of torma.

Two accumulations. (Tib. *shogs nyis*) The accummlation of merit with concepts and the accumulation of wisdom beyond concepts.

Two obscurations. There are two categories of obscurations or defilements that cover one's Buddha nature: the defilement of conflicting emotions (see *five poisons & afflictive obscurations*) and the defilement of latent tendencies or sometimes called the obscuration of dualistic perception, or the intellectual/cognitive obscurations (see *cognitive obscurations*). The first category prevents sentient beings from freeing themselves from samsara, while the second prevents them from gaining accurate knowledge and realising truth.

Two truths. Relative truth and absolute truth. Relative truth describes the superficial and apparent mode of all things. Absolute or ultimate truth describes the true and unmistaken mode of all things. These two are described differently in the different schools, each progressively deeper leading closer to the way things are.

Vairochana. (Tib. *nam par nang dze*) The sambhogakaya Buddha of the Buddha family.

Vajra. (Tib. *dorje*) Usually translated "diamond like." This may be an implement held in the hand during certain Vajrayana ceremonies, or it can refer to a quality which is so pure and so enduring that it is like a diamond.

Vajradhara. "Holder of the vajra. *Vajra* means indestructible and *dhara* means holding, embracing or inseparable. The central figure in the Kagyu refuge tree, and indicating the transmission of the close lineage of the Mahamudra teachings to Tilopa. Vajradhara symbolizes the primordial wisdom of the dharmakaya and wears the ornaments of the sambhogakaya Buddha, symbolizing its richness.

Vajrapani. (Tib. *Channa Dorje*) A major bodhisattva said to be lord of the mantra and a major protector of Tibetan Buddhism.

Vajrasattva. (Tib. *Dorje Sempa*) The Buddha of purification. Vajrasattva practice is part of the four preliminary practices. A sambhogakaya Buddha who embodies all the five families. He is also a major source of purification practices.

Vajrayogini. (Tib. *Dorje Palmo*) A semi-wrathful yidam. Female.

Vajrayana. (Tib. *dorje tek pa*) Literally, "diamond-like" or "indestructible capacity." *Vajra* here refers to method, so you can say the method yana. There are three major traditions of Buddhism (Hinayana, Mahayana, Vajrayana) The Vajrayana is based on the tantras and emphasizes the clarity aspect of phenomena. A practitioner of the method of taking the result as the path.

Vidyadhara. Holder of knowledge or insight: the energy of discovery and communication. An accomplished master of the Vajrayana teachings.

Vinaya. One of the three major sections of the Buddha's teachings showing ethics, what to avoid and what to adopt. The other two sections are the sutras and the Abhidharma.

Vipashyana meditation. (Tib. *lha tong*) Sanskrit for "insight meditation." This meditation develops insight into the nature of reality (Skt. *dharmata*). One of the two main aspects of meditation practice, the other being shamatha.

Wheel of dharma. (Skt. *dharmachakra*) The Buddha's teachings correspond to three levels which very briefly are: the first turning was the teachings on the four noble truths and the teaching of the egolessness of person; the second turning was the teachings on emptiness and the emptiness of phenomena; the third turning was the teachings on luminosity and Buddha nature. When referring to the thirty-two marks of a Buddha it is the design of an eight-spoked wheel.

Yana. Means capacity. There are three yanas, narrow, (Hinayana) great (Mahayana) and indestructible (Vajrayana).

Yidam. (Tib.) *Yi* means mind and *dam* means pure, or *yi* means your mind and *dam* means inseparable. The yidam represents the practitioner's awakened nature or pure appearance. A tantric deity that embodies qualities of Buddhahood and is practiced in the Vajrayana. Also called a tutelary deity.

Yidam meditation. (Tib.) Yidam meditation is the Vajrayana practice that use the visualization of a yidam.

Yoga. "Natural condition." A person who practices this is called a *yogi,* characterized by leaving everything natural, just as it is, e.g. not washing or cutting your hair and nails etc. A female practitioner is called a *yogini.*

Index

A

Abhidharma 5
Absolute truth 34, 84
Akshobhya 40, 83, 84, 86-88, 182
Amitabha 20, 40, 70, 83, 85-88,
    117, 182
Amoghasiddhi 40, 83, 85-88
Ananda 121, 123, 124, 126, 129,
    187
Anuttarayoga 132
Arhat 9, 105, 136
Arhati 9, 105
Arura 33, 66, 97
Aspiration 10, 14-18,
23, 28, 50, 53,
    54, 56, 57, 59, 65, 68, 70, 74, 79,
    99-112, 119, 121-123, 126, 127,
    131, 141, 144, 175-178, 183-185
Avalokiteshvara 10, 61, 74
    Chenrezig 180, 181

B

Blessing (s) 1, 7-11, 13-15, 19, 20,
    21, 22, 24, 28, 32, 36-39, 65-67,
70, 73, 75-78, 93, 94, 102, 105-
110, 114, 115, 120-126, 129,
133, 135, 137, 141, 142, 144,
156, 183
Blessing of a Buddha 114
Blessing of dharma 21, 36
Blessing of the deity 10
Blessing of the lineage 11
Blessing of the Medicine Buddha
    13, 28, 36, 67, 109, 115, 120,
    122, 124, 125, 129, 142
Blessing of mind 66
Blessings of body 66, 73
Blessings of speech 66
Bodhicitta 2, 9, 10, 11, 15, 20, 23,
    24, 39, 70, 72, 78, 79, 105,
    112, 125, 136, 184, 185
    Aspiration bodhicitta 185
    Perseverance bodhicitta 185
Bodhisattva level 55
    Bodhisattva bhumi 186, 188
Bodhisattva vow 100, 120
Brahma 17, 36, 62, 161, 169, 171
Buddha nature 8, 37, 106, 136, 140,
    145, 153, 156

Buddha realm 38, 43, 101, 164, 181, 188
Buddha Shakyamuni 14, 18, 34, 35, 62, 99, 101, 102, 112, 122, 127, 131, 132, 179, 182, 187
Buddhadharma 6, 14, 36, 51, 109, 120
Buddhahood 3, 9, 10, 14, 23, 24, 37, 39, 78, 79, 85, 102, 105, 106, 108, 123, 130, 131, 136, 137, 145, 146, 179, 184, 185, 188, 189

C

Chakrasamvara 128, 132
Chakravartin 53, 54, 71, 72, 183
  Universal monarch 71, 72
Clarity of appearance 63
Clear appearance 63, 140
Clear light nature 179, 181, 183, 185
Common vehicle 9, 61, 77, 136
Completion stage 3, 22, 69, 136, 137, 139, 140, 180, 188
Consciousness 4, 5, 6, 7, 139, 145, 146, 180
  Eight consciousnesses 4, 6
    Eighth consciousness 6, 7
      All-basis 6, 7
    Five sense consciousnesses 5, 6
    Mental consciousness 5, 6, 180
    Seventh consciousness 6, 7
    Sixth consciousness 5
Six consciousnesses 6

D

Dakini 22, 23
Deity/deities 7, 8, 9, 10, 13, 17, 21, 22, 31, 32,36-40, 42-46, 51-54, 56-65, 69, 70, 75, 76, 81-83, 98, 117, 128, 135-138, 143, 144, 179-181, 184, 186-188
  Invitation of the deity 81
  Wisdom deity/deities 9, 37-40, 63, 69, 81-83
Dharmadhatu 83, 84, 85, 180
Dharmapalas 21, 22, 128
Dharmata 28, 32, 47, 69
Diligence 2, 54, 55, 60, 105, 110, 112, 153
Dorje Chang 75
  Vajradhara 1

E

Eight auspicious signs 46, 51, 57, 91
Eight auspicious substances 46, 50, 57, 91
Eight great bodhisattvas 61
Eight Medicine Buddhas 17, 38, 39, 69, 132
  Seven Buddhas 17, 35, 38, 59
Eight offerings 45
Eight traditional offerings 57
Emotional afflictions 137
Empowerment 11, 39, 40, 58, 76, 83, 85, 87-89, 94, 124
  Abhisheka 76
Mudras for the empowerment 89
Empowerment mantra 83
Emptiness 6, 8, 30, 31, 43, 45, 46, 64, 69, 70, 82, 84, 139, 140, 181, 183, 186, 188, 189
Enlightenment 23, 78, 101, 130, 175-179

Essence mantra 82

F

Five aggregates 138, 139
Five Buddhas 40, 83, 86-88
Five families 40, 83
Five male Buddhas 40, 83, 85
Five offerings 45, 90
Five wisdoms 83, 85
   Mirror-like wisdom 84, 85
   Wisdom of accomplishment 85
   Wisdom of discrimination 85
   Wisdom of equality 84-85
   Wisdom of the dharmadhatu 83-84
Four great kings 17, 22, 35, 57, 62,
   69, 117, 125, 132
Four immeasurables 25-28
Four noble truths 35
Front visualization 18, 31, 33-36,
   38, 40-42, 44, 63-66, 69-83, 96,
   97, 137, 181, 184

G

Generation stage 3, 6, 7, 63, 64, 69,
   139, 140, 188
Guru 1, 2, 19, 21, 22, 44
Guru Rinpoche 185

H

Higher realm 15, 16,
Hinayana 121, 136, 179

I

Impure perception 7, 24, 25, 148,
   149, 180
   Pure perception 7, 24, 25, 148,
   149, 180
Impure realm 103

Indra 17, 36, 47, 62,
Innate wisdom 136
Insight 2, 54, 67, 96, 112, 115, 116,
   137, 139, 179, 180, 185, 189

J

Jambhala 76, 137
Jewel Ornament of Liberation 105,
   153, 154
Jnana 69, 171, 181-184
Jnanasattva 181, 182, 184

K

Kagyu 1, 42, 95, 147
Kalachakra Tantra 82
Karmapa 1, 95
King Trisong Deutsen 19
Klesha 6, 7, 9, 29, 54, 55, 63, 67,
   69, 95, 115, 116, 136, 138, 139,
   141, 188, 189

L

Lama 19, 144, 161, 181
Liberation 2, 6, 9, 39, 78, 102,
   104, 105, 107, 108, 122, 136,
   153, 154, 156, 179, 180, 184,
   188, 189
Lineage 1, 2, 11, 13, 19, 20, 21,
   42, 77, 80, 146, 147, 186
Lineage guru 21
Lower realm 16, 20, 120, 122, 124,
   125, 171, 176

M

Mahakala 94, 180
Mahamudra 1, 11, 180
Mahasiddha 14, 132
Mahayana 9, 61, 62, 104, 105,

130, 136, 176, 183, 185

Mahayana sangha 61, 62

Maitreya 93, 184

Major and minor marks 34, 164
Eighty signs 35, 49, 51, 102
Thirty-two marks 35, 49, 51, 102, 175

Mandala 17, 18, 22, 24, 25, 28, 38, 39, 41, 54, 56-59, 61-63, 69, 71, 73, 91, 117, 179, 183

Mandala mudra 91

Manjushri 17, 61, 100, 101, 112, 113, 117, 118, 121, 122, 126, 137, 150, 178, 180

Mantra 3, 27-30, 39-45, 50, 53, 56, 58, 60, 65, 66, 68, 69, 73, 74, 76, 82, 83, 88, 89, 91, 93, 99, 142, 180, 181, 184, 185

Mara 48, 107, 115, 135, 138, 139, 140, 146, 177
Four different types of maras 138-140

Meditative absorption 2, 46, 54
Samadhi 2, 30, 34, 46, 47, 54, 55, 121, 135

Mental affliction 6, 7, 8, 59, 138, 141, 144, 186

Middle Way School 131

Mikyo Dorje 95

Morality 15, 105, 113, 114, 117, 159

Motivation 2, 3, 9, 10, 11, 14, 15, 23, 24, 39, 100, 101, 146, 188
Appropriate motivation 101
Impure motivation 101

Mudra 1, 11, 33, 81-83, 86-92, 180, 182

Invitation mudra 82

Lotus mudra 92

Mudra of Akshobhya 86

Mudra of Amitabha 86

Mudra of Amoghasiddhi 86

Mudra of Ratnasambhava 86

Mudra of Vairochana 86

Mudras for the empowerment 89

Mudras for the offerings 89

N

Negative karma 115, 121, 122, 129, 140, 144, 186, 187

Ngöndro 71, 95

Nirmanakaya 33, 41, 59

Nirvana 145

O

Offering 24, 25, 28, 32, 41, 44-48, 50-60, 63-65, 69, 71, 82, 83, 89-93, 117-123, 137, 141, 183, 184
Inner offering 46
Outer offering 45, 46
Secret offering 46
Ultimate offering 46
Offering mudra 83, 89
Three types of offering 56
Offering of the mandala 57

Omniscience 145, 184

P

Pandita 19

Prajna 10, 41, 54, 55, 103, 183

Pratimoksha ordination 100

Pratyekabuddha 105, 176

Primordial awareness 181, 183, 185

Jnana 69, 171, 181-184

Protector (s) 17, 20-22, 35, 36, 61-63, 69, 132, 176

Pure realm 24, 25, 38, 40, 41, 65, 66, 83, 103, 131, 140

Impure realm 103

R

Ratnasambhava 40, 83, 85-88, 182

Recollection of purity 63-64

Relative truth 33, 34, 84, 85, 87, 142

Root guru 1, 2, 19, 21, 44

Root teacher 44

S

Sadhana 42, 52, 76, 93, 95, 97, 106, 128, 180, 185

Samadhi 2, 30, 34, 46, 47, 54, 55, 121, 135

Samantabhadra 69, 184

Samaya 39, 58, 69, 82, 83, 98, 181, 182, 184

Samayasattva 181, 182, 184

Sambhogakaya 33, 36, 41, 59, 131

Samsara 6, 7, 34, 35, 51, 61, 78, 105, 109, 110, 117, 131, 136, 139, 145, 184, 186

Sangha 21, 22, 33, 61, 62, 94, 125, 146, 147, 148

Exalted sangha 61

Ordinary sangha 61

Santarakshita 18, 19, 161

Self-generation 9, 18

Self-visualization 31, 32, 65, 66, 69, 70, 81, 97, 98

Sentient being (s) 14, 51, 61, 99, 125, 153, 175, 176, 177, 179, 183, 184, 185, 187

Seven articles of royalty 25, 53-57, 71, 91

Seven limbs of awakening 55, 71

Shamatha 49, 69, 79, 128, 139

Shastra 18, 99, 179

Shravaka 14, 105, 109, 121, 176

Siddha 14, 78, 132

Siddhi (s) 21, 22, 51, 137, 179, 180, 182

Two siddhis 137

Common siddhis 137

Relative siddhi 179-180

Supreme siddhi 137

Ultimate siddhi 179

Six paramitas 185

Six realms 109

Sixteen bodhisattvas 13, 17, 35, 36, 58, 61-63, 65, 69, 122, 132, 169

Skilful means 176

Stable pride 63, 64

Subtle mental affliction 6

Sukhavati 20, 86, 117, 162, 181

Supplication 1, 9, 13, 14, 17-20, 28, 70, 72, 75, 76, 91, 92, 102, 106, 114, 120, 122, 124, 135, 136, 142, 144

T

Tantra 6, 11, 14, 86, 132, 171, 172

Tara 10, 179, 180, 185

Green Tara 180

White Tara 180, 185

Ten protectors 17, 22, 35, 36, 61-63, 69, 132

Three jewels 20, 21, 62, 126, 154,

Three poisons 109, 174, 186

Three roots 20, 21
Tonglen 79, 80, 128
Torma 46, 90, 172
Twelve (extraordinary) aspirations
    16, 70, 99, 101, 102, 112, 119,
    121, 122, 144, 178
    First of the twelve aspirations 102,
        175
    Second aspiration 103, 175
    Third aspiration 103, 175
    Fourth aspiration 104, 105, 176
    Fifth aspiration 105, 176
    Sixth aspiration 106, 176
    Seventh aspiration 106, 176
    Eighth aspiration 107, 177
    Ninth aspiration 107-108, 177
    Tenth aspiration 108, 110, 177,
        177
    Eleventh aspiration 110, 178
    Twelfth aspiration 110, 111
Twelve yaksha chieftains 18, 22, 36,
    61, 62, 63, 69, 76, 124-126, 132
Two accumulations 10, 44-46, 48,
    50, 51, 53-57, 111, 136
    Accumulation of merit 28, 31, 41,
        44, 45, 53-56, 64, 83
    Accumulation of wisdom 45, 53,
        54
Two obscurations 137

Afflictive obscuration 57, 144
Cognitive obscuration 57, 137, 139,
    144

U

Upaya 10, 41, 103

V

Vaidurya 33, 61
Vairochana 40, 83, 86, 87, 182
Vajradhara 1, 2, 32
Vajrapani 17, 50, 61, 126, 171
Vajrayana 7-9, 11, 14, 20-22, 46, 58,
    75, 82, 83, 89, 91-, 98, 128, 131,
    135-137, 139, 140, 181, 183, 186
Vajrayogini 128, 179-182, 185
Vidyadhara 62-63
Vipashyana 69, 128, 139, 189
Vow of refuge 100, 147

W

Wheel of Existence 109
Wheel of the dharma 52

Y

Yaksha 18, 36, 61, 62, 69, 76, 124-
    127, 132
Yidam 10, 21, 22, 33, 69, 128, 137,
    140, 179-181

Books by Thrangu Rinpoche

The Three Vehicles of Buddhist Practice
This book gives an overview of the Hinayana, Mahayana, and Vajrayana as it was practiced in Tibet. Boulder: Namo Buddha Publications, 1998.

The Middle-Way Meditation Instructions of Mipham Rinpoche
This great Tibetan scholar who actually stayed for a while with the previous Thrangu Rinpoche at his monastery describes how one develops compassion and then expands this to bodhicitta and eventually develops prajna or wisdom. Boulder: Namo Buddha Publications, 2000.

The Four Foundations of Buddhist Practice
There are the four thoughts one should contemplate before practicing and are: precious human birth; impermanence; karma; the downfalls of samsara. Boulder: Namo Buddha Publications, 2001.

Showing the Path of Liberation.
The Dorje Chang Tungma or Short Prayer to Dorje Chang is one of the most recited supplications for practitioners of Mahamudra. Composed by Penkar Jampal Zangpo after his completion of eighteen years of solitary retreat on Mahamudra it is said to have unparalleled blessing. Because it outlines the entire path of Mahamudra Thrangu Rinpoche has used it here as the basis and outline for this profound teaching on the path of liberation. Namo Buddha and Zhyisil Chokyi Ghatsal Publications 2001.

The Essence of Creation and Completion
Every Vajrayana practice has two phases to it: the creation stage in which one creates the visualization and the completion stage in which one dissolves the visualization. Jamgon Kongtrul wrote an important text describing these two processes and Thrangu Rinpoche gives a detailed

commentary on this root text. The book includes a translation of the root text as well as Rinpoche's commentary. Zhyisil Chokyi Ghatsal Publications 2001.

The Life of Tilopa & The Ganges Mahamudra

The first section of this book is the spiritual biography of Tilopa, the Indian yogi who is considered the founding father of the Kagyupa tradition. The second section contains the Mahamudra pointing-out instructions given on the banks of the Ganges River by Tilopa to his foremost disciple, the great pandit and mahasiddha Naropa. Thrangu Rinpoche gives a detailed commentary on this text which includes the of Tilopa's text.

Teachings on the Practice of Meditation

The essence of the teachings of the Buddha, is practice. The reason we practice meditation is to attain happiness. This means happiness in both the short term and the long term. In this remarkable teaching Thrangu Rinpoche presents all the important aspects of Buddhist meditation in general and from the Vajrayana perspective in particular. In it are covered motivation, posture, mental technique, consciousness and wisdom, as well as creation and completion stages and Mahamudra. Zhyisil Chokyi Ghatsal Publications 2001.

Journey of the Mind: Teachings on the Bardo.

When one dies, the mind takes an intense and very important journey through the bardo—that intermediate state between death and rebirth in the next body. To prepare for this journey, we must understand what is happening to us in the bardo and also how we can prepare for this journey while still living. Thrangu Rinpoche discusses this complex process in lucid terms and explains its significance to every day meditation. Zhyisil Chokyi Ghatsal Publications 2001.

The Practice of Tranquility and Insight.

This book is a practical guide to the two types of meditation that form the core of Buddhist spiritual practice. An extremely detailed book which is an invaluable guide for anyone doing Buddhist meditation. (Ithaca: Snow Lion Publications, 1993)

For an updated list and ordering contact:
www.greatliberation.org or Email: orders@greatliberation.org

Meditation Centre Information

For more information and instruction
please contact one of the following centres.

Rumtek Monastery
International Seat of His Holiness 17th Karmapa Urgyen Trinley Dorje
Sikkim, INDIA

Sherab Ling Buddhist Institute
Seat of His Eminence Tai Situpa
Kangra District, Himachal Pradesh, 176-125, INDIA
Ph: (01894) 63013/63757

New Zealand

Karma Choeling Buddhist Monastery
66 Bodhisattva Road
RD1 Kaukapakapa
Ph: 09 420 5428
www.kagyu.org.nz

Karma Thigsum Choeling
PO Box 3160
Christchurch
Ph: 03 384 4626

Kagyu Samten Choling
PO Box 917
Gisborne
Ph: 06 867 1956

Australia

Kagyu Thigsum Chokyi Ghatsal
PO Box 235, Newstead
Tasmania
Ph/fax: 03 6334 9680

Karma Tashi Choling
P.O. Box 973
Bega, NSW 2550
Ph: 02 6496 7169

Kagyu E-Vam Buddhist Institute
673 Lygon Street,
Carlton North, Vic. 3054
Ph: 03 9387 0422

For a list of Karma Kagyu Centres worldwide, contact:
Karma Triyana Dharmachakra
352 Meads Mt Rd, Woodstock, New York 12498
(914) 679-5906, email office@kagyu.org
www.kagyu.org

A Long Life Prayer for the Glorious Lama, Scholar and Siddha

THRANGU TULKU, KARMA LODRO LUNGRIK MAWAY SENGE

The Youthful Vitality of Immortal Nectar

In Praise of Amitayus

OM SWASTI DZI WEN TU

The dharmakaya, free of elaboration is ever stable and never destroyed.
Amitayus, your speech is the melodious sound of the nada,
the invincible vajra.
Through an enlightened mind that sees all possible phenomena
Perfect Guide, you accomplish all goodness.

In Praise of Thrangu Rinpoche

From the golden age arose a new mansion of clouds
poised in the depth of space;
May you remain for a long, long time.
Creating festive occasions for beings to increase their merit.
May you remain for a long, long time.
Through the blooming, full lotus of your flawless knowledge,
Your writings are suffused with great kindness and compassion.
Through limitless abilities, you satisfy
a multitude of beings seeking liberation.
Guide of beings, may your life be long.
Through explaining the Dharma, you release beings
from the tangled net of ignorance and confusion
In debate, you defeat the opponents' bold stance.
Our minds are carried away with joy by the nature of your writings.
You of genuine and powerful speech, may your life be long.
Rising from the jeweled ocean of your immeasurable merit,
the white moon, clear mandala of your wisdom.
Pours forth nectar that is the light of your activity.
Lion of speech, teaching scripture and reasoning, may your life be long.

The Dedication

By churning an ocean of milk with good intentions,
These words of aspiration-a white lotus garland-come to the surface
Protector, through the merit of offering this
to all the Buddhas and bodhisattvas.
May the benefit of your life last for hundreds of aeons.
Glorious Lama, through the power of the truth of the Victorious One.
Amitayus, and the power of a good connection with this sincere,
pure intention.
May your life remain stable until the end of the world.
May the vitality of all the four, perfectly flourish.
(Dharma, wealth, enjoyment, and liberation).

This prayer was requested by the one responsible for Nenang Monastery,
Lama Tsewang Tashi, who offered representations of the Buddha's body,
speech, and mind, and was written by the
XVIIth Karmapa, Ugyen Trinley Dorje
during a fine waxing moon of Saga Dawa.
SHUBHAM.

May it be a cause for virtue.

Care of Dharma Books

Dharma books contain the teachings of the Buddha; they have the power to protect against lower rebirth and to point the way to Liberation. Therefore, they should be treated with respect, kept off the floor and places where people sit or walk, and not stepped over. They should be covered or protected for transporting and kept in a high, clean place separate from more "ordinary" things. If it is necessary to dispose of Dharma materials, they should be burned with care and awareness rather than thrown in the trash. When burning Dharma texts, it is considered skilful to first recite a prayer or mantra, such as OM, AH, HUNG. Then you can visualize the letters of the text (to be burned) being absorbed into the AH, and the AH being absorbed into you. After that you can burn the texts.

These considerations may be also kept in mind for Dharma artwork, as well as the written teachings and artwork of other religions.